Sports
Marketing

For the three most important women I know
— Jocelyn, Erin, and Hennie —
and the most important guy — Murry.

Sports Marketing

Howard Schlossberg

First published 1996

Blackwell Publishers, Inc.
238 Main Street
Cambridge, Massachusetts 02142
USA

Blackwell Publishers Ltd.
108 Cowley Road
Oxford OX4 1JF
UK

Library of Congress Cataloging-in-Publication Data
Schlossberg, Howard.
    Sports marketing / Howard Schlossberg.
        p.   cm. — (Global marketing perspectives)
    Includes bibliographical references.
    ISBN 1-55786-590-6 (pbk. : alk. paper)
    1. Sports—United States—Marketing. I. Title. II. Series.
GV716.S34   1996
338.4'9796—dc20   95-50936
                                                                          CIP

British Library Cataloguing in Publication Data

Cover Photo provided by the Sports Car Club of America, Inc.

A CIP catalogue record for this book is available from the British Library.

Typeset by Cornerstone Composition Services.

This book is printed on acid-free paper.

Global Marketing Perspectives
Series Foreword

Will marketing be different tomorrow than today? When will this change occur? What does change mean to marketing professors? How can change best be explained to marketing practitioners? Who will be crucial marketing actors? Where will marketing take place? Is marketing global, or global with national sales and distribution practices, or national with global brand names? What is marketing? Answers to these questions range from marketing euphoria to marketing realism.

Tomorrow's marketing promotes dialogues with economics, management strategy, culture and consumer behavior, and international business. Marketing has as its ultimate goal understanding the problems faced by marketers and offering them practical advice on marketing strategy, the 4Ps, sales force behavior, and value marketing. While marketing literature contains a wide variety of paradigms, each with loyal proponents, it cannot sort out which marketing actions achieve long-term competitive advantage over rivals. Nevertheless, individual marketers believe their unique solutions are the real answers to marketing's diverse global problems. That is the dead end of marketing euphoria.

Therefore, marketers must ask two fundamental questions. What marketing actions will create a sustainable advantage for an individual firm? And, under what market conditions are such actions effective? The first question is about practical advice for marketing managers. The second question is about how marketers overcome market imperfections, grow sales, and increase profits. Together, they form the basis of marketing strategy for global, national, and local markets and discussions about how firms deal with asymmetric shocks, such as, free trade agreements among countries, and computer-based telecommunication technologies within industries. Marketing team-work begins inside the firm looking out and ends outside the firm looking in. That is the road to marketing realism.

Here is our goal for this series of books. We want marketing professors and practitioners to walk (perhaps run) down the road of marketing realism. When they come to a fork in the road we want them to look at our books on global, sports, and green marketing for signs that show the way towards sustainable competitive advantage for individual firms. If read carefully, marketers find the danger signs that say caution, no entry, or dead end; because, some suggestions do not overcome price and product market imperfections. The purpose of this series is to introduce marketers to some of the marketing challenges for the next century.

Douglas Lamont
Series Editor

Contents

Preface

Why would anyone want to write a book about sports marketing?

First of all, you get asked – in my case, by Doug Lamont, the editor of the series of business books of which this text is a part. Doug kindly asked me to write this tome after I spent three years writing a column about same in *Marketing News*, the American Marketing Association's biweekly news magazine for its members.

Why pick the specific topics I did? Simple. To me, after years of observing sports and sports marketing as both participant and literary observer, these were among the hottest trends in the industry at the time I sat down to write this book.

What better entity to exemplify global marketing than the NBA? How much more intrusive does so-called "ambush marketing" have to become before it merits a book of its own? What sport already has more global acceptance than soccer? What sport is attracting sponsors and licensees more rapidly than auto racing? What activity exemplifies the fans' emotional attachments to sports that marketers can leverage better than fantasy sports participation? And what brings sports to everyone? The media, of course.

With the labor strife rampant in the other major sports, focusing individual chapters on them was not merited. Their inclusion in the introductory overview chapter is sufficient. The Olympics has been hammered to death.

It's customary here to thank everyone and anyone who helped out. So let's first thank my wife, Jocelyn, for her support and Doug Lamont, who sought me out to write this book.

Thanks also to Rolf Janke, Mary Riso, Jan Leahy, and the gang at Blackwell; the people at places like International Events Group and the National Sporting Goods Association who let me attend the conferences where I gleaned so much first-hand information; Ernie Saxton; the one and only and inspirational Tom Amshay at RFTS Productions; Dallas Branch, Tracy Schoenadel, and the crowd at *Sport Marketing Quarterly*; two guys who won't like being mentioned in the same sentence but I'm doing it anyway, Alan Friedman (*Team Marketing Report*) and Dick Lipsey (*Sports Marketplace*); Shelley Ball, late of the American Marketing Association, for her undying support of sports marketing in the face of short-sighted opposition; Kim Lee at Walker, a sports marketing fan who is one of the few people on the planet to never say a discouraging word about me; Mickey Charles at Sports Network; Seth Sylvan and the gang at the NBA; Wood Selig at the University of Virginia; Mark Andrew of the Indiana Pacers; Dennis Sandler and David Shani, the kings of ambush marketing research who kept me in Baruch College glassware; Lois Lazarus; the gang at Robert Morris College's sports management program; Bill Sutton at UMass; the guys in the Cahners Rotisserie Baseball League (CRBL); the crew at Randy Hundley Baseball Camps; and manuscript reviewers Lynn Kahle at the University of Oregon, C. B. Claiborne at James Madison University, and Richard C. Leventhal at Metropolitan State College.

And, not to forget, copyeditor Kim Field, he of the astute eye and way with words.

There's more, but they know who they are, and I'm out of time and space. Enjoy. And hold onto your wallet – sports marketers are out for it. There are some sports marketers who merit your dollar, and some who don't – be careful how you spend it.

1

Sports Marketing – An Overview

What is sports marketing, and what do we think of it? How do we react to it? Why does it work? When does it work? When doesn't it? Sports marketing is how companies separate themselves these days by identifying with athletic heroes and their prowess. We working stiffs think it's just dandy for the most part, or so we say, and it works because of our powerful emotional attachments with teams and athletes. When sports marketing doesn't work, it's usually because someone didn't match up corporate goals with the benefits to be gained of a particular sports sponsorship opportunity.

Yet, public perceptions are positive. In fact, 93 percent of adults "believe that corporate sponsorships are a good thing or are something they are not concerned about,"[1] according to a study by The Roper Organization for the American Coalition for Entertainment and Sports Sponsorship (ACESS). The study also noted that "76 percent said advertising and sponsorships are a fair price for the entertainment they provide." The study went on to say that "82 percent said corporate sponsorships benefit local communities by presenting events that attract visitors and helping to hold ticket prices down and 76 percent said that corporate sponsorship is a fair price to pay to keep sports on free television and hold down ticket prices."[1]

Corporations have responded accordingly, as shown in Table 1.1, which displays corporate leaders in number of sports sponsored. And Table 1.2 shows the ever-augmenting number of sponsorship dollars being spent over the years 1990-93.

But just what is this thing we call sports marketing? Try these pertinent examples on for size.

Sports Marketing – All Shapes and Sizes

Sports marketing is . . . being a tobacco company in a sensitive time for cigarette manufacturers. At a time when legislators and public policy groups are applying pressure to not only eliminate and restrict tobacco promotion but to eliminate cigarettes, tobacco marketers march on.

TABLE 1.1. Companies that Sponsor the Most Sports

Company	Number	Company	Number
Coca-Cola	17	JC Penney	10
Budweiser	16	Genuine Draft	10
Gatorade	16	Pizza Hut	10
USAir	16	Toyota	10
Delta Airlines	17	AT&T	9
IBM	13	Avis	9
Pepsi	13	Campbell Soup	9
Kodak	13	Canadian Airlines	9
Bud Light	12	Continental Airlines	9
Fuji	12	Evian	9
Reebok	12	MCI	9
Coors Light	11	Met Life Insurance	9
Ford	11	Nike	9
McDonald's	11	Olive Garden	9
Miller Brewing	11	Panasonic	9
Northwest Airlines	11	United Airlines	9
Sprint	11	Upper Deck	9
Chrysler/Plymouth	10		

Source: Sports Sponsor FactBook/Team Marketing Report, October 1993

TABLE 1.2. Sponsorship Spending in America

	1993	1992	1991	1990
Sports	$2.447B	$2.112B	$1.792B	$1.700B
Pop Music/Enter- tainment	$361M	$318M	$364M	$330M
Festivals, Fairs, Annual Events	$333M	$286M	$280M	$250M
Causes	$314M	$254M	$196M	$125M
Arts	$245M	$223M	$168M	$150M
Totals	$3.700B	$3.200B	$2.800B	$2.500B

B = billions, M = millions
Source: International Events Group, 1993.

Phillip Morris is one such marketer. The tobacco company, according to Ina Broeman of Phillip Morris USA, uses sponsorship, including sports sponsorship, to increase sales, entertain clients, and – most importantly – interact directly with its customers in the general public, including the building of extensive databases of consumers. How?

It sponsors everything from bowling tournaments to race cars to music festivals. Phillip Morris's sponsorship of the successful Roger Penske race car team includes signage, premiums, sweepstakes, and on-site sale of its cigarettes and licensed merchandise at races. Its Marlboro Racing News Service is the wire service of auto racing.

Phillip Morris's Virginia Slims tennis tour is a staple of American sports. For 25 years, this sponsorship has built goodwill, supported charities with funds from tournaments, boosted awareness through clinics for customers with top stars, and boosted sales through retail tie-in programs.

Phillip Morris's Merit brand bowling sponsorship is even more impressive. It attracts 800,000 people to its national tournament and holds qualifying events nationwide. A pro-am event in Reno tops off the tournament, with qualifying local winners getting to roll with the top pros. All told, Broeman claims, 40 million people are reached through Phillip Morris's sponsorship programs annually. In Broeman's words, this sponsorship "strengthens the relationship between Phillip Morris brands and the consumers who use them," and it's as easy to do right as matching up consumer demographics, psychographics, and lifestyles with each brand's objectives. It reinforces positionings, boosts awareness, builds databases, increases sales, and generates trial. For example, if a Phillip Morris brand wants to build awareness, it will be the title sponsor of an event. If just generating trial is the goal, associate sponsorship fits the bill.

Merit rolls to success in bowling, Broeman notes, reaching an audience split equally between men and women who have an annual income of $30,000, some college education, an awareness of sports and recreation, and – most importantly – a smoking habit. Bowling is a "smoker-friendly" environment, Broeman notes, and Merit holds its national roll-off in 2,500 bowling centers around the country. Forty-five regional winners advance to the national pro-am in Reno for the trip and thrill of a lifetime. National free-standing insert (FSI) support and a sweepstakes to generate database names provide promotional support. Eight hundred thousand names were added to the database from the tournament in 1993. Broeman calls this a "unique platform to talk to, in a direct way, our Merit consumers." Cigarette makers haven't been allowed to advertise on television for some two decades now, but with sports promotions like this, who needs to buy ad time on television?

Auto racing attracts American men in the 24-to-38 age bracket who like sports and music, Broeman told the International Events Group sponsorship marketing conference in March of 1994. For Marlboro, whose goals are to build sales volume, maintain and increase awareness, and build consumer databases to support all that, sponsoring the Roger Penske racing team was the answer. Penske teams give Marlboro exposure at 13 of 16 Indy car events. (See Chapter 6 for the impressive numerical parameters of auto racing.) At these races, a Marlboro trailer is parked along trailer row to sell product and licensed merchandise. Marlboro signage is everywhere. Retailers are given incentives to feature Phillip Morris brands. National advertising hammers home the sponsorship relationship. The race cars and drivers eventually make trade show appearances on Phillip Morris's behalf. In race-venue bars and taverns, Phillip Morris bar nights, including race car simulators to help consumers have a good time and build the awareness of the sponsorship association, celebrate the race.

All this comes in an atmosphere and time when the American Medical Association is asking Major League Baseball (MLB) to have its teams remove tobacco company signage in stadiums, when stadiums and arenas are increasingly outlawing smoking, and when similar actions are being taken in sporting venues around the country. And sports franchises need the sponsorship money. Virginia Slims is under severe pressure to be removed as a tennis sponsor. But Phillip Morris keeps on rolling. So do others.

Sports marketing is . . . General Mills selling its famous Wheaties brand cereal through its "He didn't have his Wheaties" campaign, which began in 1970 with a baseball slugger named Hank Aaron and continued with the great contemporary sports legend, Michael Jordan.

Sports marketing is . . . Coors sponsoring the Silver Bullets, a women's semipro baseball team that traveled the country in 1994 and 1995 playing men's teams. This was the first time a women's team played men's squads. Silver Bullet is the marketing slogan Coors uses to sell its silver-canned Coors Light.

Sports marketing is . . . Bike Athletic Company, makers of athletic supporters, among other personal equipment, providing souvenir athletic supporters to players in college football's Cotton, Sugar, Orange, Rose, and Fiesta bowls.

Sports marketing is . . . Ocean Spray reaching women through its support of Women's Athletes' Voice of Encouragement (WAVE) by providing scholarships for student athletes and funds for financially strapped athletic programs, helping women's sports reach a new level of esteem, and by using spokespersons like Olympic medal-winning swimmer Summer Sanders to support the program. Ocean Spray's primary consumers are 18- to 44-year-old women.[2]

Sports marketing is . . . the PSP sports marketing promotion agency packaging 25,000 Fan Paks full of major consumer brand samples and coupons for free distribution at major college football games – a surefire way to get beyond just plain old premium distribution.

Sports marketing is . . . Jostens, maker of student recognition products such as class rings, awarding the NCAA Division III Football Coach of the Year award.

Sports marketing is . . . AT&T (and it should come as no surprise) sponsoring NCAA football Long Distance Awards for individual leaders in rushing, passing, receiving, kickoff and punt returns, and punting.

Sports marketing is . . . Refrigeration contractor York International engineering and building a refrigeration system for luge and bobsled tracks for the 1994 Winter Olympics, part of a long history of such refrigeration systems York has supplied to build a better sales environment for itself in its commercial relations.

Sports marketing is . . . how all these companies – and many more – use the emotional attachment of the fans to their sports heroes and teams to position themselves to sell more of their products and services, to increase their awareness and goodwill as the conduit to sports for the average fan (who is increasingly being priced out of the game), and to be sure trade customers feature and promote their products and services.

Sports has become a marketing medium in and of itself, with the ability to target, segment, promote, and cast products and services in heroic lights. More and more companies you'd never think of being remotely attached to sports are using athletics to enhance and embellish their marketing.

Companies like VISA and Coca-Cola that already enjoy universal recognition and sales use sports to reinforce those positionings and to cement their position as the supplier of sports heroics for fans hungry for such and willing to plunk down their plastic to prove it. Only VISA can buy you Olympic tickets, for instance, and only Coca-Cola brings you basketball's Dream Teams. How do some of them do it? How do they tap into consumers' lifestyles and leverage the emotional attachment consumers have as fans to their favorite sports and sports heroes?

McCall's and Stratton Mountain

When the New York Times Company's Women's Magazine group wants to promote itself, it goes to the golf course. No, it doesn't necessarily take prospective clients golfing, and it couldn't possibly help its 4-million-plus readership to tee up. But it can take them to the golf course, get them closer to the golf players they worship, and get other corporations to help them do it. The Times's sponsorship of the LPGA Stratton Mountain Classic brings fans and clients together with premier women golfers for a week of fun and excitement – and a pretty good golf tournament, too. In its magazines (*McCall's, Snow Country, Golf Digest*), players are profiled, and their personal fitness, nutrition, and fashion habits are scrutinized. Associate sponsors were offered 30-second ad spots in the television broadcast of the tournament. A tie-in with a sweepstakes promoted by the 308 Grand Union grocery stores in the Northeast (Stratton Mountain is in Vermont) gave the tournament exposure in a busy retail environment. Twenty-five thousand fans were expected to attend the tournament. Billboards that would be easily viewable during the telecast were made available to associate sponsors.

For *McCall's*, a leading women's magazine, serving as title sponsor allowed it to celebrate women's achievements. One million of its female readers already play golf, a figure that represents 17 percent of all women golfers. Attracting associate sponsors wasn't difficult for *McCall's*, as it already features many of America's leading consumer marketers on its advertiser roster. Being part of the media empire of the *New York Times* made it even easier to leverage that exposure and offer it to associate sponsors. On-site sampling, trade entertainment, and coupon offerings created an opportunity to make cash registers ring at retail.

CIT Financial and Getting in the Door

The CIT Group of financial services wanted to make headway with business prospects and get their business. But how to open the door? Signatures. Signatures of famous baseball players – Willie Mays, Mickey Mantle, and Stan Musial. Targeted executives, decision-makers at prospect companies, received baseballs autographed by Willie Mays along with invitations to inquire about more CIT information. The ball came in a display box with room for two more. A request for more information got the inquirer another autographed baseball. An appointment with a CIT representative filled out the display case – the third ball was delivered by the CIT rep at the meeting. More than 92 percent of targeted respondents requested more information, and CIT garnered $60 million in revenue from the "Signature Series" campaign as well as a Direct Marketing Association Diamond Echo Award.

The University of Virginia Goes to School

The University of Virginia needed to attract sponsors for its increasingly successful football program. To do so, it had to attract fans and profile them, thus convincing prospective sponsors that the targeted customers they wanted to reach were all conveniently gathered at the school's football venue each fall. So it surveyed its fans. Thousands of them. It asked them where they ate, what travel vendors they patronized, what hotels they stayed at, how often they traveled, what cars they owned, what household merchandise they bought and used, and what business or service providers they patronized. The university learned about their fans' personal preferences for everything from airline carriers and athletic footwear to media habits and telephone carriers. They salted it with demographic information and then overlaid the University of Virginia graduate profile.

That meant a lot of masters degrees. That meant people with net worths of more than $400,000. That meant people with $200,000 homes. That meant households where at least one-third of the kids were 18 or younger, and you know how they influence purchase decisions.

Sponsors reach them through collector card game programs that sold eight times more copies than traditional programs. It also meant a Sunday night "Cavalier Call-In" radio show on 25 stations statewide and a growing licensed goods catalog. It meant the ability to tell sponsors where targeted customers around the state were and who they were. It meant a 10 percent sales increase at Hardee's when the collectible cards hit distribution and were offered in tandem with Hardee's food items and a Swatch Watch moving into UVA basketball with a free tuition program through a shootout contest promotion at home games. And it meant that UVA sports would continue to be well funded through sponsor contributions resulting from the university's ability to reach targeted customers in an era in which colleges and their athletic programs were financially strapped.

Schick Hits the Hardwood

What's the biggest tournament you can think of? How about the Schick Super Hoops? On some 800-plus college campuses around the country, Schick is bringing college-age students – who coincidentally are at a time in their lives when they're making shaving product decisions – the opportunity to play in a basketball tournament in which the finalists would find themselves playing in an NBA arena, at halftime in an NBA game. The sampling and awareness opportunities were numerous – 200,000 razors and blades one year – and there was that ever-present aura of goodwill associated with sponsoring such a fun activity. In a universe of some 13 million college students with $9 billion in discretionary income (or about $114 each per month), Schick's program plays perfectly. It's no wonder Timex has tried sponsoring a campus Fitness Week in conjunction with Reebok and that Certs and Trident (like Schick, Warner Lambert brands) hosts a campus intramural volleyball tournament, sprucing up their images on college campuses around the country in the process.

Mazda Goes to the Golf Course

When Mazda needed to address the sales slump of the early '90s (even adjusting its sales goals downward), it turned to the golf course. Like *McCall's*, it just didn't take people golfing. It reached targeted customers and achieved an air of benevolence by linking its association with golf with charitable causes. Mazda knew that women influence 80 percent of car purchases and make 47 percent of all such decisions. Enter the LPGA Women's Golf Championship in Maryland and a charitable tie-in to the Susan B. Komens Breast Cancer Foundation in nearby Washington, D.C. To Mazda, this event – and others like it – enable the company to position itself as an upscale marketer through association with upscale events. In addition, Mazda knew that women buy cars for the same reasons men do (save for, maybe, the reliability/durability factor, which weighs more heavily with men).

Sponsoring the tournament alone isn't the only such activity hosted by Mazda. The car maker sponsored an executive women's golf clinic during the week of the tourney during which 150 local women business executives got pro-level instruction. It also formed a Team Mazda golf marketing tool, with pros like Meg Mallon, Pat Bradley, Patty Sheehan, Hollis Stacy, and Beth Daniel appearing on Mazda's behalf to help Mazda meet its marketing objectives. The whole sponsorship package adds up to Mazda being a Japanese company being able to give something back to the American community to which it sells so many cars – and experience a 9-percent sales increase during its first year of the program.

Budweiser Goes to the Races

Budweiser sold 28 billion bottles of beer in 1990. Part of that was because of its association with motor sports, and sports in general. Or, as then Director of Sports Marketing Mark Lamping puts it, "A high percentage of beer drinkers virtually live and die with their favorite teams."[1] As he notes, "Sports can offer a sales environment that can allow a sponsor to become part of the action. This works particularly well in a product like beer." For Anheuser-Busch, the largest sports marketer in America, that means associations with 75 percent of pro franchises in America. But that's not all.

The Miss Budweiser hydrofoil racing boat has been around for 29 years and Lamping calls it Budweiser's sports marketing benchmark. It helps A-B "reach customers in an environment where they have a key interest in having fun." People enjoy figure skating, too, but its nonmasculine nature will keep Budweiser out of that sport. In the context of a race, Budweiser sponsorship delivers its message to a receptive audience that Lamping says is "less vulnerable to avoidance" of it. The Bud customer, he maintains, fits the "profile of the motor-sports enthusiast," which is why Budweiser is all over motor sports. All told, Busch maintains some 44 percent of the beer market, and in an otherwise static industry, it uses its various sports sponsorship mechanisms to stay in that leadership position.

Planning Makes Perfect – But It's Not Soup Yet

When Tonya Harding's associates executed the now-famous whack on Nancy Kerrigan's knee, they performed a dastardly deed – which happened to boost Campbell Soup fortunes for the first time in a decade. After the incident, Campbell, a sponsor of the United States Figure Skating Association and premier skater Kerrigan, saw a reversal in its red-and-white-can soup line, heightened all along by the buildup to the Olympic showdown and Kerrigan's ultimate silver medal-win-

---

1. Speech at the American Marketing Association Sports Marketing Conference, June 1994.

ning performance. With Kerrigan all over the tube in commercials for Campbell, and making personal appearances for the company and endorsing recipes and nutrition tips, Campbell sales skyrocketed. When the Olympic aura and the controversy wore off, sales leveled off again, and Campbell even retreated from its promotional stance. While Campbell was fortunate and smart to have Kerrigan and the USFSA in its promotional portfolio, no amount of planning could have produced the publicity it received from the wounded knee incident and the sales bump that accompanied it. Campbell was even mistakenly perceived by the general public as a full-fledged Olympic sponsor in 1994, even though it wasn't. Which all goes to show that sometimes sports marketing success goes beyond what you planned – and sometimes it goes beyond what you didn't plan.

Frequent Tri-ers

Saucony makes great running shoes – even *Consumer Reports* magazine rated one of its shoes the best. But the company's sales are still less than half of what Nike spends on advertising. So, to build and maintain loyal customers – customers who want the best shoes when they're new on the market – Saucony works with upscale retailers through its Extra Mile Club, providing incentives for retailers to sign up customers to come back to them for Saucony running shoes by enrolling them in the club and giving the consumers $30 worth of aftermarket products and a $5 rebate on their next purchase. A quarterly newsletter keeps club members posted on new product developments. Saucony reinforces this positioning with its hosting of the Danskin Triathlon series for women and sponsorships of well-known triathlon competitors. In the first three months that it announced the Extra Mile Club in 1992, 800 retailers signed up, as did 6,000 consumers. Saucony uses the back-end information it gained from club members – demographics, psychographics, lifestyle habits – to develop more and better marketing programs and offers to reward its frequent customers and attract others.

Publishing Punch

You've seen *Sports Illustrated* give away every sports video ever made to build circulation. So how do you break into the sports publishing business against all that? If you're *The Diamond*, you position yourself as the history of baseball, tying the great moments of the past into the great thrills of today in baseball. That's what the new monthly did to break in in 1993. After becoming a Major League Baseball licensee, it immediately targeted subscribers from the season ticket holder lists of the league's franchises, hitting the market with a 250,000 circulation guarantee and planning to increase it to 400,000 within one year. With a strategy to get into mailboxes as well as skyboxes and hit the serious baseball fan, the magazine also tied into America's 163 minor league teams – even Little League squads. For an advertiser or sponsor, the magazine will reach into the Major League Baseball Players Association (MLBPA) to arrange to have a legend of the game appear at corporate golf outings or the like. In exchange for their cooperation, *The Diamond* will donate funds from such outings to the retired players' organizations.

Will *The Diamond* be a hit? Does America love baseball?

Ever Hear of Us?

Fortis is not a household word in insurance, but it is a $2-billion company that provides insurance services to businesses around the country. Fortis wasn't an Olympic sponsor in 1992, but when the U.S. Olympic Committee needed coverage for what it describes as its "core" 2,500 athletes, it turned to Fortis, which stepped in to provide coverage above and beyond what official supplier Blue Cross/Blue Shield provided for the 30 days before and after the games. Fortis took advantage of the opportunity to leverage this coverage into its promotional pitch to business clients and to spur its agents to recommend its coverage over competitors. It even motivated the firm to do national television advertising. And Fortis took the package it specially designed for the Olympic Committee and rolled it into a package for its business clients. The new product, according to Fortis, energized its brokers and took off in sales because, in part, of the brokers' abilities to now market it as the package of the Olympics. Now Fortis more regularly advertises on television, especially during special events like the Olympics, which is what gave it the impetus to spread its new wings in the first place and take it beyond being the least known $2-billion company in the insurance industry.

Who Are the Pitches Thrown at – and Why Are They Strikes?

Sports marketing is huge – sponsorship is a $4-billion business in and of itself, according to the International Events Group. Sports marketing, consequently, has become a mainstream portion of major corporate marketing programs. In 1993, sports, according to the consulting/publishing concern, commanded some $2.5 billion of such marketing expenditures.

Coca-Cola is not only a sports sponsor – it's a producer and televiser. Its $1.6-billion Big TV project includes the works of well-known sports personalities like Ted Shaker and appears on networks like Madison Square Garden and SportsChannel. Coke also sponsors locally, from high school all-star games to local 10K races.

In fact, according to *Team Marketing Report's Sports Sponsor FactBook*, Coke sponsors more sports (17) than anyone. Anyone. Budweiser, Gatorade, and USAir were each one sponsorship behind.

Why do companies continue to sponsor at these breakneck paces? A quick look at America's top sports and sporting events tells why. The big four – baseball, football, hockey, and basketball – offer a good view of why corporate sponsors use them as the conduit to fans' hearts.

Baseball

Despite itself, despite its ongoing perception problems caused by ongoing labor strife between owners and players; despite games that can be long and tediously boring games; despite a halving of its leaguewide television revenues; despite all the egos that have combined to give the game a high-priced, overpriced image; the fans continue to patronize baseball and the corporate sponsors continue to court the fans through the game.

In skyboxes – the financial manna from heaven that has owners building new stadiums frantically – corporate sponsors entertain key trade clients and/or consumer winners of sweepstakes. Fans are handed premiums – everything from jerseys to bats to balls to caps to key rings to posters – nearly every time they enter a ballpark. Signage throughout the parks reminds them who the corporate sponsors are that really make the games possible. In game programs (remember when they were just folded pieces of cardboard on which you kept score?) fans read about all their favorite players but primarily view ads inviting them to patronize the sponsors of the team and the league.

Corporations gather retired major leaguers and pit them against fans who win sweepstakes or pay out of their own pockets to compete against and learn from these veterans at week-long fantasy camps. Or they send their favorite trade clients or their suddenly motivated, top-selling field reps to such events.

Why? Attendance numbers in the 60-million-plus range each year is the answer, although, by some estimates, that's not 60 million individuals but the 20 million who can afford to go to increasingly expensive games and ballparks. (See Chapter 8 for indexes of the cost of attending major sporting events.)

In 1991, baseball attendance surpassed that 60-million mark for the first time ever. Along with minor league attendance, baseball was up 9 percent that year. Even with most of the teams out of their respective division races, an average of 36,201 people showed up for all major league games in the last weekend of the 1993 season. The Baseball Hall of Fame in Cooperstown draws crowds pushing a half million each year, even in its remote location in upstate New York. When Miami was poised to receive baseball's blessing for an expansion team (at an entry fee of $95 million), more than 67,000 fans showed up in 1991 for the first exhibition game ever played in the new Joe Robbie Stadium in Miami.

And the Colorado Rockies, based in Denver, have been baseball's busiest team at the turnstiles, recouping their entry fee. Nearly 5 million showed up to watch the sometimes sorry expansion franchise play in 1993, its initial season. Although there is something to be said for winning, sometimes it's just the novelty of being there, and with a new stadium coming on line in 1995, the team's attendance strength is expected to easily continue. The Braves, who began a three-year championship run in the National League West in 1991, started pushing and then breaking their attendance records in Atlanta after more than 20 years there. Yet, in Pittsburgh, where the Pirates were matching that divisional championship feat over roughly the same years, attendance slumped. Maybe fans knew the financially strapped team's best players were headed for more lucrative money in bigger markets and the winning ways were about to go by the boards. Which they did.

Yet, the Chicago White Sox, after a slow attendance start in 1993, picked up momentum as they charged toward a division championship and their first playoff appearance in 10 years. Fans are simply hungry for winners or the novelty of the game, or both. In Colorado and Florida, the two expansion franchises in 1993, attendance approached 8 million combined. Crowds of 70,000 per game were not uncommon at Colorado Rockies games.

This is despite the cost of going to a game being right around $80 for a family of four.

Despite the ongoing labor problems, baseball created – or tried to create – more excitement about itself in 1994 by realigning its divisions from a dual to a tripartite arrangement and by expanding the playoffs to add two teams, including a best-record wildcard team. This is sure to generate more fan interest in more cities where more teams will stay playoff-eligible for longer periods of time in a given season. That should only enhance marketing opportunities, yet the new Baseball Network partnership between MLB and networks NBC and CBS guaranteed only that television revenues to baseball would be half of what they were during the overpriced, billion-dollar years of the CBS contract.

Baseball remains in trouble with the general public, though, despite the ticket prices people pay and the flocks who keep showing up to pay them. An ESPN poll revealed that among kids, the next generation of fans, football is number one, basketball is number two, and baseball is number three in popularity, with only 18 percent expressing the opinion that the national pastime is their favorite game. With owners looking to max revenues now instead of build for the long term, they started nationally telecast playoff games, their most critical television product, at increasingly late hours, alienating the fans of the future who couldn't stay up to watch the conclusions, let alone the fans of the past and present who didn't want to stay up, either. Will maxing out ad revenues now backfire later in eroded fan support? Probably, if it hasn't already. Will it erode corporate sponsor support, pegged at as much as $9 million per team per year? Maybe, if the sport no longer serves as the conduit for the corporation to reach the consumer.

So how do marketers leverage this conduit? Blockbuster Video, with an ownership interest in the Florida Marlins, is the official distributor of MLB home videos. Blockbuster has more than 1,000 stores nationwide. The Score Board, a national marketer and distributor of memorabilia products, has been granted exclusive rights by players like Cal Ripken and stars from other sports to market and distribute memorabilia products with their likenesses and signatures everywhere from national retailers to home shopping television stations. The company has similar rights for many MLB and MLBPA collectible items. Everything from equipment to certain trading cards is covered as The Score Board brings the game closer to the fans and hopefully helps retailers generate more traffic and sales, too.

USA Today – "the nation's newspaper," as it bills itself – tries to solidify that title in part through an agreement with MLB to provide live radio broadcasts of games in progress to airplane passengers, thus enhancing its in-flight entertainment package to travelers, airlines, and its advertisers, too. (Travelers often pay a premium to get a headset; this is primarily to get the movie, but the features and ads accompany the film.)

It goes on and on. MLB trademarks appear on everything from Christmas ornaments to stuffed animals, decorative items to clothing, sporting equipment to personalized gifts. The Chicago White Sox, the Colorado Rockies, the Los Angeles Dodgers, and the New York Yankees traditionally lead the way in licensed merchandise goods sales each season.

Fans snarf up the goods and the chances to get close to the players through these and virtually any other opportunity. Fanfests are increasingly popular, offering offseason weekends celebrating the team and its players and offering sponsors opportunities to introduce and/or reintroduce themselves to fans and media. To be closer to the game, fans pay hundreds of dollars to be wired for interactive television systems that enable them to electronically play along with live games in progress. Of course, why anyone wants to do this instead of just playing along without the system hooked up is beyond this writer. But people want to prove their baseball knowledge, have it electronically stacked up against other armchair managers, and have the opportunity to do it over and over again.

As a sponsor, you don't necessarily have to go to those extents to market your association with the game. Pizza Hut did, offering fans three tiers of prizes for each of three fly balls caught by preselected lucky fans in a pregame promotion. Fans were presented in-store coupons for that day's game that identified the contest and the prize levels, which ranged from free toppings to a free pizza pie altogether. The coupons, assuming there was a winner, had to be redeemed within a few days of that day's game.

Leaf Candies, with its relationships with 20 of MLB's 28 teams, consistently, market to market, offers tickets in exchange for candy wrapper redemptions to push sales, generate retailer in-store feature support for their lines, and motivate their salesmen to pitch retailer participation even harder. Similarly, Kellogg's has handed out many thousands of tickets to games through redemptions by fans of proof-of-purchase seals off cereal boxes. That promotion was so popular that teams often couldn't comply with the specific ticket locations promised because the overwhelming fan response for tickets bumped against actual tickets sold beyond the promotion.

So, increasingly, the corporation becomes and maintains itself as the conduit for the fan to get to the game and get closer to the game, however that may be.

Chicago-based Florsheim helps the Chicago Cubs and its fans honor its great players over the years through a "walk of fame," allowing fans to vote players into it, giving them team posters in return for their completed ballots, and offering them discounts on Florsheim shoes, all in one offer, while also collecting the fans' names and addresses and thus building their database.

The success of such licensing and sponsorship opportunities in great part depends on baseball's marketing and positioning of itself. So, increasingly, the game is reaching out to more and different kinds of fans as much as it can, although the starting times of nationally televised playoff and World Series games might belie that notion. Women's clinics with players and coaches are helping women understand the game better in hopes they'll become better fans – or at least not bother their husbands and boyfriends too much for explanations of what's happening when they accompany them to a game or watch one with them on television.

Knowing it needed to win over kids and that it was about to alienate them through far-too-late-at-night telecasts, MLB let marketers reach out to them. In 1992, Toys'R'Us used not-so-great role model Jose Canseco, then still with the Oakland A's, as the hook in a sweepstakes. To boost store traffic and sales of the Canseco baseball board game, the kids retailer offered extended weekend trips to spring training with Canseco and the A's.

Another marketer offered an MLB birthday kit that included a taped birthday message from the popular player selected by the fan who purchased it. A limited number of star players participated; the kit also included a collectible card and an autographed photo in the kit. It was offered at retail for $7.99.

Then there's sophisticated marketer Nabisco, which, through its Better Cheddars, Oreo, and Wheat Thin brands, offered collectible cards personally autographed by retired star players via redemption of proof-of-purchase of its participating brands. It's one way Nabisco offers its customers ways to be closer to the game and offers retailers chances at more traffic and sales by boosting their participating brands with the pull-through sales power of sports card marketing.

On and on, corporations use the game to let fans feel closer to it through them. One company did it with kids, marketers, databases and a sponsorship with nearly unlimited potential. Chicago-based Ron Berryman, through his Amateur All-Star Baseball Inc. (AABI), enabled marketers to reach young baseball players and their families, and perhaps help these kids grow up to be the baseball fans that the game so sorely needs. Simply put, AABI organized first-ever national tournaments in 1993 for various youth age groups and even got the finals onto ESPN. What AABI offered to national marketers, subsequently, was access to information about a hoped-for half of the nation's 89,000 youth teams, stocked with kids aged 5 to 18 – some 1.6 million of them.

Marketers tagged along. Leaf Candies, already a MLB sponsor, helped teams raise money for equipment by offering a rebate of 15 cents per wrapper. Think about that as a community goodwill builder. Kids literally scoured neighborhoods for wrappers and the promotion helped drive sales and establish goodwill for the company, for the kids' leagues, and their families. One community turned in 27,000 wrappers and received $4,100 for their efforts. Associate sponsors *USA*

Today and Donruss (collectibles) also gained exposure to youths and their families with visibility at league sites all over the country. More importantly, AABI built a potent database of names of kids and families for associate sponsors to latch onto.

That's the kind of marketing power the game of baseball can offer, at its grass roots best, enabling marketers to build customers for life. If MLB can once again build kids' interests and support at that level, maybe its future will be more secure too. Right now, it seems to be collecting immediate profits but trading off long-term uncertainty in return.

Basketball

Basketball is covered more fully in Chapter 3, but a brief overview here will express the marketing power the game has established in its now relentless pursuit to overhaul soccer and become the world's favorite game, which it is near to doing, according to some. More than any other popular American sport, basketball offers the best opportunity to market along with it on the road to global business success.

The power of the NBA is enormous. Its super-star-stocked Dream Teams dominate international competitions and attract enormous amounts of sponsorship dollars and subsequent promotional support. Truly, its sponsors ride its coattails into international markets. Such luminaries as the esteemed writer Frank Deford believe basketball, more than any other game, has a chance to surpass soccer as the world's number one sport. It's already on the way. Licensed merchandise sales of $2 billion for the NBA include its fastest-growing segments – international sales and children's goods sales. Licensees are helping the NBA build the next generation of basketball fans, something baseball has slipped on.

NBA arenas generally operate at some 90-percent-plus capacity. Its stars, without hats, helmets and other hefty gear to mask them, are more recognizable than other sports stars. Attendance continues to grow, even if only nominally in the wake of the retirements of the three greatest stars the league has ever had, if not its three most marketable stars ever: Larry Bird, Magic Johnson, and Michael Jordan. Now, Shaquille O'Neal, the 7-foot, 300-pound slam-dunking rap star, is leading the way as the league's most marketable star, helping the league's identity as well as nearly doubling sales in some segments for manufacturers like Spalding, for whom he endorses products and makes promotional appearances.

NBA-licensed outdoor hoops adorn suburban driveways all over America. When Michael Jordan was active, you could hardly go anywhere in America without seeing someone wearing a red number 23 Bulls jersey. And sponsors and licensees use the full houses at games to distribute premiums that they hope will help endear them into the hearts and awarenesses of potential customers. During games in arenas, you're likely to see the AT&T long-distance shootout for fans selected from the stands during timeouts, and you definitely see it live during the All-Star Game weekend, where the NBA's best long-range shooters battle it out from three-point range. Also that weekend, you'll see the Schick All-Rookie game, which was preceded for years by the game it replaced, the Schick Legends of the Game contest, which featured retired league stars. And there is the Schick's Super Hoops intramural basketball tournament held on college campuses around the country that we mentioned earlier.

What else could you ask for from the NBA? Read all about it in Chapter 3, which is dedicated to the league's marketing prowess. But as Commissioner David Stern says, "Sports is marketing," and the NBA *is* sports right now.

Football

In the aftershock of the implementation of the salary cap that topped off team salaries at some $34 million plus per team, the National Football League rolls on, still scoring licensing success.

Total attendance hit 17,784,354 in 1993, breaking the 1991 record (but just barely). What the league faces is the reality of marketing a product where the components – the teams – are griping and groaning already about not being able to sign the players they need to win, to have depth, and to satisfy fans. Salary-cap demands have forced the retirement of some favorite personalities (Phil Simms, for instance), pay cuts for some established veterans, and new teams for others, whose former teams' fans are angrily awaiting any slipoff in performance because of that player's departure.

Yet, the 1992 trial in which the players achieved free agency only to bargain it away again revealed that some teams were making as much as $8 million or more at the end of the last decade. To make sure that figure holds, the league has tampered with the game again, putting in a two-point conversion after touchdowns that it hopes will generate more excitement for fans. How important a move was that? As the headline in the *Honolulu Advertiser* cried out in announcing the rule change, "The point is, the game had gotten boring."[3]

Trying to generate more excitement is new Philadelphia Eagles owner Jeff Lurie. He paid an all-time sports record $185 million for the franchise and is trying to do everything to please the fans, including guiding the team back to the Super Bowl. He hasn't hesitated speaking personally with fans around town.

Just north up the New Jersey Turnpike, on the other hand, the New York Jets have begun selling games to corporate sponsors to try to squeeze revenues as far as possible. For an extra $60,000 on top of their already-paid sponsorship fee, corporations could have a game in their own name at Giants Stadium, including a scoreboard message, stadium signage, and a program ad announcing the event.

Maybe it's better to do things through NFL Properties (NFLP), the licensing and marketing arm of the league. In fact, speaking of program ads, the NFL is the only league that publishes its own programs leaguewide; this is part of its tripartite principal business areas, the other components being retail sales and corporate sponsorships. In 1991, NFLP had retail sales of $1.5 billion through 400 licensees selling and distributing 3,000 products. In fact, that year NFLP was retailer Foot Locker's number three supplier, trailing only sports shoe heavies Reebok and Nike. Five years before, NFLP had zero sales with that retailer.

Want to catch on with NFLP? Here are some of the categories you can do it in: adult merchandise; kids' merchandise; back-to-school supplies; linens; tailgate accessories; the automotive aftermarket; swimwear; pet supplies; baby merchandise; and bowling gear. NFL Team Shops can be found in major retailers, through which the league has marketed "tee boy and girl" contests (another database-name builder). It even got MLB teed off at it by using all-star pitcher Orel Hershiser in an ad (which was quickly pulled) endorsing NFLP merchandise.

And while then NFLP Vice President Don Garber admits that "people aren't breaking the doors down to pay the NFL $1 million to become a sponsor," league sponsor revenues were $50 million that year.[2] Tie-in marketing also allows NFL sponsors to bask in a positive glow through the league's $65 million or more donation raised through its activities for United Way.

But don't think you have to market leaguewide only. Things can be customized. The league's largest sponsor, Coca-Cola, has each of its ads customized for all 28 markets. Using stock footage from the league, this is usually easy and inexpensive to do.

Sponsors like Coca-Cola are on board because the NFL reaches women – 39 percent of its television audience is female. That's why NFL-sponsored, free-standing inserts in your Sunday newspaper are so popular.

But nothing replaces winning. The Dallas Cowboys catapulted back to near the top of the heap in licensed merchandise sales after getting back into the habit of winning Super Bowls in the '90s. The Los Angeles Raiders retain their seemingly eternal position as number one, though.

The silver and black of the Raider is just one of America's best-known trademarks that belong to the NFL. Its trademarks, according to surveys, are recognized by some 95 percent of American men. The "Monsters of the Gridiron" promotion with Coca-Cola last year was one of the NFL's largest ever and generated hundreds of thousands of phone calls from fans calling in to try to win prizes after qualifying by checking symbols on the inside of bottle caps. To get those gifts, of course, they had to purchase the bottles. Talk about building a database, store traffic – and sales.

The NFL offers companies opportunities to market themselves in a healthy aura. It allows Apex-One to market its Anti-Shox athletic shoe insert as the insert in the shoes of 550 NFL players (which it is).

But nothing symbolizes the NFL more than the Super Bowl. Every year it seems to provide some $50 million or more in economic benefits for the host city and to knock down incredible television ratings. The 1994 Buffalo/Dallas game was supposedly viewed by 134 million people. Every year, therefore, the nation's major consumer products marketers

---

2. Speech to the American Marketing Association Sports Marketing Conference, May 1991.

choose the Super Bowl to unveil new products and/or marketing themes and campaigns. Yes, the Bud Bowl continues to be as watched with as much interest as the Super Bowl it helps sponsor. And yes, ad time on the game will soon hit $1 million per 30-second spot.

It's also the place where Campbell serves soup out of a 600-gallon vat. It's where 81 percent of the game attendees are there on some corporation or another's tickets. It's a game where advertiser recall runs high (three times what normal television programming gets) and sponsors get lots of free publicity through media coverage of their marketing plans. Nike, Frito-Lay, Anheuser-Busch, McDonald's, Pepsi and Coke make their year's worth of awareness at the game. It's where Frito-Lay kicked off its challenge to see if anyone could "eat just one" and where the game program contains nearly $3 million worth of advertising and hits $1.9 million in circulation revenue. And the game is broadcast everywhere from Scandinavia to Russia. Each year, fans tell marketing researchers they only have more interest in the game than they did the year before.

But football has to get past its own financial problems, many of which were created by the new salary-cap and free-agency arrangements and fallout from the now-famed Freeman McNeill free-agency trial of 1992. For some reason, the league is still trying to generate international interest through the World League of American Football, its offseason breeding ground for talent that is played primarily in European metro hubs. The NFL's resurrection is on the heels of its failure earlier this decade. And the league does play exhibition games in Japan and Europe, although attendance actually declined for its European exhibition in 1994.

But the Canadian Football League likes America. Seeing opportunity where two previous leagues failed against the NFL, the CFL has opened three American franchises and installed its wide-open, free-wheeling style of play in Sacramento, Baltimore, and Shreveport, Louisiana.

Maybe, just maybe, it's following on the heels of the suddenly rejuvenated National Hockey League (NHL).

Hockey

The year is 1980. The United States has just won the Olympic hockey gold meal. A guy named Wayne Gretzky is emerging as the greatest magician to ever lace up ice skates – and we don't mean figure skating. A National Hockey League dynasty in Edmonton is about to be followed up by one in New York.

Hockey is on a roll, right? The game will earn its share of the sports market dollar from fans and corporate sponsors alike, right? It has earned a spot right up there with football, still-slumping pro basketball and – dare we say it – the national pastime of baseball, right?

Not. The game disappeared. It struggled to get national television coverage. It tried local pay-per-view. It kept home games off free television. It watched basketball race by.

Since then, slowly but surely, hockey has struggled back. It has opened for business in former unheard climes, from northern California to Florida to Texas and other Sun Belt markets where fans have shown great support for the teams, which have racked up beyond-your-wildest-dreams licensed goods sales. It has gotten itself on TV and has had the privilege of having at least one of the United States' two biggest markets represented in its Stanley Cup finals two years in a row. It has lost its hard-to-understand divisional names and replaced them with more understandable divisional alignments – like East and West. And it brought in a former NBA executive to be its commissioner (its first ever), who was there when that league and that sport rose to popularity beyond belief.

Regardless, hockey still has a long way to go. Fighting continues to be a debate in terms of the game's marketability. So is the puck – its visibility, that is – in terms of the game's television potential. Hockey remains hard to televise. Not only that, like its sports brethren, it faces potential labor strife and image problems. But it's addressing them – all of them – and is making headway. How much and how much room to grow exists are the questions facing the league as it aggressively markets itself and marketers face up to latching on – and to what degree.

Hockey was definitely on the way up as the '90s rolled on. Former NBA general counsel Gary Bettman became the league's commissioner. League attendance averaged 13,417 per game, ticket prices averaged $25 per and player salaries had soared to an annual average of $650,000. The league needed to clean up its fighting-marred image and expand its fan base through expansion and television.

Those were all Bettman priorities as he tackled the 75-year-old league. He brought in an NBA crony to help work on television. San Jose, Ottawa, Dallas, Tampa Bay, and Miami became franchise locales. Bettman immediately stated he wanted to keep the game affordable to fans and clean up its fight-marred image.

San Jose, with its black-and-teal uniforms, became a smash hit. It immediately soared to the top of the licensed-goods sales pile. NHL licensed-goods sales got a shot in the arm when rap singers, seeking new twists to their funky outfits, began showing up and performing in hockey duds, an unplanned boost to NHL popularity.

Still, problems persisted. Bruce McNall, the aggressive owner of the Los Angeles Kings, has had to sell his interest in the team due to business problems. The Minnesota North Stars, in one of America's most hockey-crazed states, folded up shop there and moved to Dallas. (Despite crowds of 14,000 regularly, the team claimed to have lost $24 million in about three years.) And the Stanley Cup-dominant Pittsburgh Penguins were a bargain basement sale at $31 million plus.

Fighting still prevailed. Instant replay was booed and debated. Unpopular shootouts instead of overtimes were floated as an idea for game tiebreakers. And with expansion came not only new audiences and fans, but diluted talent and charges of a hold-and-clutch style of play that limited scores and scoring opportunities. Hockey fight videos were advertised as gift ideas.

And in 1992 the players went on strike just before the playoffs, angering fans and nearly forcing a playoff cancellation. In 1994, contract talks between players and owners centered around a salary cap, the very thing that put the baseball players into strike mode that same year. As Blackhawks owner Bill Wirtz put it, success for hockey in the '90s "will come down to one thing – how we do at the bargaining table with the players," a hint that a good, solid collective bargaining agreement in the owners' favor would maintain the profitability, marketability, and longevity of the game.[3]

That notwithstanding, hockey, an international game, is still not a global marketing force. There are former and future NHL players in the Olympics, but no Team USA/NHL or Team Canada/NHL. Russia and other countries send touring teams over to North America only to

---

3. Speech to business breakfast club meeting, Chicago, October 16, 1990.

have NHL owners gripe and moan over having the regular season broken up by the exhibition contest. But with Bettman in charge, the NHL is starting to play international exhibitions; when it went into London in 1993 it was greeted enthusiastically by the Brits. If other sports can sell overseas, hockey wants to get its share there, too.

Hockey thinks it's on a roll now. With the tremendously exciting Stanley Cup finals of 1994, fueled by the presence of a New York-market team, the league is making rumblings in the media that its popularity can approach that of the NBA. While that's a stretch, NHL collector cards are only in the households of 9 percent of collectors, according to the research firm Market Facts's Telenation poll in April of 1993, ranking it far behind basketball, football, and number-one baseball.

Expansion teams in the Sun Belt, roller hockey, and minor league hockey may have ridden to the rescue of the NHL, however. In-line skating, popularized by Rollerblade, was a $243 million industry in 1992, up 13 percent from 1993 according to the National Sporting Goods Association. Now, the suddenly popular roller hockey is commanding a strong percentage of those sales, up to 50 percent at sporting goods retailers. Roller Hockey International is now a league, with former NHL stars playing and cable television broadcasting it. Regardless of small crowds and limited television, hockey is capturing some fans out of this, fans who were previously just in-line skaters but got attracted to the game on wheels and translated that into ice hockey interest.

All this despite the Federal Consumer Products Safety Commission declaring in-line skating a very dangerous sport in July of 1994. And despite the NHL's New Jersey Devils suing their roller hockey counterparts in an attempt to get them out of their arena in the Meadowlands on the grounds that they draw fans away from the Devils. (A judge threw out the 1993 suit.)

But no one can throw out the undeniable strength of the expansion franchises, particularly in California and Florida, and the Dallas Stars, relocated from Minnesota. The best of the expansion bunch, the San Jose Sharks, immediately became a sellout smash in northern California. They sold 8,300 season tickets in their initial season. They accounted for $100 million worth of NHL licensed-goods merchandise sales in their first year. But there was still a lot to be learned about the game there. When a fan threw a hat on the rink after a player scored a third (hat trick) goal, an usher began to throw him out for littering.

The Florida Panthers also exploded. Based in Miami and playing to an audience of obviously relocated hockey fans in south Florida, they too became an immediate, near-sellout hit and played to 95 percent capacity their first season, in which they challenged for a playoff spot. The team set a record for most wins by a first-year expansion team and with owners like Wayne Huizenga (Blockbuster Video), an aggressive team can be expected continually. The team has been a marketing success, scoring sponsorships from local corporations, including south Florida-based Alamo Rent-A-Car's hat-trick savings rate for Panther followers, which included free perks and premiums with the cars.

The Mighty Ducks of Anaheim, of course, were a movie and a sequel before they were a hockey franchise. They sold 12,000 season seats before they ever hit the ice. And they have the Disney Company ownership behind them, which made and marketed the Mighty Ducks movies. If any marketers can turn hockey into family entertainment from brawling, Disney and Blockbuster can.

If they can't, they can turn to minor league hockey, like the International Hockey League, based in Indianapolis. With average ticket prices in the $10 range, team associations with NHL clubs, Prime Network television coverage, and an image for entertainment rather than fighting, leagues like this have exploded in popularity, playing as well in Sun Belt (San Diego, Las Vegas) towns as in traditional hockey markets.

Can, or will, hockey overcome itself and become the marketing success that baseball, football, and basketball have become – and that soccer wants to be in the United States?

With all the media options approaching, with all the problems and potentials facing other event marketers, and with all the discussion you're about to find about in this book, you'll probably be able to make up your own mind.

References

[1]   Ernie Saxton's *Motorsports Sponsorship Marketing News*, December 1993, p. 5.

[2]   "Playing the New Game of Sports Marketing," *Food Business*, Jan. 3, 1994, p. 9.

[3]   "The Point Is, The Game Had Gotten Boring," *Honolulu Advertiser*, March 23, 1994, p. 1.

Ambush Marketing

"Ambush marketing" is that which gives the appearance of an official association with an event when no such contracted or official association actually exists.

An example are the American Express advertisements that give consumers a feeling that its credit card is an integral part of tourists' Olympic Games' experiences when in fact it is VISA that is the official card of the games and the only one accepted at official games' venues. American Express has gone to great pains in the 1990s to give the appearance that it has an association with the Olympics. This is an explicit attempt to thwart VISA's official sponsorship and its promotional positioning that it is accepted at desirable places that American Express is not.

But the reigning definition of ambush marketing is that of professors David Shani and Dennis Sandler. In 1989, while at New York City's Baruch College Department of Marketing, they defined it as: "*A planned effort (campaign) by an organization to associate themselves indirectly with an event in order to gain at least some of the recognition and benefits that are associated with being an official sponsor.*"[1]

Research Shows that Ambush Marketing Works

Shani and Sandler's study of the impact of ambush marketing reveals that it works. Ambush marketers can create an aura of being an official sponsor by sponsoring the telecast of the event as opposed to the event itself. A survey by Shani and Sandler – part of their study of the 1988 Winter Olympics – showed that 20 percent of the respondents recalled official sponsors. Thirty-nine percent recalled sponsors in general. The more the respondents watched the games on television, the more likely they were to respond correctly to official sponsor identification inquiries.

But there was not much difference, they found, in the ability of respondents to separate official from ambush sponsors. While Shani and Sandler concluded their study by saying "official sponsors were able to achieve significantly higher levels of awareness than nonsponsors who attempted ambush strategies," they went on to note that "in only four of seven product categories studied were the correct official sponsors identified more than nonsponsors."

While Shani and Sandler recognize the value and awareness levels established from official sponsorship, they do note that ambush marketers can cause confusion, and later in this chapter we'll see how some have done that. Especially during Olympic competitions, shrewd marketers have utilized carefully crafted advertising and marketing to emit an aura of being an official sponsor, even though they're not one in any way, shape, or form.

In 1993, meanwhile, the professors updated their work. (Sandler was still at Baruch College, but Shani had moved to Kean College of New Jersey.) Their subject was the 1992 Summer Olympic Games from Barcelona, Spain. Their mission was simple: How well can consumers correctly identify official sponsors of a major sports event? What effect do ambushers have on identification? Does sponsorship affect consumers' attitudes towards sponsors or influence their purchase intentions?[2]

One hundred and eighty-nine respondents broke down this way: 126 correctly identified VISA as the official credit card, but 50 said it was American Express; 64 respondents said AT&T was the official long-distance sponsor, while 70 split their vote between ambushers MCI and Sprint; 31 said United was the official airline, while 35 improperly identified ambusher American; 143 correctly identified Coca-Cola as the official soft drink, while no one identified anything else; 59 remembered Jeep was the official auto, but 41 said Chevrolet;

and 137 recalled McDonald's as the official fast-food restaurant, with *zero* naming anyone else.

Explanation? Did some official sponsors leverage their sponsorship positions better than others? Obviously. Did some ambushers leverage their opportunities better than others and nearly as well as official sponsors who paid millions and millions of dollars more to wear that title? Obviously, as well.

While respondents to the study also expressed the sentiment that they do not mind corporate sponsorship of athletic events so that they can be brought to American television and the public eye, that attitude obviously did little, in some cases, to separate official sponsors from ambush marketers.

Respondents told Shani and Sandler that, as consumers, *ambushing did not appear to be of much concern*. Only 20 percent said they were angered by unofficial sponsor attempts to portray themselves as official sponsors through ambush tactics. Only 25 percent said they would like to see a mechanism in place that would enable them to differentiate more easily between ambush marketers and official sponsors.

Those kinds of attitudes are the stuff ambush marketing campaigns are made of, as both professors would agree. Back to American Express, for instance. Since the 1992 Winter Olympic Games in Albertville, France, the firm has quite loudly declared its value in its marketing communications to consumers who want to attend the games at any of its locations. Calling VISA's campaign "misleading,"[1] American Express proceeded to try to undercut its rival's approximate $20 million expenditure as an official Olympic sponsor with a new campaign. The point? American Express is as accepted around Olympic venues as VISA is (everywhere but the ticket gate, that is).[3]

A newspaper insert just prior to the Games' commencement headlined "American Express Cardmember's Guide To The Winter Games" declared "we'd like to take a moment and let you know all that we're doing to support you . . . Rest assured, we're there for you. In addition to our 42 travel locations throughout France, we recently opened six new customer service centers around the Games."

Did the tactic pay off? You decide. You've read about the Shani/Sandler research. Another study released shortly after those games by Performance Research, Inc., a sports-marketing tracking firm out of Newport, Rhode Island, revealed that 55 percent of its respondents correctly identified VISA as the 1992 Winter Olympics Games credit-card sponsor. Yet, 30 percent said it was American Express.

The same survey turned up interesting numbers in other categories. Both Kmart and Sears far outdistanced JC Penney as being recognized as official games sponsors, even though Penney it was. United Airlines doubled the count on recognition as official sponsor over rivals American and Delta, but combined, the ambushers virtually dead-locked United. Tylenol was identified by 41 percent of respondents as official pain-relief sponsor. Unfortunately, Nuprin was the official sponsor in this category, but only 15 percent of respondents recalled that. Chrysler/Jeep was double-digit percentage points ahead of rivals Buick and Subaru in official-sponsor recall. But combined, the two ambushers equaled Chrysler/Jeep's recall as an official sponsor.[4]

Is there consumer confusion out there? You bet. And so ambush marketing goes on and on and on, like a certain bunny that ambushes its advertising rivals but can't stand to have itself mimicked.

Even though Pepsi has been unable to even dent Coke in awareness levels as an official Olympic sponsor, the firm has taken its ambush potshots. For instance, it got Coke up in arms shortly before the 1992 Summer Olympic Games in Barcelona by using its pro basketball all-star spokesperson, Earvin "Magic" Johnson, in an ad promoting its signature brand in which he's being encouraged to do well by supporters. Johnson, of course, was a member of the U.S. Olympic "Dream Team" that year, of which Coke was the official soft-drink sponsor.[5]

That same kind of marketing relationship initially kept NBA super-star Shaquille O'Neal off Dream Team II, which played in the World Championships in 1994 in Toronto. O'Neal has an agreement to endorse Pepsi, while the team – again – is sponsored by Coke. Only such a conflict or an injury could keep a player of O'Neal's stature, profile, and talent off the greatest team money could assemble at a time when the NBA was establishing him as its next great worldwide superstar representative on the heels of the retirements of Larry Bird, Johnson, and Michael Jordan.

Meanwhile, the debate rages on whether official sponsorship is better than ambush marketing. The research to date, presented here, is inconclusive at best, depending on your product or service category. Another Performance Research study, completed prior to the 1994

Winter Olympics in Norway, showed that 43 percent of respondents could not (unaided) name official Olympic sponsors. Thirty-four percent were unaware it was an Olympic year. Sixty-eight percent "confirmed VISA's sponsorship role," but "more than half (52 percent) indicated that AMEX [American Express] was also involved."[6]

The evidence, and the tracking thereof, is compelling in two ways. On the one hand, true sponsorships are noted by the consuming public. On the other hand, ambush marketing attempts at establishing true-sponsorship positionings also are effective. Much further study is obviously called for to determine the effectiveness levels. But truly, the research reveals, it has an impact.

And it can get expensive. And involve lawyers. And courtrooms. And judges. And official judgments. And so the National Hockey League (NHL) and Pepsi did square off – or should we say face off – a few seasons ago.

The National Hockey League versus Pepsi

The National Hockey League is a lumbering, slumbering giant, rolling in money but stuck a few decades behind most other sports in marketing expertise and muscle. While expansion into new, lucrative markets has keenly enhanced its position, and while it is trying to make new television arrangements and clean up its image on and off the ice, hockey remains a marketing mystery despite its periodic successes (see Chapter 1). That perception came through loud and clear when Pepsi/Canada unveiled an ambush-marketing campaign that truly caught the league with its collective shorts down. Not only that, but it took a Canadian judge, as opposed to any marketer or promoter, to lay down the definitive rules and parameters that make an ambush marketing attempt successful.

Sometimes the true effectiveness of an ambush promotion can be seen in how long it takes the ambushed party's legal department to respond. In the case of *NHL v. Pepsi/Canada*, it was pretty quickly. Here's the scenario:

The NHL brought suit in 1992 against Pepsi-Cola/Canada, claiming the firm's "Diet Pepsi $4,000,000 Pro Hockey Playoff Pool" and "Pepsi

Shoot and Score Pro Hockey Draft" promotions in 1990 and 1991 violated the league's registered trademark usage.

Specifically, the promotions offered consumers chances to win cash (up to $10,000) and free soft drinks by collecting game pieces inside bottle caps. As with standard promotional procedures, Pepsi-Cola/Canada clearly printed the odds of winning, prizes, dates, parameters, and so forth. More importantly, its literature for the promotion included the following disclaimer: "Diet Pepsi's $4,000,000 Pro Hockey Playoff Pool is neither associated with nor sponsored by the National Hockey League or any of its member teams or other affiliates."

Hockey player images were used, as were NHL franchise city names, but not team names. To win the playoff pool, fans had to have bottle caps denoting the winning team of a given best-of-seven playoff series and the number of games it took to win. Prizes were redeemed by mail.

While granting that Pepsi had not used any NHL trademarks, the NHL contended in court that "the promotions confuse the public into believing Pepsi has an official relationship with the league [and] the league also claims Pepsi benefited from the falsely perceived association, while official league sponsors [Coke] and the league itself were damaged."[7]

NHL attorney Gil Stein told this author in an interview at the time of the lawsuit that Pepsi's marketing tactics made their promotion suspicious. "When you decide to use a disclaimer," he said, "it's an admission you're misleading the public. It's a passing off (Canadian terminology for a false or deceptive presentation), which shows that the basic thing is misleading. People don't even see them (disclaimers). Pepsi very clearly put on the promotion indicating a tie-in with the NHL. We asked them not to do it. They refused. They left us with no choice but to go to court."

Oh, to what lengths marketers and trademark holders will go to protect their trademarks. But what did the court think? And what did Pepsi garner, if anything, from the alleged trademark-violating promotion?

The British Columbia Supreme Court in Vancouver, in a ruling from Justice Stephen Hardinge, clearly ruled in Pepsi's favor, albeit grudgingly. A hockey fan himself, Hardinge was clearly disgusted that the integrity of Canada's national game was dragged through the mud in his courtroom. Where the NHL alleged the promotions were "an unlawful interference with [its] relations with Coke," Hardinge ruled that "the plaintiffs' [NHL] sole product is hockey games while that of the defendants is soft drinks. There is no possibility therefore, that the Contest could have misled the public into believing the defendant's product was that of the plaintiff."[8]

Hardinge also contended that the NHL's complaint that the advertising supporting the promotion indicated a direct connection between the NHL and Pepsi was not substantiated by the NHL in its presentation to the court. Even though former NHL coach Don Cherry was the promotion's pitchman on television during "Hockey Night In Canada" broadcasts, Hardinge did not budge on this point.

However, because official NHL sponsor Coke does not have exclusive advertising rights during those broadcasts among soft-drink companies, and because Cherry was not a paid NHL employee or endorsee, again, Hardinge said, the NHL/Pepsi connection could necessarily be implied or inferred. "Having viewed the T.V. advertisements several times and read the printed material relating to the Contest, I am unable to say that the Contest suggests, to my mind, that the plaintiffs approved, authorized or endorsed the Contest in any way or that there was some form of business connection between the defendant and the plaintiffs," Hardinge said in official court documents.[9] In essence, he ruled, "there is neither evidence nor the appearance of passing off."

Hardinge similarly dismissed the NHL's contention that the disclaimer usage in and of itself was an admission of guilt, especially since league attorneys went on from there to say the disclaimer was inadequate. Well, which is it?, he wondered in court documents. "In the present case," he said, "the wording of the disclaimer was unambiguous. Anyone reading the disclaimer could come to no reasonable conclusion but that the NHL and its member teams had nothing to do with the Contest," although he went on to state that he would have liked to have seen the disclaimers displayed more visibly and for greater lengths of time, particularly in the supporting television advertisements for the promotion.

Furthermore, Hardinge ruled, with the NHL having failed, in his ruling's view at least, to have established that Pepsi falsely created a link between itself and the NHL in an official sponsorship capacity, then the NHL's contention that any of its trademarks had been violated held no water at all.

Slowly but surely, Hardinge continued in his opinion to partially rewrite ambush marketing rules, regulations, and law in Canada – if not everywhere else.

As to the NHL's contention of economic damages, Hardinge said there was no interference with Coke's ability to do its contracted business as an NHL licensee, and that Pepsi had not deliberately tried to block that contractual license, which would have been grounds for him to rule otherwise. While the Coke/NHL contract, Hardinge noted, protects Coke from ambush marketing, it does not protect Coke (or the NHL) from lawful marketing exercises like the one Hardinge was ruling on.

That Pepsi interfered with future business opportunities for NHL licensee Coke was also dismissed because the promotion, in and of itself, was not illegal.

In short, Hardinge summed up, "The Contest did not constitute the tort of passing off, it did not infringe any of the plaintiff's registered marks, and did not interfere with the plaintiff's business relations."

Pepsi also had argued that its promotion was based entirely around the results of officially completed games that were in the public domain, and that while its contest was a game of chance, it was not a form of gambling. Plus, no trademarked NHL team names, or anything else, were used. And "if I don't use it, how can I have violated it?", a prominent trademark law attorney (who declined to allow his name to be used because of his and his firm's close ties to the actual case) told this author. That same lawyer did say, though, that the disclaimer, while clearly not associating the promotion with the NHL, was a "circular argument" that the judge ostensibly could have dismissed and that the NHL's position that the disclaimer's use was a virtual admission of guilt by Pepsi/Canada was pretty much as on target as the NHL was going to get in this case. Still, he welcomed the ruling as defining a body of law and operations in promotional marketing for trademarks and sports entities.

The NHL, for its part, had argued that the "hundreds of millions of dollars" in annual revenues it receives were in part generated from agreements like the one it has with Coke, and that Pepsi, albeit without mentioning Stanley Cup or NHL, clearly identified itself with those named playoff games. In other words, there weren't any other pro hockey playoff games that match up to the cities that the Pepsi promotion highlighted. Therefore, any association with such was a violation of NHL trademarks and a "passing off" of an official tie-in with the league. In addition, the NHL contended, Coke – not Pepsi – was the only soft-drink company licensed to take such marketing.

Pepsi's action, in effect, did not therefore "dilute the exclusive license to [Coca-Cola Ltd.] and [does] diminish the rights of [Coca-Cola Ltd] and therefore the market value thereof to the plaintiffs." The contest and the commercials to support it, the NHL contended, were "clearly designed to tie into and trade upon the goodwill and reputation of the Plaintiffs and to thereby misrepresent or create confusion with the public as to the Defendant's relationship with the Plaintiffs."

Through all of this, "the Defendant will be unjustly enriched thereby," the NHL said, and is "undercutting the rights of [Coca-Cola Ltd.] in a manner calculated to cause and in fact [is] causing loss and damage to the plaintiffs." The NHL suit never specified the amounts of loss or damages sought, other than declaring its desire to have the contests halted immediately at Pepsi's expense.

Pepsi countered that because the games were in the public domain, their results were eligible for contest usage like this, and that while an NHL association may indeed exist, "No reasonable person would either consider it relevant or be confused as to whether or not the contest was sponsored by the Plaintiffs," namely the NHL. Pepsi claimed nothing more than using officially published game results as the crux for its promotional campaign. And, without specifying amounts, it countered that the NHL and Coke suffered no loss or damage because of Pepsi's promotional activity.

While Pepsi did win the case, lawyers at the Heenan Blaikie law firm, which has offices throughout Canada, assured business/promotion clients that there was no carte blanche on ambush marketing in Canada, despite the ruling.[10] "Property owners," began an article in the firm's newsletter, *Marketing and Advertising Law,* "and sponsors needn't panic too much; although Pepsi won, it doesn't mean 'ambush marketing' is legal. Ambush marketing refers to a whole range of activities and may include a panoply of executions. Each case will have to be judged on its own merits."

The lawyers cited the importance of Pepsi's disclaimer in winning the case, and a significant NHL *faux pas*– that of submitting a consumer survey showing that fans clearly associated such a contest with an official NHL sponsorship position. But because the survey was conducted only among fans in greater Vancouver, the judge promptly disallowed it, regardless that its findings were obviously slanted in the plaintiff's favor.

Right down the line, point for point, Pepsi won the case by proving that properly conceived and administered ambush marketing efforts are permissible. The NHL, which netted $2.6 million from Coke for the sponsorship agreement according to the Heenan Blaikee article, obviously was going to vigorously prosecute any perceived-to-be illegal association with its trademarks.

The NHL did file an appeal after the final ruling. And in May of 1993, it got part of an answer. An unwelcome one.

The British Columbia Supreme Court, which had already been decidedly unimpressed with the NHL's prosecution of its original case a year earlier, ruled that the NHL had to pay some $225,000 in legal fees to Pepsi for its costs incurred in originally defending the case. The amount was escalated because the NHL was accused of (and found liable for) trying to withhold testimony by its own Wayne Gretzky, arguably the game's greatest player. Gretzky was going to be called as a Pepsi witness. Hardinge, ruling on the Gretzky portion of the case, said the "misconduct of the Los Angeles Kings [Gretzky's club] in seeking to avoid an order of this court is scandalous, outrageous, and reprehensible conduct deserving of chastisement."

Above all else, said yet another Canadian attorney, "If you're going to ambush, avoid use of trademarks, and do use a disclaimer."

Yet, sometimes all of those precautions and the best intentions can't avoid a lawsuit. MasterCard, official credit card of the World Cup 1994 soccer tournament's first-ever appearance in the United States, sued long-distance carrier Sprint and the event organizing committee for infringement when Sprint issued a calling card with the World Cup logo. MasterCard claimed such use was only allowed on the plastic it issues. In its defense, Sprint said its card and the usage of the World Cup logo thereon was within its sponsorship rights as official long-distance carrier of the tournament and that the card to which it applied the logo was a calling card only, not a credit card, as MasterCard's is.

In summary, ultimately, ambush marketing remains in vogue. Marketers will continue to rely upon it regardless of rulings like the one in the Pepsi/NHL case and regardless of which way that ruling went. Marketers and lawyers in the United States claim that trademark enforcement statutes are more vigorously enforced and interpreted by American courts than by those in Canada, but most marketers are expert at skirting such guidelines until they caught or legally barred from doing so. In fact, ambush marketing and trademark infringement are so rampant that they are nearly impossible to police, let alone enforce.

"There is no way to legally stop ambushing," Professor Shani told this author in an interview with his research partner Sandler in 1991. "We think the best thing these [event] organizers can do is educate these sponsors how to best or better use their sponsorships."

"The initial advantage is to the sponsor," said Professor Sandler, "if he's doing the right thing with it." And that is? Leverage it, to the max. "Match and exceed the sponsorship fee to make the sponsorship work. Being an official sponsor is a purchase to spend more money."

"Being a sponsor is always better than ambushing," said Shani, noting that at another level, "The sponsors in local events are doing tremendously. They have a higher percentage [of] recall than Olympic sponsors." The professors concur that there is a goodwill halo from sponsoring events, and that even if consumers can't identify the specific event you sponsor, they will probably, at the very least, associate you with the sport. That leads to better trade relations too, they said. In their words, while most "consumers can't say specifically what event they sponsored . . . [they can] associate you [sponsor] with the sport."

Shani and Sandler believe that official sponsors and event-rights' holders will increasingly tighten the ways in which they control their trademarks and monitor any infringements. They suspect that a movement toward European methods could occur. Many European pro soccer and pro basketball teams bear the names of their sponsors rather than typically American use of animal or symbol nicknames and monikers, thus automatically protecting that trademark in every way, shape, and form. Both Shani and Sandler predicted that the 1996

Atlanta Summer Games won't become the Coca-Cola Olympics (after all, they will be held in Coke's geographic backyard, in great proximity to its international headquarters). "Where it will stop, I don't know," Shani said, in terms of extent of sponsorship and extent of trademark protection and making oneself ambush-proof.

American attitudes may not lag far behind those methodologies. In the 1994 Performance Research survey on American attitudes toward the Olympics and sponsorship, 25 percent of respondents said they wouldn't mind specifically titled Olympic events in sponsors' names, but 34 percent were dead set against it. Respondents also said they'd make a point of buying Olympic sponsors' products and services, but not where the sponsorship was perceived to be pursued only for promotional purposes and not to help the United States win more gold medals.

Then again, sometimes you don't have to do very much work to be a successful ambush marketer. Sometimes your official sponsor will do it for you by not leveraging it well, or at all. In the Performance Research survey, only eight percent of respondents properly associated Home Depot with its official sponsorship position for the 1994 Winter Olympic Games. Nonsponsors Sears (39 percent) and Wal-Mart (25 percent), and 1992 sponsor JC Penney (33 percent) all received considerably more awareness as official sponsors – at considerably less expense.

The 1994 Winter Olympics – Ambush Redux

Post-1994 Winter Olympic surveying confirmed what expert marketers already knew: leverage your sponsorship or be vulnerable to ambush.

Again, Performance Research measured consumer perceptions and attitudes about sponsorship, and again hit home with the aforementioned message to marketers. Consumers consistently did not get the message when it came to sponsorship – namely, who the official sponsors were – in several categories. Much of this was attributed to the official sponsors doing a less-than-credible job leveraging their sponsorships, and/or ambush marketers doing a terrific job creating an aura about themselves that said "official sponsor."

If nothing else, Performance Research's work showed that Olympic sponsors could be doing a better job with their sponsorships, especially since many consumers responded that they were likely to purchase sponsors' products because some percentage of the sponsoring companies' sales went toward helping the United States win more Olympic medals, a powerful testimony to the emotional pull and appeal of the games.

Among consumers who said they watched at least three nights of the televised coverage of the 1994 Winter Olympics, 17 percent could not name any official sponsors in unaided recall. Only four percent could name six or more.

Sears, JC Penney, and Wal-Mart were identified as being closely associated with the Olympics by 37 percent, 28 percent, and 23 percent of respondents, respectively, despite the fact that none of them had a sponsorship position.

American Express (which clearly used its advertising during the games to establish that it has had a long-time presence in Norway, the host country) was "associated with" the games by 52 percent of respondents in aided recall, a strong showing. However, official sponsor VISA leveraged its position handsomely, giving it a 72-percent recall rate. Apparently, "they won't take American Express" went further than "you don't need a VISA" in advertising recall, although American Express did score points. (See Figure 2.2.)

But the biggest surprise came in reflections of official sponsorship among fast-food restaurants. McDonald's it was, right? Right, but not among the survey respondents.

Respondents told Performance Research that it was Wendy's that was the official fast-food restaurant sponsor of the games. Sixty-eight percent of them said so in aided recall, versus 55 percent for official sponsor McDonald's.[11] (See Figure 2.1.)

Wendy's hit home with a striking ad campaign that featured its founder and chairman, Dave Thomas, on a quest to find an Olympic sport, from bobsledding to figure skating, in which to compete. 1992 gold medal-winning figure skater Kristi Yamaguchi was also featured in the campaign.

McDonald's, meanwhile (according to an ad agency executive), didn't leverage its sponsorship well at all, advertising its super-value meals and Double Big Macs instead of its Olympic sponsorship.

Wendy's, without ever saying it was an Olympic sponsor, associated itself with the Winter Olympic events closely enough to ambush McDonald's effectively.

It's all a keen lesson: You've got to hit consumers over the head with your message of sponsorship, or don't do it. Wendy's got what McDonald's was seeking for about $20 million or so less than what McDonald's spent.

Thirty-eight percent of consumers and fans, meanwhile, told Performance Research that they were "all for it" when it came to companies spending up to $40 million to be games' sponsors, although 54 percent said that sponsorship had no effect on whether they purchase that company's products. Both before and after the games, some 85 percent of fans told Performance Research that Olympic sponsorship predominantly kept a firm's products on a level playing field with others' when it comes to product-purchase decisions. More than half the respondents said they'd be either "not very" or "not at all" likely to purchase a company's products because of its sponsorship of the games.

Yet, 34 percent of consumers – the number one response – said they are "somewhat" more likely to support Olympic sponsors if it would help the United States win more gold medals. And fans are in

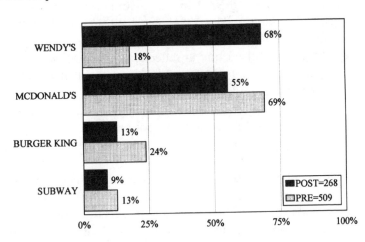

Figure 2.1. Ambush Marketing: Many consumers believed Wendy's, not McDonald's, was the official fast-food 1994 Winter Olympic sponsor.

Source: The 1994 Winter Olympics sponsorship graph is courtesy of Performance Research, Newport, Rhode Island.

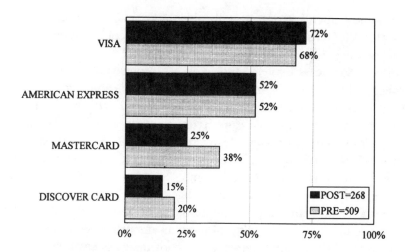

Figure 2.2.   Ambush Marketing: Many consumers believed American Express was an official 1994 Winter Olympic sponsor, instead of VISA.

Source: The 1994 Winter Olympics Sponsorship graph is courtesy of Performance Research, Newport, Rhode Island.

favor of Olympic sponsors and their products if they can help defray the costs of the athletes' participation.[11]

However, the bottom line is that both official sponsorship and ambushing can work. Forced to select one or the other, 63 percent of respondents identified official sponsor VISA while 32 percent picked American Express as the official credit-card sponsor of the games. Meanwhile, 57 percent, in answering a similar question, selected Wendy's as the official fast-food restaurant sponsor versus 37 percent who chose McDonald's.

For its part, Wendy's told researchers for this book that it was pleased with its campaign and the results. American Express, on the other hand, said that in no way could its campaign be construed by any "reasonable person" as "trying to present an image as an Olympic sponsor."[1]

American Express specifically asserted that its campaign was not an ambush per se, but a response to VISA advertising that it said implied that American Express was simply of no use in traveling to Olympic venues. It even had survey results to back it up: nearly 54 percent of

---

1. Interviews with Wendy's and American Express representatives, March 7, 1994.

consumers intercepted at a mall told American Express researchers that the VISA ads implied that American Express could not be used in such venues.[12][2]

Both American Express and Wendy's representatives said they specifically used no Olympic trademarks in their campaigns and did no specific promotions around the games or their campaigns. In fact, said Wendy's, its campaign came at a time when nationwide weather conditions were awful, but sales were up year-to-year for the quarter in which the campaign ran. Wendy's primary promotional activity in that quarter was a push for its "combo" meal at a special price that had no Olympic-related overtones whatsoever.

Both Wendy's and American Express said it was not their intent to ambush and that any labeling of them as ambushers was inaccurate and unfair. "The creative definitely took advantage of a widely known television event" (namely the Olympics), said a Wendy's spokesperson. But, "we weren't the only ones that had creative tied into the events."

But Wendy's was the only one with a creative campaign tied into the events that so smashingly outscored the official Olympic sponsor in terms of consumer association with the games. The Wendy's spokesperson said that the ad campaign deal was inked with CBS six months before the games, so there was no way the campaign was linked to any Nancy Kerrigan/Tonya Harding figure skating controversy (for those with short memories, the attack on Kerrigan, contrived by Harding associates, that kept her out of the U.S. national competition). In fact, said a Wendy's spokesperson, "The Dave Thomas campaign is going into its fifth year," so using him in Winter Olympic-related events was not out of character with long-running advertising for the chain.

However, American Express said its campaign, while not an ambush per se, was in response to VISA advertising that "we've said in the past

---

2. In a Custom Research Inc. mail intercept survey conducted for American Express in November of 1993, two hundred and fifty-six consumers were asked about VISA's advertising before the Winter Olympics in Lillehammer, Norway. Specifically, they were asked, "Based on what the commercial told you, could an American Express card be used at places like hotels, restaurants, and shops in cities hosting the Winter Olympics?" Thirty-five (13.8 percent) answered "yes," 137 (53.9 percent) answered "no," and 82 (32.3 percent) answered "don't know."

we will not stand for," according to a corporate spokesperson, "so we launched our own Norway ads. They contain no Olympic imagery. They don't show the games. They don't show any Olympic events. They talk about how American Express is accepted at 20,000 places in Norway. They talk about our services for travelers in Norway."

If anything, American Express believes VISA has used what the spokesperson called its "$40 million for the rights to use the Olympic rings" to attack American Express, over and over, ever since the 1988 Seoul, South Korea, Summer Olympics." But, "they haven't acquired the rights to attack American Express with impunity. Our advertising was to let our customers know we're there for them [and] to set the record straight for our customers."

As to Wendy's intent, "Dave (Thomas) is an ordinary guy," continued the Wendy's spokesperson. "The idea for the creative for the Olympics is, 'Who hasn't had a dream of competing in the Olympics?' The humor is instantly there. He (Dave Thomas) doesn't have an athletic body. We took advantage of that." And was it so effective that more consumers identified Wendy's as an official Olympic sponsor than identified McDonald's, the actual sponsor? "I guess so," said the spokesperson. No guesswork, just fact, actually.

So, to ambush or not to ambush, that is the question. The answer depends upon who you are, what you do with it, why you do it, and to whom you're doing it.

"It depends on the product category. It depends on the situation," says ambush-guru Sandler, who has moved on to Pace College in New York City. In a follow-up interview, he said he was impressed with the numbers scored by American Express and Wendy's in terms of consumers thinking they were official Winter Olympic sponsors in 1994. But he's still not sold completely on the value of ambush.[3]

"In the past, it hasn't shown to be that successful, if the sponsors correctly leveraged it," Sandler said. Ultimately, "the problem still comes down to measurement issues" – namely, tying ambush marketing or sponsorship positions to specific sales achievements. Consumers don't always do what they say, as any good marketing researcher will tell you, so believing that consumers will buy sponsors' products just because they're sponsors is not completely trustworthy.

---

3. Interview with Dennis Sandler, March 7, 1994.

VISA, for its part, relies heavily on its positioning as being accepted where American Express isn't. Vice President of Marketing Services Bob Pifke told a Strategic Research Institute audience in January of 1994 that "since 1985, we have featured merchants who do not take American Express. We do this to prove our superior merchant acceptance, one of the most important benefits a credit card can offer a cardholder."[4]

"From an advertising perspective," Pifke continued, "the campaign has dramatically improved consumer *perceptions* toward VISA. Today, VISA is considered the most accepted card, the best overall card, best card for retail purchases, best card for personal travel and entertainment, etc."

VISA promotes heavily around its sponsorship and guaranteed a $2.5 million donation to the 1994 U.S. Winter Olympic Team. "VISA is supporting this . . . with television and print advertising, statement inserts, and a major public relations campaign."

It's all "a single thought," he said. "Use VISA and help the Olympic Team." You can't ask for a more sports-oriented, emotional appeal than that.

"It's all *perceptions*," said Sandler. "It's an interesting question as to whether it's deceptive. Consumers miscomprehend, that's really what's happening."

Sandler's partner, Shani, feels the same, if not more strongly. In the wake of the success scored by Wendy's and American Express, "we'll see more and more" ambush marketing, he said in an interview.[5] "They [Wendy's and American Express] were very successful."

However, combating ambush marketing is as difficult – if not more so – than pulling it off, Shani believes. When a company ambushes and plays by the rules without violating trademarks in any way, shape, or form, the official sponsor and the event-rights' holder have few alternatives.

Between the camp of the ambushers and the camp of the rights' holders/sponsors, the opinions turn 180 degrees. VISA's Pifke, in a follow-up interview, concurred with the International Olympic Committee's view condemning the so-called ambush campaigns. Specifically, he said, any kind of ambushing is next to unpatriotic.

---

4. Speech to the Strategic Research Institute Tie-In Forum, Jan. 20, 1994.
5. Interview, March 7, 1994.

Ambush campaigns, he alleged, take money right out of the pockets of the athletes, not necessarily the license-granting body. That scenario plays out because VISA promotes its sponsorship, for example, in part around its donation of a percentage of sales from goods purchased by consumers with their VISA cards to the U.S. Olympic team, with some $2.5 million guaranteed for the 1994 Winter Games. Ambushing, Pifke feels, takes some of that money away because it violates the official sponsors' abilities to raise funds and will make it harder for governing bodies to negotiate future sponsorship rights fees for monies for the athletes.[6]

Regardless of all that, "you can't prevent someone from showing a picture of Norway in their advertising, or a picture of someone skiing," Shani said in a direct reference to the 1994 Winter Olympic ambushing. "All they [the International Olympic Committee] can do is educate the consumer that these are companies that are ambushing and they're not official sponsors. There's nothing legally they can do."

An educational campaign is needed badly, Shani says, because, like his research partner, he believes that "consumers don't know the difference" between ambushers and official sponsors much of the time. "To them, it's a sponsorship," whether it's of the event or the telecast thereof. "That's why ambushers reap the same benefits as sponsors." Shani believes some sort of official, public logo campaign would help differentiate ambushers from official sponsors.

You can fight ambushing all you like, he says, from the positioning of an event-rights' holder or an official sponsor, but in the end, "I don't think you can eliminate it."

---

6. Interview, March 10, 1994.

References

[1] Shani, David and Dennis Sandler, "Olympic Sponsorship versus Ambush Marketing." *Journal of Advertising Research*, August/September 1989, p. 11.

[2] Shani, David and Dennis Sandler, "Sponsorship and the Olympic Games," *Sport Marketing Quarterly,* Vol. II, No. 3, p. 40.

[3] "Amex Card Takes On Visa Over Olympics," *Wall Street Journal,* Feb. 4, 1992, Sec. B, p. 1.

[4] "Circle the Rings, Ambush Ads Hit," *Atlanta Constitution/Journal,* March 3, 1992, Sec. A, p. 6.

[5] "Magic Ad Upsetting, Uh-Huh, *Chicago Tribune,* July 14, 1992, p. 2.

[6] Performance Research Olympic Sponsorship Study, Feb. 2, 1992.

[7] "NHL Files Suit Against Pepsi-Canada Alleging 'Ambush' Promotion Tactics," *Team Marketing Report,* January 1992, p. 6.

[8] Supreme Court of British Columbia, Vancouver Registry No. C902104, "National Hockey League v. Pepsi-Cola Canada," June 2, 1992, p. 25.

[9] Ibid, p. 38.

[10] Heenan Blaikee, *Canadian Marketing & Advertising Law,* Heenan Blaikee, July 1992, p. 3.

[11] Performance Research Olympic Sponsorship Study, February 1994.

[12] Custom Research Inc. survey for American Express, November 1993.

3

The NBA
Takes Over the World

Even without three of the most recognizable personalities in the world – Magic Johnson, Larry Bird, and Michael Jordan – the National Basketball Association (NBA) in 1993–94 continued its amazing growth.

Attendance overall was up. New stars, particularly Shaquille O'Neal, emerged as marketing vehicles. And the league continued its ever-onward push toward international conquest as the world's most popular game with expansion franchises in Canada and the momentum provided by its stars playing in formerly amateur championship events under the heading "USA Basketball."

As the esteemed writer and author Frank Deford claims, "I honestly believe, in a few generations, basketball will supplant soccer as the number one sport in the world."[1]

You may or may not disagree with this, but the facts support it. NBA merchandising has exploded, with sales going from about $65 million ten years ago to some $2 billion in 1993. The NBA truly is global with its "Dream Teams" competing in international tournaments, its franchises competing in an annual European tournament on a rotating basis, its attendance driving upward despite the loss of household-

---

1. Speech at American Marketing Association conference, June 1992.

name superstars, and its teams competing more and more in palaces instead of just arenas and stadiums.

How has the NBA achieved all this? How has it gone from what Deford calls a "game perceived . . . for blacks on drugs" in the '70s to a game that he says now has more recognizable stars off the court than any other in America. The players, literally and figuratively, are "larger than life," he proclaims, so that even with the loss of Johnson and Bird and the premature retirement of Jordan, the game has outshone its stars, or, in his words, "the show will outdistance the game."[2]

This chapter will explore how the NBA has become the "larger than life" entity that it is. It will discuss how it has overcome its perception problem with a marketing approach that has produced an unparalleled positioning and booming licensed merchandise sales around the globe. And it truly is the globe that the NBA dominates, or is trying to dominate. Television, talent, and international tournaments have made the sport of basketball a global entity. Basketball is exploding in popularity with fans across demographic and international boundaries.

Here's how marketers have latched on and made the most of the ride the NBA is providing to establish and leverage the emotional link pro basketball creates for them with fans all over the world – fans who also happen to be the customers they want to reach.

Globalization

Canada, with Mexico on line. Europe in its back pocket. The Pacific Rim falling in line, particularly Australia.

All of these are the international territories that the NBA, to different degrees, is invading and conquering. Stealing the thunder right out from under soccer's feet, if you will. Along for the ride? McDonald's, Nestlé, and any number of multinational marketers and manufacturers who see the game's popularity, feel its emotional grip on fans in countries around the world, and want to use an attachment to it to achieve their global marketing goals, especially with ultracompetitiveness and saturation in most categories in the U.S. marketplace.

---

2. Speech at American Marketing Association conference, June 1992.

North America

Vancouver and Toronto have become the first NBA franchise cities outside of the United States proper; their teams competed in the 1995–96 season. With the North American Free Trade Agreement comes the NBA, eh?

Toronto has already been Americanized. It is already one of the world's most truly intercontinental cities, and North America's most expensive city in which to live. That's not an NBA qualification, but greater Toronto has about one-fifth of Canada's population and the demographics marketers love. Now it will have the Raptors, the dinosaur age nickname that has been selected for the team, and an NBA great – recently retired, perennial all-star guard Isiah Thomas of Detroit Pistons fame – as its director of basketball operations.

Vancouver, in the province of British Columbia, is generally known as the "Southern California of Canada" for its climate, culture, and location on the Pacific coast. Achieving the Southern California success that has been attained by the Los Angeles Lakers will be another story.

The investors owning these new teams put up respective $125-million fees just to join the NBA, and they obviously feel that it was worth it. They see the NBA's marketing success in partnering with multinational manufacturer marketers and sponsors as the big key to success and the ability to generate huge television ratings and revenues, let alone fan support. Even the lowly Minnesota Timberwolves, strapped with facility debt problems, constant losing records in their first five years, and public opinion polls that showed general apathy toward them, played to average crowds around 17,000 in the Target Center.

The NBA and the Toronto ownership group obviously felt the investment was important enough and the market critical enough to deal with one other significant, adverse factor: the Province of Ontario's Pro Line Lottery, which allowed legalized gambling on NBA games. But a $10-million contribution by the NBA and the Raptors' owners to civic and charitable groups in the province erased the woes of the $6 million in losses that would have occurred if basketball betting had been eliminated from the Pro Line inventory.

Although it's a country enraptured with hockey and even lacrosse, Canada is still prime territory for the NBA. Canada is nearly a mirror reflection of the United States, so much alike are the countries in culture and population demographics. If baseball can fly in Canada, so can basketball. Pro hockey has proven it can fly in San Jose, St. Petersburg, Miami, and Anaheim, but it washed out in Minnesota.

Most U.S.-based sponsors of the NBA have Canadian operations and sales to a good extent anyway and have reorganized operations to reflect NAFTA and the ability to market better to that country. Now they can ride along with the NBA, too, using NBA telecasts, promotions in two prime local Canadian markets, and the star power that the entire league carries to market products and services directly to Canadian citizens and businesses. Now their banners can hang in NBA arenas in Canada, their coupons and consumer sweepstakes can carry the NBA's blessing, and they can entertain their trade customers with tickets and attendance at NBA games, with opportunities to get up close and personal with the world's greatest athletes. They can do the local clinics with NBA stars, where trade customers get to bring their kids in for free, personalized instruction from NBA stars, with the parents looking on and getting a chance to meet the players, as has been done all over the NBA's U.S. markets. It's a feeling that can only be transmitted through such close, personal contact with stars of this magnitude, and it's worth is almost immeasurable.

Expansion into Canada created NBA fever in the country. Bruce McNall, owner of the Canadian Football League's Toronto Argonauts and the NHL's Los Angeles Kings, declared that he was eager to get an NBA franchise in Canada. Considering he's the man who traded for and signed the great Wayne Gretzky and had partners like the late John Candy, his clout and profile were huge. Then the rest of his financial empire collapsed and he put his share of the Kings on the block.

But the expansion fever spread to the south end of the NAFTA agreement, too. Mexico will not have an NBA franchise soon, but it is providing a testing ground for the NBA. The Continental Basketball Association (CBA), a sort of minor league proving and holding ground for NBA players, added an expansion franchise in Mexico City in 1994–95, and with the NBA already having declared its desire to get in there, you can bet the big brother league will be watching closely, as are its marketing partners and sponsors, who are licking their chops anxiously in anticipation of getting a better foothold in Mexico than they already might have. The Mexico City market has a population of

21 million, and Mexico is expected to have a burgeoning middle class evolve over the years as NAFTA takes hold.

Europe

NBA Commissioner David Stern has a question about today's increasingly global economy. What makes very, very good television programming and travels well across the economic boundaries that are coming down?, he wants to know.

You know the answer. The economic boundaries that are coming down are ones like those involved in NAFTA and the European Community (EC). It is there that the NBA has moved beyond the foothold stage and into the mass popularity stage. Its sponsors know that and have successfully hitched along for the ride, bringing their own marketing goals with them.

The NBA has been sending its franchises, on a rotating basis, to an international tournament featuring Europe's best teams since 1987. It is sponsored by McDonald's, which earns an incredible 47 percent of its systemwide sales outside of the United States, which accounts for 45 percent of its profits. In case you think the U.S. marketplace really is saturated and the growth opportunities for U.S. manufacturers and marketers really is overseas, there's the proof positive. Perhaps like no other sponsor, McDonald's has visibly enjoyed its ride with the NBA to overseas markets.

The NBA helps McDonald's achieve its international goals, and vice versa. Two of the world's best-known brand names complement each other nicely in international markets. In markets where foreigners hunger for American culture and snatch it up faster than it can be served up, the NBA and McDonald's set the pace for paving the way not only for each other but for Americanization in general. The McDonald's in Rome, bordering the Vatican, is one of its highest grossing and most popular locations worldwide. Not coincidentally, the McDonald's tournament has been held in Italy and Americans stock the teams that compete in the Italian pro league, regularly playing one year with an Italian league team and the next with an NBA franchise, or vice versa.

American players are household names in Italy and all over Europe. So is McDonald's. The firm's growth rates overseas far, far outpace sales growth in the United States. In the United States, in flat growth times, fast-food restaurant sales growth increased by 6 percent – or $3.6 billion in 1993, according to Nielsen Marketing Research. That makes the growth-rate prospects overseas for U.S. vendors like McDonald's and the NBA full of nothing but upside potential.

Sponsorship, of course, is not a foreign concept in Europe. In fact, it outpaces U.S. efforts in some respects, so seeing corporate names from the United States show up in Europe in sponsorship postures should come as no surprise to sports-eager Europeans. In the Italian league alone, teams go by their corporate sponsors' names rather than Hawks, Pacers, Bulls, or Lakers.

It's no coincidence then that the McDonald's tournament in Europe, held each fall during the NBA exhibition preseason, has expanded. What used to be a four-team tournament will become a six-team event, with an NBA franchise and five other European champions gathering on an every-other-year basis. It's all part of the NBA's global thrust, which included the Dream Team of the 1992 Olympics and the Dream Team II that was in the world basketball championships in 1994 in Toronto.

This thrust includes the possibility that teams other than NBA franchises and European champions will compete in the McDonald's tournament. (McDonald's international is not limited to just Europe either, you know.) The NBA has already been playing preseason exhibition games all over the globe and regular season games for the first time in Japan to open the 1993–94 season.

Europeans have simply embraced the game. You don't have to look any further than the NBA rosters themselves to spot many Eastern Europeans – from Sarunas Marciulionis with Golden State to Toni Kukoc with the Bulls to Dino Radja with the Celtics. They've even had a marketing impact: The Grateful Dead, the legendary San Francisco-based rock band, helped sponsor, through their connection with Marciulionis, warm-up uniforms for the Lithuanian Olympic basketball team in 1992, which finished third. That enabled a lot of publicity for Mike Fitzgerald, proprietor of Phoenix-based Fitzy's, who supplied the warmups and whose small business became a hot property after the surrounding publicity of the event. Now a Grateful Dead licensee, he manufacturers and sells warmups, sweats, T-shirts, and other Dead apparel to colleges around the country.

Kukoc, a key cog for the Bulls in 1993–94, received endorsements galore from U.S. companies upon arriving in Chicago after becoming generally regarded as Europe's best player. He kept on endorsing multinational, multidiscipline Bennetton products after arriving here, as part of the contract negotiation release he received for leaving the Bennetton team in Italy to play for the Bulls. His exploits, and those of Marciulionis, Radja, et al., are closely monitored by European basketball fans, which heightens their interest in the American game, which is continually being exported in greater amounts to Europe.

No one can say how much is derived in sales from a particular athlete's endorsement, but their association with your product or service surely will heighten its profile because of the attention the athletes garner among fans and media reporters. It's no wonder then that Kukoc and his European brethren in the NBA continue to attract the attention of sponsors, especially those who want to sell product into the competitive but always lucrative American marketplace, let alone maintain and increase their sales paces in Europe.

But when you see how the NBA is so well accepted in foreign countries, especially in Europe, it's easy to understand why the league continues its focus there. Europeans gobble up licensed merchandise. They relish slam dunks. They often pay scalper prices for tickets to games featuring American touring teams. And now they'll be able to see more and more of the NBA on television. SAT 1 of Germany will televise NBA highlights into that country. That puts NBA television into 100 countries worldwide, where it was in only one – the United States – ten years ago.

Meanwhile, American-style problems have also been encountered by foreign leagues. The Italian League suffered financially after a bidding war for American players escalated salaries – and expenses. Strict financial controls are being instituted. Don't think the NBA doesn't keep close tabs on all that. Former Alfred College coach Kevin Jones was named NBA Europe manager of basketball operations in May of 1994. The NBA is serious about Europe.

And the rest of the world. And the sponsors know it. To leverage their presence, they come up with programs like Nestlé's "Sweet Moves Across Europe." This promotion enabled the brand to maintain good visibility here for five of its products. The program included a sweepstakes with a travel prize to Europe plus trade sales incentives to move product and enable the brands involved to increase sales by getting more display and point-of-purchase promotional support at the retail level. Nestlé already produces chocolate bars emblazoned with the logos of all 28 NBA teams.

With the world as its oyster, it's easy to see why the NBA's attitude about international expansion is summed up so well by Commissioner Stern. In a 1992 interview with the Associated Press, he told them: "Domestically, I think we're close to our limit. We can't televise too many more games, and we can't sell too many more seats. The average fan is not going to see a game in person. There aren't that many seats ... I'd say we're at about 85 to 90 percent of what our domestic potential can be. Internationally, we're probably not at 3 percent or 5 percent."[1]

Down Under

To fulfill the rest of its international potential, the NBA is not stopping in Europe. It had two teams play regular season games in Japan during the 1993–94 season. Its presence in the Pacific Rim is ever increasing.

The Isotonic Beverage Company used a trip to NBA games in the United States to help introduce and push its new sports drink product in Singapore in 1994. The NBA opened a merchandise store in Melbourne, Australia, in 1992, its first overseas. Of course, it came on the heels of NBA overseas revenues having increased by triple-digit percentages the previous year. As we've said, NBA merchandise is gobbled up overseas by adoring, sports-hungry fans wild for Americana.

That's not all the NBA has done in Australia. It has sent two Jam Session tours to that country that have been greeted by large, enthusiastic crowds. The tour didn't play games against Australian all-star teams per se, but it put on a demonstration of NBA skills and wizardry of the likes that has helped catapult the NBA into international popularity.

"The Jam Session was about increasing the awareness of the NBA Australia, but also lending further credibility to the brand. No other sport, or league, does anything along these lines. What we set about to do was bring a part of the league to Australia," according to Ian Campbell, vice president and managing director of NBA Australia.[2]

Players, media personality Ahmad Rashad, and team mascots were on the tour, drawing large crowds to halls and malls where they showed up, demonstrating skills, and signing autographs. Clearly, the audiences were into it. Fans showed up decked out in NBA-licensed merchandise. Australian television covered the appearances. Players from superstar Hakeem Olajuwon to far lesser known reserve guard Jim Les were either recognized immediately or quickly achieved adoration. Tour stops included everywhere from a Kmart store (yes, Kmart) to 20,000-seat arenas in Melbourne and Sydney. With each stop playing to overflow crowds, you can bet the retail stops on the tour were most grateful for the traffic generated and the awareness and goodwill built.

The NBA clearly has a presence and awareness level that is enormous in foreign countries, making latching on to the league as a sponsor a natural choice for manufacturers and marketers interested in reaching global markets. Michael, Magic, and Larry may be gone, but the game's popularity extends beyond their retirements.

The Dream Teams

It was the three legends – Michael, Magic, and Larry – along with Charles Barkley, Karl Malone, Patrick Ewing, and others, who composed the U.S. Olympic basketball team in 1992, the first time the United States had sent its pros – and its very best pros at that – to the Olympics. U.S. citizens practically screamed for such a move after the country lost in international competition more frequently in the late '80s and early '90s with teams stocked with college all-stars.

Of course, the first "Dream Team" blitzed its way through the competition to win the gold medal, leaving the marketing story as its legacy rather than its victories. Those were assumed, and they happened.

The marketing story was marred by Nike's refusal to allow Michael Jordan's likeness to be used on licensed merchandise. The players accepted their medals, many of them draped in American flags to hide the Reebok logo on their warmups, especially the guys with contracts with Nike or Converse. They had announced they would not participate in promotions sponsored by companies with which they are not associated.

Those attitudes almost broke up the team. They struck again with Dream Team II just prior to the World Championships in Toronto in the summer of 1994. Superstar Shaquille O'Neal of the Orlando Magic almost didn't play until a spat was settled involving team sponsor Coca-Cola and his own soft drink sponsor, Pepsi.

Of course, there was the flap over Magic Johnson's HIV positive status, which would force him into retirement not once but twice, once before and once after the Olympics. The Australian team said it didn't want to play against a United States team with Johnson. And teammate Malone was outspoken against Johnson's active status from the time of Johnson's original diagnosis until his second retirement announcement.

Yet, the sponsors lined up to participate with the Dream Team, to advertise their good luck wishes, to sponsor trips to the Olympics in 1992 to Barcelona to see the Dream Team play, to buy advertising time on NBC during Dream Team game telecasts, and generally to bask in the glow of the team's success. (Thank goodness they won – they briefly trailed a Croatian team stocked with NBA-level talent in the gold medal game.)

As the *Los Angeles Times* put it: "Advertisers viewed the team as the marketing opportunity of a lifetime. Many still do because it seems to be a no-lose proposition: Superstars Michael Jordan, Magic Johnson and Larry Bird all on the same team."[3] Despite marketer concerns that the team would have so easy a time that no one would watch, the fans watched anyway, and sponsors scored right along with the team.

For a fee in the range of $1 million to be an official sponsor: Quaker ran a sweepstakes sending someone to Barcelona for the 1992 summer Olympics, McDonald's served drinks in Dream Team cups, Kraft sold posters and caps tied into their merchandise, and Sheraton offered special Dream Team merchandise to its hotel guests.

The overcommercialization was not enough to deter the sponsors, all 15 of them, from participating. They saw numbers – big viewership for games the Dream Team was playing. Big viewership means the biggest audience a sponsor can reach, an audience rooting for the pros to recapture what the collegians surrendered – America's supremacy in world basketball, which, in its own way, is a tribute to the popularity of basketball around the world.

The rest of the world, including and especially South American and Eastern European nations, were so taken with basketball that they developed the talent to compete in it. While U.S. pros represent their country in basketball now, how long will it be then before other nations develop their expertise up to that level, as they did against U.S. amateurs? Just look at the NBA rosters stocked with foreigners, especially from Eastern Europe, to make your best guess at the answer.

That notwithstanding, sponsors line up for USA Basketball sponsorships, knowing they'll bask, for now, in the glow of the U.S. basketball talent that will surely bring home gold medal after gold medal from World Championship and Olympic competitions.

As the *Chicago Tribune's* Sam Smith observed in 1992: "It's the first time NBA players will compete in the Olympics, and perhaps the principal area of expansion on the NBA agenda is international. The NBA wants to sell its game and its merchandise overseas. So why not bring its biggest stars? It's a walking billboard for the NBA. And are they going to lose? . . . The talent is overwhelming and the opposition dubious. And the corporate sponsors who hire these people will be wearing the widest grins."[4]

The sponsors were especially smiling after the Olympics, we believe. A Bruskin Goldring Research survey revealed that Americans thought the Dream Team winning the gold medal was the number one memorable moment from the 1992 Olympics, outranking the gold-medal-level achievements of swimmer Summer Sanders and other standout athletes, including Gayle Devers, Mark Lenzi, Jackie Joyner-Kersee, and even Carl Lewis.[3]

In terms of marketing, the NBA was not only thrilled that it sold out its USA Basketball/Dream Team sponsorships to its 15 corporate sponsors in four months, but was thrilled over the prospects of expediting its marketing internationally, truly one of its goals.

"I think it's the single most important thing to happen to basketball. Markets that had never expressed an interest before were captivated by the Dream Team. It could have moved up our timetable by at least five years," said Rick Welts, president of NBA Properties.[5]

"Sports is an enviable position to be at the intersection of a phenomenon," according to Commissioner Stern, making it the single

---

3. BW Sportswire release, Aug. 10, 1992.

most significant way to market products and services around the world. World trade barriers are dropping, he notes, and sports is partly responsible. Any reference to EC or GATT makes him think about sports as marketing, he says.[6]

And, he adds, "In many ways, we are ahead of the organizational flow at these corporations as they try to deal with the phenomenon." But "all sports now are global events, attractive to global marketers trying to get their message through the exploding media of the '90s. Professional sports leagues and global marketing are a marriage. We have this unique opportunity . . . to break new ground. We're using our marketing partners to help us develop global awareness. It's expertise we don't have. Basketball has the opportunity to become the number one sport in the world."

Tell that to Frank Deford.

Marketing and Merchandising

Make no mistake about it – the NBA is the epitome of the emotional marketing power of sports.

Consider: before Michael Jordan's *first* retirement, his personal sponsor, Nike, experienced a 900-percent earnings increase from 1987–1993. Consider: when NBC televised a Chicago Bulls game featuring Jordan, ratings were 38 percent higher than other NBA games; when cable's TNT network televised Jordan and the Bulls, ratings soared 49 percent above other games.

Think you couldn't do well tying in with the marketing power of the NBA that Jordan once represented and again, represents?

Here are its parameters: licensed merchandise sales hit $2 billion in 1993, up from $10 million in 1981, and NBA arenas operate at 91-percent capacity and 17,000 average attendance, up from 10,000 over the same period.

• Want to reach youths? Twenty-eight million people between 7 and 17 play basketball in the United States, making it the number one participatory sport, according to the NBA. The American Basketball Council estimated in 1993 that 12.2 million women played basketball at least once that year, an 11-percent increase over the figure measured six years earlier. Seventy-five percent of the females playing in 1993 were 17 or under.

More than 40 percent of high school players now are females, and the Amateur Athletic Union (AAU) reported a 23-percent increase between 1993 and 1992 in individual female registration to participate in its various national championships for age groups up to and including age 18. The more than 58,000 players in 1993 represented an eightfold increase from 1983.

Women may still only represent 30 percent of all basketball players, but between ages 11 through 17 they represent 38 percent. And in the 12-to-17 age bracket they account for 40 percent. These women grow up to be the coveted marketing targets in the 18-to-34 age group.

Want to reach them – and their male peers – at the ages where they're impressionable and are making the decisions that will dictate their adult lives? Try basketball.

Ever drive down a suburban street and marvel at all the backboards adorning garages and driveways? Some 300,000 officially licensed NBA backboards were sold in 1981. Some 3 million were sold in 1993, in all shapes and sizes, for small balls and regulation size, "smush" balls and nerf balls, mini and street balls. "Different size balls for different size people," is how Bill Marshall, NBA Properties group vice president and general manager, likes to put it.

And, he adds, unlike soccer, these "participants grow up to be season-ticket holders."[4] If all of soccer's equivalent participants had grown up to be season-ticket holders today, soccer wouldn't be grasping for life in the United States as it is. It's at the point where, during the 1994 NBA playoffs, McDonald's, an official sponsor of both the NBA and World Cup Soccer, ran commercials specifically geared to calling attention to its participation in the upcoming World Cup tournament.

The NBA does have a way with kids. Sales of licensed merchandise to kids skyrocketed 140 percent in 1993, with electronic video game sales quadrupling. Licensed goods sales are growing 100 percent annually around the world and represent 12 percent of NBA Properties' total volume.

---

4. Speech to National Sporting Goods Association, August 2, 1993.

The NBA is simply ubiquitous. And it is closely monitoring its own growth. Marshall says it plans to maintain its growth by driving more sales from the same number of licensees, rather than adding licensees just to drive sales and possibly diluting the licensee base. "Less is more," he says, noting, however, that "sports licensing will not slow down in the near future." The key to its success is prime-time exposure on television and strong relations with the retailers that sell the product.

Keeping the number of licensees basically stagnant helps the NBA maintain quality control, above all else, and helps it build better relationships with its licensees, creating the family-type marketing partnerships it wants. It will also help the NBA grow its licensed sales the way it wants to.

That way is: more mail order, through more and enhanced cataloging; more of its own stores, building on the two it had open in 1993; more electronic and interactive relationships with consumers, as it has through Disney and Warner communication outlets and its TV video catalog through Prime Sports Network; and more phone orders tied into ticket sales opportunities.

The Age of the Database

In this day and age of database marketing, when firms everywhere are scrambling to acquire the names of customers and potential customers so they can build direct, one-to-one relationships with them, the NBA offers a direct route.

No less than 29 companies put goodies, coupons, and the like into an NBA gym bag that was distributed to media, VIPs, and corporate guests at the league's showcase one-game event, its annual all-star game – in this case, the 1993 game at Utah. These firms ranged from long-distance telephone suppliers to contact lens vendors to trading card manufacturers to restaurant franchisors to shaving product makers to magazine publishers. They knew the NBA's great following mandated their presence before an audience that contains many of their existing customers and many potential customers.

Sweepstakes, coupons, special discounts, premiums, and incentives are all used in connection with the NBA by marketers trying to maintain and augment business.

TNT cable, part of the Ted Turner cable television empire, is paying $350 million over a four-year period ending in 1998 to televise NBA contests. To leverage that and its telecast of the McDonald's tournament games in Europe, TNT sponsored a match-and-win sweepstakes around the tournament's Paris stop. Advertised in a nationally distributed free-standing newspaper insert (FSI), it offered a trip for two to the tournament as the grand prize, NBA videos, NBA encyclopedias, NBA jackets, and a trip for two to the on-location filming of a Turner feature movie.

To win, consumers had to leaf through the FSI (exposing them to even more manufacturer offers), which carried pictures of NBA team jerseys. Entering and winning depended on matching the picture in the FSI's various coupons with pictures on merchandise displays at participating grocery stores, driving traffic in specific categories. A second chance drawing offered opportunities to garner thousands of names.

Dr. Scholl's, "the official footcare products of the NBA," offered 50 cents off, via bar-coded traceable coupons in FSIs, on its athlete's-foot products, all of which carry NBA logos on the package. American Airlines, attempting to build traffic, offered a sweepstakes to its frequent-flyer registrants offering them, and guests, a chance to win flights to and special accommodations and amenities in any NBA city and tickets to a game as a means to build awareness for its role as official carrier to NBA "Ultimate Business Meetings," where NBA and team officials would help corporations and organizations generate the kind of business momentum the league has. For American, it was a great idea – at least until the meeting program was scrapped for lack of corporate participation, which pushed it back to the drawing board for retooling.[7]

Of course, there's always the irresistible Michael Jordan mug – his face, that is – not only on boxes of Wheaties cereal, but on the 50-cents-off coupons the company offers.

• The NBA, in fact, appears to work with anything. In 1993, the NBA and Warner Bros.' Looney Tunes hooked up, allowing licensees to manufacture NBA products with Looney Tunes characters on them and Looney Tunes character merchandise with NBA trademark logos on them. Youth, infant, and adult apparel, from pajamas to bathrobes, T-shirts to sweatshirts, from Josten, Wormser, and Changes – all were eligible to participate and use the magnetism of these two tremendously popular trademarks to market their products.[8]

Castrol became the "Official Motor Oil of the NBA" for three years beginning in 1993, reinforcing its already strong media position during NBA contests. The company not only planned to do national marketing, but local programs, too, in various NBA markets. With the NBA's nine-month-long season, this gave Castrol a chance to reach consumers outside of its traditional race-car marketing and during its peak selling seasons in spring and fall.[9] The tie-in allowed Castrol to use NBA merchandise and events as incentives to drive consumer and retailer participation.

In many cases, local-area promotion is the key to driving national programs or testing national programs-to-be. It helps establish the more personalized link that national promotion only builds awareness for. That's why so many companies execute like this in conjunction with the NBA.

Keebler proved that. As one of the dominant snack-food producers, it set a goal to reach its prime markets in a way its competitors were not. That put the family snack-food producer into a sponsorship role with the NBA. It had great success in localizing its "Kids Club" promotion and in extending it all the way through adult demographics.

Keebler sprang the club in Cleveland, through the "Cavaliers Kids Club." Television advertising announced the program. In-game promotion reinforced it by getting club members involved in in-game participation programs during timeouts and breaks. In-store promotion drove the program at the retail level, spotlighting participating products in the Keebler line with special packaging, display, and features driven by a now more motivated sales force able to communicate the traffic and draw benefits to retailers. Finally, a special insert in a local television magazine went into 92,000 Cleveland-area homes, explaining the program, announcing it all over again, and offering participation and special bonus opportunities, and premiums and incentives for enrollment.

The promotion enabled Keebler to establish a direct dialog with the youth market that consumes its cookies, the teen market that is partial to its salty snacks, and the adult female market, aged 24 to 44, that purchases those products for the household. The program was expected to be expanded into other NBA markets, and why not.

Twenty-one of the NBA's franchise, three-quarters of the league, have official retailer sponsors by market. Keebler's involvement with the NBA franchises only enhances its mutual goals along with those of retailer sponsors in each market. Traffic, sales, database name accumulation, enhanced promotional opportunities, and the opportunity to establish ongoing communications with each individual household that had club members were the benefits of the club, for both Keebler and retailers.

Schick, and its parent Warner-Lambert, is another consumer products manufacturer that has ridden a trail of success through its relationship with the NBA. Annually, it sponsors the world's largest intramural basketball tournament at college campuses around the country, with local, regional and finally national championships played at NBA arenas, with NBA-related prizes. The tournament enhances the firm's role with the college-age participants, who are at an age where they are making the shaving product-usage decisions they will probably carry with them for life. For the schools, there is an equipment enhancement program from Schick, which they need desperately in these financially strapped times, particularly in the athletic and physical education departments. Those same athletic department representatives who benefit from the equipment and financial endowment from Schick serve as the company's on-campus liaisons and coordinators for the tournament, becoming the firm's goodwill ambassadors on campus to help promote it.

The tournament offers not only exposure and awareness for Schick, but opportunities to distribute product samples to those critically aged consumers. With local retailer tie-ins at stores frequented by students in the college markets, the program comes home at the cash register with special offers on Schick products to generate trial and sales. With college budgets ever tightening, expect programs like these to expand for Schick, not just via enhancements to basketball but through volleyball and softball, which are other popular college campus activities. And similarly structured high school-targeted activity is in the offing.

Schick doesn't stop there. The company annually sponsored the NBA's old-timers' game during the NBA all-star weekend, with the greatest legends of the game parading up and down the court in an abbreviated game in uniforms with the Schick logo all over them. That game became the Schick Rookie Game in 1994, with the premier rookies who were not in the league's all-star game participating in virtually the same format as the old-timers once did.

Schick promoted the game loudly. An "advertorial" – an ad presented in editorial format – appeared in *USA Today* on weekends preceding the all-star weekend events. Outdoor billboards in the specific market (in this case, Minneapolis) drew local attention to Schick's sponsorship. Advertising during NBA telecasts on TNT also announced the program.[10] While sponsoring the old-timers/legends game was a good marketing vehicle for Schick, latching onto the rising stars at the rookie level is probably a better one, making for an association with these stars who will carry the NBA banner for years to come.

In addition, students are a terrific market. Many work and have more money than students of years gone by. Many commute rather than live on campus, and many are adults who have returned to school to enhance their careers or train for career changes. More and more, students eligible to compete in or with an interest in a tournament like Schick's or the basketball-related programs Schick sponsors are a more lucrative marketing target.

The tournament generates media coverage too, particularly critical local market coverage, which generates free publicity for Schick, and all contestants in the Schick tournament receive free T-shirts to commemorate their participation. Having the event on the school's intramural calendar as far in advance as possible also builds anticipation, participation, and more promotional support planning and activity. And Schick uses a shootout like the NBA's three-point contest to enhance the tournament, getting shoe supplier K-Swiss to sponsor that portion in a tie-in and offering shoe prizes for winners.

The possibilities are endless.

Spalding knows that. The official supplier of basketballs for USA Basketball, the NBA partnership producing the "Dream Teams," leverages its NBA relationship to the point that its "NBA-endorsed merchandise continues to grow at double-digit rates," according to John Doleva, the company's director of marketing. The firm also produces balls with the individual logos of each of the 27 NBA franchises, in full and mini sizes, and has worked hard to make the logos as large and visible as possible by using what Doleva calls "energized color schemes."[11]

IBM, as it tried to struggle back from the adversity that hit it in the computer marketplace in the late '80s and early '90s, used sports – and the NBA in particular – as one of the vehicles, becoming the league's official computer. IBM equipment became the software and computers that tracked NBA statistics and performances, and helped teams develop scouting reports. The firm worked personally with individual team coaches and managers to establish customized criteria and parameters. IBM also supplied teams with convenient laptop PCs and notebook PCs.

IBM also attained the right to sponsor interactive, multimedia computer kiosks at NBA arenas and events that enabled fans to review statistical information, event highlights, and special promotional opportunities. That aspect enabled the firm to leverage its NBA presence on-site with fans. An initial IBM Award was created and given to the player who had the best overall performance as determined by the IBM statistical system. IBM also sponsored Coach of the Month and Year awards and contributed to the NBA's "Stay in School" programming to youths, a good tie-in for the firm that has educational and promotional initiatives of its own among school-age children.

Dollar Rent A Car got into the act too, becoming the league's official car rental company and promoting this status through special offers to consumers and fans. It's "Three Point Play" promotion during the 1993 playoffs rewarded customers with up to $40 of NBA merchandise when they rented a Dollar vehicle three times within a specified 90-day period. Five rentals in that same time period earned the renter up to $80 of merchandise, with the selection ranging from backboards to Spalding basketballs to duffel bags, all available for customizing by favorite team logo.

Dollar's tie-in to the NBA and its 27 major-market teams enabled it to enhance its popularity and visibility among travelers in and between those markets, increasing its preference among them. No wonder the company set a goal to become the preferred rental unit of sports fans.

But McDonald's emerged as the sponsor with the largest, one-time promotion with the NBA when it unveiled "NBA Fantasy Packs" in 1993. The program, hubbed around merchandise sales and trading cards, incorporated virtually the full spectrum of NBA licensee resources and rewards. Prizes included: a one-on-one game with Michael Jordan; honorary ballboy status at the all-star game; a trip to the McDonald's tournament in Europe; a cruise on Norwegian Cruise Lines; vacation trips to the NBA finals and all-star game; tickets to regular-season games; NBA "fantasy" contracts and uniforms; licensed merchandise; collector cards; and a trial sample of Bausch & Lomb disposable contact lenses.

The whole promotion, of course, was geared to enable McDonald's to generate more traffic and sales, and generate trial, sales, and exposure for other NBA sponsors who tied in. McDonald's promoted the event, in part, with coupons from other participating sponsors printed on food packages and placemats.

Companies representing all different categories of product become NBA sponsors for all different reasons. Bausch & Lomb is an NBA sponsor because of the findings of a public opinion poll that showed that more people try contact lenses because of sports participation than any other reason. Aligning with the NBA allowed Bausch & Lomb to directly and more aggressively market its product to a younger male audience than it traditionally courted. The company immediately jumped into a media schedule that included "NBA Inside Stuff," the youth-oriented, 52-weeks-a-year television program on NBA news and features, and into NBA publications. The firm also arranged to entertain eye-care professionals at games and clinics – professionals whose endorsement, preference, and reference they require.

AT&T became an NBA sponsor to leverage its long-distance tele-communications services, immediately becoming sponsor of the NBA Long Distance Shoot-Out, the three-point shooting contest held during the NBA's All-Star Weekend festivities. The firm also received rights to use NBA team logos in conjunction with its telecommunications products and to provide telecommunications services to the league and the media that covers it. AT&T has also used its sponsorship to do local-market promotions around fan participation in long-distance shoot-outs during NBA games. And the company also became an official sponsor of USA Basketball and the Dream Teams.

But even if you're not an NBA sponsor or big enough to be one, you can still benefit from and use the equity of the NBA. Tony's Pizza did in 1989. The frozen brand, which didn't have nearly deep enough pockets to afford to be an official NBA sponsor, used NBA player

Figure 3.1. Sponsorship Spending In America
Source: The 1994 Winter Olympics Sponsorship graph is courtesy of Performance Research,
Newport, Rhode Island.

Figure 3.2. Hoop-It-Up: Slam dunking is part of the show. Photograph is courtesy
of Streetball Partners International, Dallas, TX.

posters and videos and *Sports Illustrated* subscription gift certificates to garner premium display position for itself in the freezer cases at participating grocers. The fact that consumers, trade customers, and the sales force were all eligible for these prizes served as a motivating tool.

Product packages featured collectible NBA posters and opportunities to get full-size posters and magazine subscriptions and videos. Tony's, which had never tied in with entities like the NBA or *Sports Illustrated* before, generated brand switching and multiple-package purchases by consumers, enabling the period of the promotion to generate more sales in a food category than in any comparable period in the company's history, which was then – and is now – ultracompetitive.

It's all testimony to the power of tying in with pro basketball and the NBA. But it gets more creative and more sophisticated all the time, with rewards to match.

Think about this: if NBA licensing didn't work, then why do NBA stat crews at games wear Nutmeg sweaters and sweater vests? Why do ballboys and floor sweepers wear Starter satin jackets, warm-ups, polo shirts and hats, and Converse team shoes? Why are McArthur towels and Starter polo shirts and team travel bags found along NBA benches at games? And why do the players use Spalding basketballs and wear Champion uniforms and warm-ups, Spalding socks, and Bike compression shorts?

Because they're all part of the "NBA Authentics" line that you see your friends and your kids and your friends' kids wearing every day. They're what your kids want for Christmas, and they're endorsed in advertising by Larry Johnson of the Charlotte Hornets, one of the league's young stars who keeps the younger generation of fans focused on the game and its merchandise. Authentics is one of the league's top properties.

Hoop It Up

Where sophistication and creativity are the name of the game now in NBA licensing, merchandising and marketing, the Hoop It Up three-on-three streetball national – no, international – basketball tournament is now one of the NBA's leading ambassadors of goodwill, excitement, and participation. And the sponsors, following the NBA's lead, know it.

Three-on-three is testimony to the popularity of basketball as a year-round game. All summer, with the NBA season over, kids all over the country play half-court, three-on-three games on blacktop in schoolyards and parks nationwide.

Hoop-It-Up started as a charity tournament called Hoop-D-Do in Dallas, raising money for Special Olympics in 1988. Four hundred eighty-seven teams raised $7,000. A year later, those numbers quadrupled.

Organizer Terry Murphy, seeing the event's potential, quit his full-time job as a magazine publisher and set out to make this big. But only Pepsi and its restaurant affiliate Pizza Hut signed on as sponsors. Three years and 31 cities later, the Pepsi/Pizza Hut three-on-three tour had lost $300,000. Pepsi and Pizza Hut disappeared.

NBC Sports rode to the rescue. Looking for a way to "extend the link" it now had with the NBA through their new television contract, NBC became a partner, and Murphy's Streetball International was born. The NBA fell into line shortly thereafter and saw how the tournament "over-delivered" for sponsors, according to Murphy.

Coke, Foot Locker, and Converse came aboard. AT&T, Upper Deck, Champion, and Spalding were right behind. In 1993, Hoop-It-Up became a 49-city tour. A 13-city European tournament exceeded everybody's wildest dreams: 20,000 fans watched as some 1,600 played in the first seven cities on the tour alone. NBA Entertainment produced two television specials about the tour.

Licensed three-on-three merchandise started showing up. "We've now become a licensed product," Murphy said of his tour. In all, seven international teams competed in the international finals held in the United States.

The sponsors found new ways to leverage their marketing communications messages. AT&T, perceived by some as a stodgy old company, saw an opportunity to give itself a more contemporary image among a younger audience. Gatorade, which came on, saw opportunities to raise awareness for its retail partners who sell its product, promoting the product and the tournament in in-store displays. Converse and Foot Locker worked together to promote discounted streetball product to generate sales and trial. Spalding became the official tournament ball, as much as it was the official ball of the NBA.

So explosive was the growth and sponsor support, with extension far beyond the 27 NBA markets, that Murphy says "we're pretty much maxed out in the United States." He turned his focus even more to Europe, the Pacific Rim, and even South America, which Murphy describes as a future "hotbed" for his game and basketball in general.

Jeep came on too as a sponsor. If streetball is the ultimate game, Jeep is the ultimate vehicle, was its tune. Sponsors used on-site coupon distribution and product sampling to reach thousands on every stop of the tour. Murphy kept the marketing fresh, positioning the event as a fest, not a tournament, to maintain sponsor interest and activity.

Soon, a free-throw-shooting contest, an AT&T long-distance shoot-out, and an Upper Deck slam-dunk contest were included in the festivities, as well as other sponsored special events. Cokes were served to fans and players off the back of Jeeps. Shooting contest winners got official tournament Spalding balls or Converse streetball sneakers.

Tournament divisions started at 10 years old and up for both male and female divisions. Some 150,000 people took part in 1993. Murphy's estimate is that each player is responsible for some 11 fans showing up to watch. It doesn't take a rocket scientist to see the numbers involved in this sponsorship opportunity.

Eighteen individual NBA teams, in addition to the league itself, are involved in promoting, endorsing, and sponsoring the tournaments.

Hoop-It-Up now has a staff of 36 working on its basketball promotions. Its four-pronged mission is to provide fun, provide a success environment for players and sponsors, be sure a worthwhile charity benefits from each event, and make money. Murphy reports that 1993 events raised $600,000 for charity. The tour has never raised less than $300,000 for charity in a single year. Murphy expects that the tour will at last be profitable in either its sixth or seventh year of operation.

"I have the greatest job in the world," Murphy says,[5] proving it by reeling off dates of rounds of golf with Prince Albert of Monaco, dinners with Michael Jordan and David Stern, tennis with Charles Barkley, and basketball with Roger Staubach and Tom McMillan.

---

5. Interview, July 1993.

The tournament has other attractive facets as well. Certain winners get dream games against NBA Legends. Venues are often spectacular spots in metro areas, overlooking the ocean in beautiful Virginia Beach, Virginia, or under the famous Gateway Arch in St. Louis. While the tour is national and international in scope, it offers local marketing promotional opportunities, local retail tie-ins, and local charitable visibility.

And what Streetball International Partners have done for basketball, they're also trying to do for football and the NFL.

Michael and Shaquille

Michael Jordan's retirement, although not permanent, was the top sports story of 1993, as voted by the Associated Press. And well it should have been.

He earned $4 million a year on the court and another $39 million off it because of his great athleticism, charisma, and achievements. But gambling allegations and his father's death put him over the top, and he quit to play baseball, where he spent 1994 packing minor league stadiums across the south.

Jordan was responsible for television ratings skyrocketing when his Chicago Bulls were on, which was just about every Sunday if NBC had its way. He had America singing "Be like Mike" after switching from Coke to Gatorade. He opened a Chicago restaurant that played to SRO crowds. He hosted "Saturday Night Live." The State of Illinois passed a tax on income for pro athletes who play road games in Chicago, specifically in retaliation for a California law that tried to take advantage of Jordan's high profile – personally and financially.

He was the reason Chicago Bulls merchandise paced NBA sales for years.

Until a 7-foot, 300-pound rap singer came along. Shaquille O'Neal of the Orlando Magic has a performance contract that makes Jordan's seem minuscule. His rap albums are top-sellers. And he almost didn't make "Dream Team II" for the world championships in Toronto in the summer of 1994 because his soft-drink sponsor wasn't the same as the one sponsoring the team.

Spalding claims his endorsement has increased one segment of its basketball sales by 20 percent. He's on driveway backboards, mini basketballs, and stationery. He was Shaq-A-Claus in Christmas promotions for the company, a life-size cutout of his hulking frame driving people to Spalding product displays.

What Jordan did for the game – transitioning it (from the '80s into the '90s as Bird and Johnson faded) – O'Neal will do, only this transformation will take basketball into the next millennium. The only question is who is O'Neal bringing with him in terms of fan profile?

When Jordan left, not long after Johnson and Bird had departed, some had fears about NBA attendance, its TV ratings, and its popularity in general. These were short-lived. League attendance was up in 1993–94, despite Jordan's retirement and despite the fact that neither Los Angeles team did well in the nation's second-largest TV market. While attendance around the league started slowly, it built steadily, and success from teams in Houston, San Antonio, and Seattle offset the Los Angeles dropoff. Chicago continued on a sellout pace.

The NBA appears to have lost little, if any, momentum, and may even perhaps have gained some.

So Sez the Commish

All David Stern has done since taking over as NBA Commissioner in ten years is to turn $65 million in licensed merchandise sales into $2 billion, produce gate receipts exceeding $700 million, put in a salary cap that revolutionized team sports, and install a drug policy that is clearly the most progressive in team sports.

The Sporting News called him sport's most powerful person in its top 100 list in 1992. NBA attendance has increased every year since Stern's arrival, and 100 countries (or more than 250 million households) get NBA telecasts, an audience second only to that for Olympic telecasts.

"Professional sports leagues and global marketing are a marriage," Stern says. "We're a tremendous brand [with] enormous awareness. Most of it we get for free. The consumer has our brand reinforced wherever they happen to be."

It used to be, he says, that league sponsors used the league profile to gain awareness and sales for their brand. Now the NBA is partnering with them, using their marketing expertise and garnering those same

Figure 3.3.   David Stern: The commissioner of commissioners. Photograph by Larry Graff, courtesy of American Marketing Association Publications Group.

benefits for itself. "We're using our marketing partners to develop global awareness, an expertise we don't have," Stern says. He acknowledges he is both league commissioner and a brand manager as well.

It doesn't bother him that there's expansion and longer-lasting playoffs that go almost to the end of June now. Television ratings for those games have been strong, he says. In fact, the Chicago Bulls-Phoenix Suns final series in June 1993 scored the highest ratings ever. The final game of the series drew the second-highest ratings for any NBA telecast.

CBS knows that. It acquired baseball and yielded basketball to NBC, and lived to regret it. "It was a wonderful ride in the '80s for the NBA" on CBS, the network's vice president, Len DeLuca, told the American Marketing Association's Sports Marketing Conference in May of 1992. Putting tongue in cheek, he called NBC's contract "temporary custody . . . and then we'll get our baby back."

But in the NBA, where the players get 53 percent of the gross, the league needs more revenue generators, Stern says. That's where international marketing comes in, and Stern has paced the growth with the Dream Teams, the McDonald's Tournament in Europe, international television, operations in Australia, and licensed merchandise sales all over the world. (Foreign sales, the fastest-growing aspect of NBA licensed sales, represent 12 percent of its gross and this share is increasing all the time.)

Sports is the single most significant way to market products and services around the world and through specific domestic barriers, Stern maintains. It makes him say that sports *is* marketing, as opposed to believing in the traditional sports marketing moniker. With triple-digit channel capacity, Stern sees the need for both domestic and international programming. The league's international exposure, awareness, television, and merchandise sales already testify to its transportability internationally. And the trend in marketing – away from mass media and toward segmented, splintered media outlets and methods reaching specifically targeted audiences – also bodes well for the NBA. Sponsorship is one of those alternate avenues, and the NBA is the king of sponsorship.

The NBA is a 50-year-old brand, Stern notes, as is its marketing partner, McDonald's: "It stands for a certain thing, as everything in sports does." No entity besides sports has the marketing opportunity to make the impact in cause-related or consumer-related marketing that the NBA does.

The NBA is the clutter-breaker marketers seek, Stern maintains. Proof? "Each fad will end," he says, "but the sports property will continue to grow. Sports becomes the continuum. As our brand grows, we invest it back in your brand."

By the same token Stern acknowledges that the glut of sports on TV translates to a plethora of consumer viewing options. He believes that the NBA's strength – its current and coming superstars – will carry it through, as they are doing now. And while he says that "it's not our manifest destiny" to plant the NBA and U.S. flags in international territories, the NBA does have offices in Melbourne, Australia, Barcelona, Spain, and Hong Kong. Stern is all in favor of the CBA's recent expansion into Mexico City and its market of 21 million. "I'm a big fan of the CBA," he says.

Everyone is a big fan of the NBA, he claims – even Nike, which withheld Michael Jordan's likeness in 1992. Even they see "the power of basketball down the road," says Stern.[6]

When you put his words to the test, you see their power. Playoff TV ratings soared in 1993, but even in 1992, with Magic Johnson retired and Larry Bird all but gone, ratings were up 15 percent. NBC paid $600 million for its four-year ride with the NBA. TNT paid $275 million for four years, then reupped for another $350 million.

Even without the national telecasts, the game is ubiquitous – to the point that the NBA had to defend itself in court against the charges of a television superstation that the league is trying to restrict its ability to televise games and make money. A lower court ruled that the NBA's actions were a restraint of trade.

What a problem to have: too many games on TV at a time when television station capacity is about to explode and international television markets are hungry for NBA telecasts.

Individual teams have their own networks that make money. The San Antonio Spurs put some of their games on pay-per-view to generate additional revenue. The Philadelphia 76ers tried to remove all their games from public television and go completely cable and pay-per-view. For 14 years running going into the '90s, the Portland Trail Blazers had the highest local market ratings of any NBA team.

The fans keep coming and watching. Despite no more Michael, Larry, and Magic. Despite no playoff team in Los Angeles. Despite the rash of fighting and physically more brutal play on the court. Despite the cost of attending a game rising 8 percent, to $27.12 a ticket on average, in 1993.[12]

If he knows nothing else, Stern knows one thing. "At some point," he says, "even *The Cosby Show* will stop, even in reruns. But I promise you the Boston Celtics will open the season."

And the one after that, and the one after that.

---

6. Speech to American Marketing Association Sports Marketing Conference, May 1993.

References

[1] *Daily Herald* (Paddock Publications), Sports, Nov. 5, 1992, p. 14.

[2] "Jam Session Visits Australia," *Hoop,* February 1994, p. 28.

[3] "Glut of Corporate Sponsors for U.S. Olympic Basketball May Blunt Marketing Edge," *Los Angeles Times,* July 8, 1992, p. 54.

[4] " '92 U.S. Basketball Team Should be Greatest Ever," *Chicago Tribune,* Sept. 18, 1991, Sports, p. 1.

[5] "Return of the Globe-trotters," *American Way,* March 15, 1993, p. 49.

[6] BW Sportswire release, Aug. 10, 1992.

[7] *AAdvantage* newsletter, March/April, 1994, p. 5.

[8] NBA Properties release, Nov. 17, 1993.

[9] NBA release, June 29, 1993.

[10] NBA News release, Nov. 22, 1993.

[11] Company release, Aug. 1, 1993.

[12] *Team Marketing Report*, Fan Cost Index, November, 1993.

Media as You've Never Seen It Before

(and if You Don't Have Enough Money, You Never Will, Either)

Here it comes. Sports as you've never seen them before on television as you've most likely never watched them before.

It's called "pay-per-view," and it means just what it stands for: you pay for it, you get to watch it. It is getting mixed reviews from event rights' holders, fans, politicians, and networks. For sports moguls, otherwise known as owners, it is the lifeline to restoring at least some of the monies lost to an expected reduction in rights' fees from the networks.

In plain, simple terms, pay-per-view means that fans shell out the kind of money to watch an event on the tube that they used to pay to watch the game in person. To politicians wary of their constituents in these budget-sensitive times, it is a battle cry to take to the voters.

Sports league commissioners and executives can't promise that in the next decade even events as big as the Super Bowl and the World Series won't be shown on a pay-per-view basis. Already, some events have enjoyed great success with pay-per-view. The Los Angeles

Dodgers have reaped benefits. So have the San Antonio Spurs. So has pro wrestling and boxing, the two sports that have consistently pulled in big numbers from pay-per-view events. Even shock jock Howard Stern of radio fame enjoyed success bringing his schtick to pay-per-view in the form of a nationally telecast New Year's Eve party.

Fans, in surveys, say that they'll watch the Super Bowl and the World Series on pay-per-view, even if it is their only option. They may have to. Not only have officials of the parent leagues of those events testified to Congress that such could be the case come the next decade, they are already starting to examine how to pull it off.

Pro baseball's new contract with ABC and NBC, plus the expanded major league playoffs, will begin to force pay-per-view down fans' throats. Expanded playoffs will mean that some postseason games will not be telecast nationally. That will mean fans in one locale who want to see a game that is only being regionally telecast elsewhere will probably eventually be able to pay a fee to get the feed for that game.

College football already is experimenting with such a notion, too. Some schools have their own pay-per-view networks that their fans and boosters latch onto readily, almost regardless of cost, for games that aren't telecast otherwise. In addition, the ESPN/ABC system has made regionally telecast games available in other areas for a fee for the last two years – allowing, for example, the Georgia Tech alums living in Los Angeles to watch their alma mater play North Carolina State in an Atlantic Coast Conference clash that they otherwise would not have seen.

Is this the future of pro sports, let alone amateur competition? Or is the lasting image of NBC's 1992 Olympic Triplecast that flopped so miserably the image of pay-per-view in the future? Will fans reject pay-per-view outright as the money-grubbing scheme that it is, or will they continue to open their pocketbooks more readily, as they appear to be currently?

Do you want to pay $15 to watch sports on TV at home? Or just certain events? Would you pay $40 to see Howard Stern's next New Year's Eve party, but not $12 to have your regional college football telecast switched out to that week's Notre Dame game, which is not available on network television?

You're not the only one who wants to know the answers to those questions. So do congressmen, senators, sports moguls, network executives, and various event rights' holders. What events will pay-per-view work for? Which won't it work for? Who will it work on? When won't it work, no matter what the event or price? Is pay-per-view good or bad? Where is the threshold that the public will draw when they want to get the message to all of the aforementioned groups that pay-per-view has become pervasive enough? Or will all those groups ignore the public's pleas and continue to spread the easy-money format?

How is pay-per-view being thrust upon you? What other factors drive it? What other factors cool it? In this chapter, we'll explore all those questions, trace pay-per-view's history and performance, and offer fact-based conclusions about its future. Depending upon who you are and who you work for, you may not like the answers.

Pay-per-View: An Overview

How big is the pay-per-view television market? Nobody knows exactly for sure. Figures on how many dollars the fledgling industry is garnering per year are strictly estimates.

Its marketplace appears to be huge, though. *Sport Marketing Quarterly* magazine reported in 1993 that *the number of U.S. households with addressable (pay-per-view) converters increased from 17.6 million to 20.1 million in 1992.* But the magazine quoted the Showtime cable network as saying that gross revenues from pay-per-view in 1992 were $329 million, or $2 million less than in 1991.[1]

The report went on to say that the Jimmy Connors/Martina Navratilova "Battle of the Sexes" tennis match, rock concerts, ABC's college football, and even pro wrestling all checked in as disappointments. Add the NBC Olympic TripleCast, and the pay-per-view industry got off with a dud rather than a bang in the '90s. Boxing remained strong, as events like the George Foreman/Evander Holyfield fight garnered more than 1 million orders. Does this mean that only boxing and the occasional wrestling match will pull in the results necessary to make pay-per-view viable?

Probably not. In fact, the market will probably grow whether we want it to or not. First of all, new stadiums with higher ticket prices and new and higher-priced amenities will force many fans out of the ticket market. But sports moguls and event rights' holders have no intention of letting those people "skate," if you will. While those who can afford it continue to pay the freight at the stadiums, one way or another those watching at home will be charged for the privilege of just viewing the game on the old TV box. Count on it.

While NBA Commissioner David Stern believes pay-per-view, on a broad scale, is "not in our best interests," he does realize that individual teams on a market-to-market basis have achieved at least a modicum of success with it, and that in all likelihood commercial establishments in those markets will be able to purchase NBA pay-per-view telecasts at what he calls a "modest fee" so they won't have to pirate it.[1] The game of pro basketball is so popular now, he knows, so why screw up a good thing by alienating the very fans who are responsible for its surge to a position of supremacy among world sports.

In Sports Poll '91, conducted for *Sports Illustrated*, two of three adults responded that they would buy the top sporting events on pay-per-view if there were no other way to watch them. In particular, 42 percent said that without question they would buy the Super Bowl on such a basis if no other options were available. How far behind can a pay-per-view Super Bowl be?

But pay-per-view is a sensitive subject. At the same conference at which NBA Commissioner David Stern made his comments, White Sox/Bulls owner Jerry Reinsdorf and Congressman William Lipinski (D.-Ill.) both canceled appearances at the last minute as part of a panel on pay-per-view. Lipinski has proposed legislation in the U.S. House of Representatives that would restrict pay-per-view telecasts of sporting events. More on that shortly. That both these high-profile, prestigious speakers would cancel appearances on the same panel on the same topic speaks to the sensitivity of the matter.

And just because NBC tried and failed at its Olympic TripleCast effort in 1992, investing lots of dollars in a losing effort, doesn't mean the networks are gung ho about pay-per-view. In fact, they continue to gripe about it, all the way to Capitol Hill in Washington, D.C. They're claiming that the pay-per-view boys are siphoning off events they might otherwise telecast for free, guaranteeing big bucks for the event rights' holders. Their arguments may be passé before they're ever credible.

---

1. Speech at the American Marketing Association Sports Marketing Conference, May 1992.

Or, as Skip Desjardin, World Wrestling Federation manager of pay-per-view marketing, told the *Chicago Tribune* in October of 1991, it's only a matter of time until the networks come around. "Let's face it," he said, "if there are 50 million basic cable subscribers out there and the Super Bowl currently draws about a third of the populace, if you could get 30 percent of the 50 million and charge 50 bucks, that's three-quarters of a million dollars. The potential payoff is mind-boggling."[2]

How are the networks going to resist being the conduit for that? How will football resist putting its product there? Peter Gent, author of *North Dallas 40* and other sports novels, and a former pro football player himself, believes the resistance wilted away a long time ago. He believes that the technology and logistics for such Super Bowl and even regular-season and playoff telecasts are all in place, awaiting the pay-per-view converter household demand and penetration levels to catch up. Gent has alluded to such schemes in his books, and he believes that even putting pro football on cable TV, in and of itself, is a form of pay-per-view that skirts legalities and antitrust laws. But the big money, as the WWF's Desjardin said, will win out.

The sports moguls agree. In 1989, NFL Commissioner Paul Tagliabue told a congressional hearing that the league would not put its showcase Super Bowl onto pay-per-view – before the end of the century. Then Major League Baseball (MLB) Commissioner Fay Vincent reiterated Tagliabue's stance, telling Congress that while MLB was putting some 175 games onto national cable distribution that year, the World Series wouldn't be immediately following onto pay-per-view format. Members of Congress used the opportunity to remind Vincent that his sport enjoys antitrust exemptions that give it basically monopolistic authority in governing, marketing, and distributing its games, and any hint by either football or baseball toward betraying the general public in the way of removing games from free TV would be frowned upon by Congress.

A year later, Tagliabue and Vincent were reiterating their respective positions on behalf of their respective sports before a congressional committee. Again, they both said their crown-jewel events (Super Bowl and World Series, respectively) were not going to be on any form of pay cable before the year 2000. Even the NBA's Stern joined the chorus in front of Congress this time, singing the same tune.

That kind of uncertain sentiment about the direction of sports and pay-per-view telecasts from the men who run the games has raised the ire of some fans already. In 1992, the *Chicago Tribune* reported that an organization called Television Viewers of America, or TVA, had spoken out vehemently against pay-per-view, especially the then-upcoming NBC Olympic TripleCast, proclaiming that the more successful the TripleCast, the more likely other pay-per-view events would pervade the airwaves. As the group's spokesperson, Gary Frink, said at the time, "Advertising-supported free TV has served professional teams and the fans very well. The teams take in millions. . . . Greed is the only reason to change this successful system."[3]

Mr. Frink didn't think of everything, though. For one thing, what makes him think that advertisers aren't going to flock to pay-per-view? If those WWF hypothetical projections about the Super Bowl ever come to pass, and if pay-per-view converters continue to proliferate, pay-per-view will become advertise-per-view too. Let's face it – if 30 percent of the 50 million fans who are wired for cable buy the Super Bowl pay-per-view telecast at $50 a pop, or three-quarters of a million dollars, do you think the advertisers are going to stay away from an audience that large? This whole book is testimony to the fact that advertisers will spend megabucks to reach much smaller audiences through sports.

For another thing, Mr. Frink, even though the TripleCast flopped, it still is the harbinger of things to come. Pay-per-view is coming, whether we want it or not. NBC was ahead of its time in introducing this on so broad a scale, but it chose the wrong event. You have to have the right event to make pay-per-view happen successfully. And for one last thing, Mr. Frink, somebody did hear you. Congressman Lipinski, as alluded to earlier, is still pushing legislation that would change the face of pay-per-view. But nothing will ever make it go away altogether.

Legislation

Congressman William Lipinski is sick and tired and has had enough. And he's standing up and shouting about it. Loudly.

Introduced in the summer of 1993, his legislation to restrict pay-per-view sports telecasts has been pending since. Lipinski's idea is to prohibit pay-per-view events from facilities that are taxpayer subsidized and to prohibit nonprofit and public organizations from telecasting events on a pay-per-view basis. As he said in a letter to his congressional colleagues, urging their support for the bill: "Tax-exempt status is granted to these [nonprofit and public organizations] by the federal government. It's unfair to allow those who take advantage of this government granted status to engage in pay-per-view telecasting, forcing taxpayers to pay again. We have a right to public viewing access if taxpayer money is used to make the event possible."[4]

Supplemental legislation Lipinski has introduced simultaneously would liberalize access of pay-per-view to commercial establishments by making them available at what the congressman called "reasonable fees." Basically, these establishments are the bars and restaurants that attract patrons in part through the many television monitors they have that seemingly carry nothing but sporting events. Complaints by many of these proprietors in part prompted the congressman to sponsor the legislation. Event rights' holders and networks gripe that too many of these establishments pirate the signal for these events. The Chicago Blackhawks SportsChannel pay-per-view carrier even had special investigators patrolling Chicago-area bars during the playoffs to monitor establishments that were pirating their pay-per-view home game signal.

But that's not enough to deter the congressman, who says he is fighting for the common man with this legislation. In an open letter in an issue of *Time Out*, the newsletter of the National Sports Fan Association based in Plymouth, Massachusetts, Lipinski notes: "Professional sports leagues see pay-per-view as a new revenue source that can help bridge the difference between what the networks pay them, and the sums they need to keep pace with escalating player salaries. Why should the average sports fan pay for the greed of professional athletes and team owners? It troubles me that working-class families might not be able to afford to watch an American tradition like the World Series! We cannot take free access away from low- and middle-income citizens. It is simply not fair."[5]

The Congressman goes on to cite in the letter that the number of homes estimated to have the ability to receive pay-per-view in 1996 will grow to 35.9 million. He sees this continued wiring of America as the mitigating factor in the inevitable march of pay-per-view to prominence.

Fans agree. In the same issue of *Time Out* that carried the congressman's letter, a fan poll revealed that 59 percent strongly disagree with the statement that pay-per-view is the best way for fans to be ensured access to professional sports. Another near 26 percent flat out disagreed, while only 5.1 percent agreed and 10.3 percent had no opinion. In other words, some 80 percent of respondents said pay-per-view is just not a good idea.

Fearful that sports moguls, leagues, and event rights' holders – and even networks, eventually – might disagree, Lipinski pressed on with his legislation. To support it, he used research showing the rate and scope of sports programming that had migrated from free TV to cable and pay-per-view. He gathered the information directly from the FCC, which interviewed, among others, cable programmers, sports entities, and the Association of Independent Television Stations, known as INTV. The association claimed that the migration revealed in the FCC findings as part of its charter from the Cable Act of 1992 will leave some 40 percent of the U.S. population without access to pay-per-view because their homes aren't even wired for cable.

To alienate such a major portion of the population, INTV told the FCC, was insufferable. Also, INTV "expressed concern that cable television's dual revenue streams, advertising and subscription revenues, will enable it to consistently outbid broadcasters who are supported by only a single revenue stream, advertising revenues, for sports programming." Despite that, the FCC found little evidence of an overabundance of sports programming migration from free to cable TV, which would lead to pay-per-view increases as well. However, the FCC reserved final determination. Fans will want to reserve it also, as the pay-per-view onslaught is still not upon us. It is only in the planning stages, as tests and tests and more tests of it continue to try to find the right mix of events, programming, and audience.

Still, the report's highlights included the finding that from 1981 to 1992 the number of Major League Baseball games on local cable per annum increased from 215 to 1,157. The number of games on broadcast television increased just four percent, from 1,488 to 1,547.

In measuring this sport plus football, basketball, and hockey, the FCC found mixed results.

It also found arguments representing special interests in the pay-per-view debate that drew obvious lines in the sand – and the debate. Interestingly, the NBA, MLB, and the NHL told the FCC that superstations such as WGN and TNT should be considered local broadcast stations because of their commitments to their home communities, despite their national distributions on cable and even national advertising. Gee, what direction do you think the leagues are going in with that argument?

The NFL showed its colors when it responded to the FCC by telling the commission to examine whether "programming that was otherwise available on broadcast television has moved to nonbroadcast television as a result. . . . If television rights are sold to basic cable networks because they cannot be sold at a reasonable price to broadcasters that cannot be considered migration."[6]

The FCC, in summary, basically concurred. "Most commenters," it said, "contend that there has been no significant migration of sports programming from broadcast television to subscription media," which would be an indication of movement eventually to pay-per-view. "They argue," the report continues, "that cable carriage of sports has not decreased the number of sports events shown on broadcast television, but rather has supplemented broadcast television so as to increase the quantity and diversity of sports events available to the viewing public."[6]

Table 4.1 displays FCC findings in its research of the migration of games from network television.

The report continues on to contend that cable simply enabled the broadcasts of events that otherwise might not have been shown at all. College athletics, in particular, was cited as a beneficiary of this. The report notes that commenters to the FCC also said that broadcast television remains the outlet of choice, as evidenced by the fact that most major sports championships are telecast on broadcast television as opposed to cable.

For now. Remember what the league commissioners said to Congress more than once.

Yet, INTV contends the migration is becoming more and more of a problem. CBS, as could have been expected, told the FCC that during

TABLE 4.1. Locally Telecast Regular Season Baseball Games (1981-1992)

Year	No. of Games	Cable	Total
1981	1,488	215	1,703
1982	1,494	400	1,894
1983	1,484	659	2,143
1984	1,426	1,032	2,458
1985	1,461	740	2,201
1986	1,505	815	2,320
1987	1,521	891	2,412
1988	1,566	933	2,499
1989	1,575	968	2,543
1990	1,552	1,103	2,655
1991	1,574	1,148	2,722
1992	1,547	1,157	2,704

Source: Federal Communications Commission, Inquiry Into Sports Programming, July 12, 1993.

the 1993–94 season none of the three New York-area pro hockey teams would have any of their games available on local broadcast television, that very few of the New York-area basketball teams' games would be available on broadcast television, and that only congressional pressure enabled seven Philadelphia 76er games to be shown on broadcast television.

The report cites that any significant migration of events to cable and pay-per-view "is due to the indifference of broadcast television." In other words, broadcast television often ignores events that don't have the necessary size and demographic scope. The networks want protection from pay-per-view; by the same token, they also are accused of creating the opportunity for its existence.

As the WWF contends, it probably won't be long before the networks come around to recognize the capacity and penetration of pay-per-view and participate in it, as NBC tried to do in 1992.

Still, Lipinski's office contends that even Notre Dame games wouldn't be exempt from his bill's exclusions, because although the school is a private institution, its athletic program receives a corporate income tax exemption. Therefore, all the bill does, according to

Lipinski's office, is keep the games available for all people, not just those who can afford them. Detractors of the proposed legislation say that pay-per-view won't take anything off free television that might have been there anyway.

In fact, because television networks are shying away from some sports because of demands for high events rights' fees and subsequent mounting monetary losses, supporters of pay-per-view say it will supplement sports television by offering events that broadcast might not pick up otherwise, especially on weekdays. The slashing of production costs at the networks may force a paring of broadcast network sports almost exclusively to weekends; pay-per-view will supplement that with weekday offerings. Pay-per-view might even save collegiate sports, say some supporters of the discipline, who see it as a way to bring games to people they might not otherwise see. So what if it comes with a cash box.

Lipinski's bill follows a "Fairness to Fans Act" that had been proposed that might have eliminated some pro sports antitrust exemptions if too many games were shifted to pay-per-view.

Meanwhile, somebody tried to shift the Olympics to pay-per-view, and failed miserably.

The Olympic TripleCast

It was, singularly, the boldest pay-per-view effort ever. Like the starship Enterprise, it was attempting to go where no pay-per-view telecasting had ever gone before. But it never got there.

Despite its optimistic tone, despite the modest numbers it needed to reach, despite the event (1992 Summer Olympics), despite the NBA Dream Team showcasing in the event, despite the broadcast network-cable partnership creating the pay-per-view telecast – the NBC Olympic TripleCast in 1992 flopped badly, falling far short of recouping the $100 million invested in it as part of NBC's $401 million investment in broadcasting the Olympics.

Maybe it was the pricing. NBC originally rolled out the TripleCast at three different pricing tiers – $95, $125, and $170 – for three different levels of service and types of events, respectively. Even Howard Stern's gross-you-out New Year's Eve Party was only $40 on pay-per-view.

Maybe it was the timing and the hours. With the games in 1992 in Barcelona, Spain, who was going to spend that kind of money to watch events in anything other than prime time? And who was going to watch the 1,080 hours of programming available, at any price?

Maybe it was the value. NBC claims it cost $90 for a family of four to attend the U.S. Open Tennis matches or an NFL game, and $75 to attend an MLB game – yeah, but at least you're *at* the game. If, as NBC stated, its TripleCast worked out to 11.5 cents per hour to watch, you'd have to watch a lot of hours to get your full dollars' worth.

Maybe it was the arrogance. The NBC executives in charge of the operation repeatedly insisted that the public wanted this, that they had research to show that after the 1988 Olympics in Seoul, fans told them they wanted more – much more. They stood by this research all the way to the lowering of prices right up to and even during the games in 1992 to gain a few incremental dollars and viewers.

Maybe it was the numbers. NBC had to get 2.8 million homes to sign up to break even, and you've already heard here that somewhere in the vicinity of 20 million homes are ready for pay-per-view. Some 16 to 17 million were ready when NBC popped this prize. Unfortunately, the number of homes NBC needed just to break even was close to twice as many as the largest pay-per-view event had ever captured. In addition, NBC had to assuage cable carriers everywhere who kept professing that they didn't have the channel capacity to carry the three networks NBC was proposing.

What happened? Like you have to guess. Response started low and got lower. Eight months in advance of the games, with lightweight promotion just beginning, NBC received 20,000 inquiries regarding the package. That's inquiries, not orders. NBC started a $40 million ad and promotional campaign to back the effort. NBC offered a Super Bowl package in the campaign to some lucky TripleCast subscriber. With the number of subscribers, the odds of winning were better than in the Publisher's Clearinghouse multi-million-dollar sweepstakes.

NBC claimed it had some 80 to 85 of the top 100 cable operators in the country signed on to carry the TripleCast channels. Of course, the ones *not* signed on represented the bulk of cable viewers around the country. Resistance to clearing the necessary channels was strong among key cable operators.

A few months before the games, with subscription rates still running dismally low, NBC announced a price change, eliminating its Bronze or $95 level package in favor of a $29.95 daily package. At the time of the price change in response to cable carrier griping and low subscription rates, NBC was still predicting it would break even on the pay-per-view telecast.

As the games were at hand, it was becoming clearer and clearer that NBC wouldn't even come close to getting the number of subscribers it needed to break even, let alone come close to the largest pay-per-view event of all time – to that date, the Evander Holyfield-George Foreman fight, which pulled down 1.5 million subscribers. In fact, despite promotional pushes for the TripleCast package, marketing research surveys revealed low public awareness for the package.

It may have been doomed from the start, according to George Bryant of *Satellite TV* magazine: "You know, I have to work for a living. If I was going to be home those two weeks and had a chance to watch all of it, it would be great, but I'm only going to be home on weekends when the majority of the stuff is on free broadcasting anyway."[7] All he saw when he looked at the package was more coverage, not different and better coverage. Without that, the TripleCast didn't have a chance.

Even the Dream Team – the greatest basketball team of all-time that won a gold medal despite itself – couldn't save the TripleCast. Subscriber rates continued to lag, as they would through the end. NBC, which once boasted of the venture's expected success and how the fans who told them they wanted it would gobble it up, got gobbled up itself instead. Chicago White Sox/Bulls owner Jerry Reinsdorf and Congressman William Lipinski weren't the only scheduled speakers who canceled appearances at the American Marketing Association's 1992 Sports Marketing Conference – so did NBC's Marty Lafferty. One of the executives in charge of the pay-per-view operation, Lafferty canceled less than 48 hours before his scheduled speech to an audience of sports/marketing executives eager to hear his spiel. It is believed the pay-per-view operation was in so much trouble that Lafferty, at the direction of higher-ups, could not pull himself away from NBC's New York offices just two months before the games to make a speech, even one to so pertinent an audience.

Just prior to the games, subscription rate estimates ranged from 5,000 to 100,000. However, NBC was in a bind, a bind it had created itself. It had to stick with the pay-per-view venture rather than sell partial rights to TNT for some $75 million and wind up in a situation where its affiliates would've been selling time against Ted Turner's Olympic non-prime-time telecasts. NBC had to show its affiliates it wouldn't betray them, and that it was willing to take the financial risk, rather than let the affiliates take it. It was almost an admission of being in a no-win situation.

Which it was. In the end, estimates of the number of subscribers ranged from 165,000 to 300,000. Regardless, it was far short of the 2.4 million NBC needed just to break even. NBC Sports President Dick Ebersole, once upon a time the creator of the network's fabulously successful "Saturday Night Live," was saying a year after the TripleCast debacle that he was against it from the start and had known that it would flop. He told a business luncheon audience in Chicago that to do pay-per-view you've got to have the right event. So far, wrestling and boxing have had the right events. Everyone thought that pay-per-view would come into its own in 1992, he said, what with the Olympic TripleCast, the Navratilova/Connors tennis match, the advent of college football pay-per-view on ABC, and all the success boxing and wrestling have already enjoyed and continued to enjoy.

Instead, the big events flopped because they were just that – the big events, not pay-per-view events. Ebersole apparently will go to his grave believing that pay-per-view's potential is limited at best. Football, because of a limited schedule of games, he believes, has a chance for some success at pay-per-view, because of the switchout possibilities from a boring game or a regional game to a more exciting one or one of simply greater interest. But for pay-per-view to work, he maintains, you must have the event, and it must be exclusive to pay-per-view (which the TripleCast wasn't).

After that, Ebersole asserts, don't look for pay-per-view to explode. There are those around the sports world who would disagree with him, including and above and beyond the already aforementioned Mr. Desjardin of the WWF, he of the almighty, grandiose Super Bowl estimates.

The Rest of the Sports World Disagrees (Well, Most of It)

For so many sports, and so many sports events, pay-per-view is the hoped-for future. So many successes have been scored, and huge numbers don't have to be necessarily achieved to make a success. Just ask the promoters of Holyfield-Foreman and Howard Stern's New Year's Eve Party. Only about a million subscribers were needed to make a killing.

Boxing and wrestling have scored the greatest consistent successes in pay-per-view. Boxing keeps coming at you on pay-per-view, fueled by Time Warner Sports' TVKO, the pay-per-view service that keeps lining airwaves with the events. What it does is get the right events.

For its "People's Choice Night of Champions" in 1993, TVKO got $24.95 per subscription. When Riddick Bowe fought Evander Holyfield for the heavyweight title in November of 1993, subscribers paid some $38 each for the event, generating some $33 million in revenue. The Mike Tyson/Razor Ruddock fight in 1991 just missed surpassing the Holyfield/Foreman bout for the number one spot of all time in subscriptions. Even Buster Douglas, who was a bust after taking the title from Mike Tyson, drew big numbers for pay-per-view. His duel with Evander Holyfield drew some 7 to 8 percent of the then available pay-per-view-capable universe and grossed $19 million. Even ancient Larry Holmes was able to attract 800,000 homes or so for his comeback fight with Evander Holyfield.

But the boxing world had one thing going against it, or so it seemed: Mike Tyson, supposedly its biggest draw, went to jail. But he was never the biggest draw, as the Holyfield numbers later proved. As Ebersole said, you've got to have the event. Boxing does.

College football has made its runs at pay-per-view too, trying to capitalize on the emotional attachment of fans to the school, its colors, and its national championship chances. The sport saw the potential that Ebersole spoke of. ABC/ESPN has been switching games out now for two seasons, offering tradeouts of regional telecasts at about $10 or so per game. It figured to be easy, much easier than the TripleCast. As newsletter publisher Barry Gould told the *Chicago Tribune* in 1992, "For cable operators who have the channel capacity, this is a no-brainer."[8]

Maybe not. Previous pay-per-view networks have struggled in college football, even with games featuring the most popular teams with the most rabid of fans. Of course, a national championship game in college football could pull down the kind of pay-per-view numbers that the WWF's Desjardin referred to in regard to the Super Bowl, especially in a day and age when there seems to be a college football game a minute during the holiday season and when pro football is increasingly taking time and viewers from college football with more games, more weeks, more dates, and its own playoffs.

Yet, there are success stories. Louisiana State's "Tigervision" makes a half million or so a year at $29.95 per game at about 6,000 subscribers per game.[9] Again, it's the event. LSU is in a basically noncompetitive situation in its market, as far as its home fans go. Notre Dame would probably do well with it, but the school already has a long-term contract for its home games with NBC and the rest of its games are on one national network or another.

But college football didn't prove to be the pay-per-view draw ABC/ESPN imagined. Switchouts of between 15,000 to 25,000 nationally were being reported during 1992, the first year of the deal. ABC/ESPN didn't anticipate, perhaps, the power of the regional networks around the country, which offer competitive games tailored for their specific broadcast regions. Or, as columnist Prentis Rogers of the *Atlanta Journal/Atlanta Constitution* says, "A game between Stanford and Oregon has no chance of selling in Alabama when paying to see the Crimson Tide is an option" (as it is sometimes, on the regional SportSouth network), even if the cost is more than the ABC/ESPN offering.

That can't be said about hockey. When the then Minnesota North Stars (now the Dallas Stars) miraculously made their way to the Stanley Cup finals in 1992, their fans watched the home games on pay-per-view in increasingly greater numbers from round to round as the lowly overachievers made their way closer and closer to pro hockey's ultimate prize. It wasn't enough, though, to keep the team from moving a year later to Dallas, where they've been selling out their home game tickets on a regular basis. It's testimony to the power of winning – the more you win consistently, the more likely you are to be "the event" that Dick Ebersole says you have to be to sell pay-per-view subscriptions.

Not one to pass up a good thing, the Chicago Blackhawks got into the act too. Owner Bill Wirtz, known to be tight-fisted with a buck, had never televised home games until he introduced "HawkVision" in 1991 during the playoffs. The Blackhawks, who have had some playoff successes but no Stanley Cup championships since 1961, have been selling the postseason package very handsomely ever since. At one game for $16.95 or an entire series at $19.95, the Blackhawks felt they were offering a bargain. They even offered the linkup to commercial establishments such as bars and restaurants for $100.

The Blackhawks projected subscriptions to be anywhere in the 10,000-to-30,000 range, which it just managed to achieve. They knew that if the team did well in the playoffs, the subscription rate would multiply quickly. The whole venture was a difficult go-ahead for the Blackhawks, who lost millions on their initial pay-per-view effort, which went on to become the basic cable SportsChannel/Chicago station (sans Blackhawk home games). In 1993, the Blackhawks doubled their first-round subscription rate from 1992, hitting 9,000. In 1994, the team had 11,000 on line to witness its first-round dismissal by archrival St. Louis.

Playoff hockey seems to be another example of "the event" that Ebersole relishes. Even regular season sells, however, as the then North Stars and even the Detroit Red Wings will tell you. But in 1993 the Blackhawks backed up their claim to the necessity of pay-per-view when they claimed that a nationally televised playoff game on ABC from Chicago Stadium was not completely sold out, although rumors swirled that the team had withheld tickets to make its point that free home TV would hurt ticket sales. In the end, Blackhawk pay-per-view carrier SportsChannel sued 68 commercial establishments for pirating the 1992 playoff signal. As the team advanced round by round through the playoffs that year, operators reported subscription bumps of up to 50 percent – again, winning meant everything in creating "the event."

Clearly though, cable and pay-per-view are the vehicles of choice for pro hockey, which has regional interest and which is difficult to televise because of the small but quickly moving puck and all the fighting that mars the games – not to mention the few opportunities for commercial breaks. If any major sport leads the way into pay-per-view, it may be hockey.

Outside of boxing and wrestling, special events have had their problems on pay-per-view. The Jimmy Connors/Martina Navratilova tennis match did not approach the largest pay-per-view audience ever. Neither did the Julius Erving/Kareem Abdul-Jabbar one-on-one legends basketball matchup. Neither had to, though, to break even or to achieve the participants' share fees and winner pots. The NBA successfully barred Magic Johnson from playing Michael Jordan in a one-on-one contest while both were still active players, leaving the world to wonder not only who would've won but just how high the pay-per-view buy-in fee would've been and how many would've bought the one-on-one basketball matchup of all time. Now that they're both retired, who cares?

It all goes back, once again, to having *the* event – that right event, with the right timing, the right participants, and the right availability to pay-per-view, the right audience, and the right price.

Thank you, Dick Ebersole.

Speaking of Ebersole's Comments . . .

The Olympics are not ruling out pay-per-view as a carrier in 1996 in Atlanta. In a report in the *Cleveland Plain Dealer* shortly after the 1992 games and the TripleCast bust with its estimated $100 million in losses, the U.S. Olympic Committee said that the games have to be made available to as wide an audience as possible, and that with all the events going on, broadcast television couldn't handle it all. That is despite an apparent International Olympic Committee rule that prohibits pay-per-view in the host country. But in this case, the host country is the lucrative United States market.[10]

The powers behind the Olympics are searching for a way to make pay-per-view a viable option for 1996. This is typical of the greed of the American event rights' holder, typical of what MLB has in store for America with its expanded playoffs and its new television network with expanded regional coverages, and typical of the college football experiments and pro football hidden plans to do the same. Milk as much money out of fans as possible, at the ballpark or through the boob tube.

Meanwhile, NBC came back with a winning, record $456 million bid to televise the 1996 games in Atlanta, although it would not commit to pay-per-view plans this time around.

And TripleCast flop notwithstanding, pay-per-view does appear to be the wave of the future. Flip on your television – if you have a converter box, chances are your cable carrier greets you with an initial screen advertising pay-per-view offerings before you switch over to the channel you want to watch. At hotels, pay-per-view movies are rampant; previews for these are the first thing to come on your screen when you flip on the set.

Baseball believes it has found its way into pay-per-view happiness, although owners downplay the possibility. These are the same owners who expanded the playoff and regular-season formats to include more games and teams, respectively, for more money, hopefully. Their new TV contract with ABC/NBC, which created the Baseball Network, establishes regionalizing as a principal trend. This means that regional games not available in one market will eventually be made available in another via pay-per-view. Pay-per-view will become a necessity in the new network – the new contract and partnership with NBC and ABC are projected to yield some one-half the revenues over four years that the former inflated and overpriced billion-dollar contract with CBS did. Pay-per-view will be looked to to help make up the difference.

Boxing and wrestling continue to pull down big, profitable numbers. Hockey continues to see success with playoff telecasts. Some pro basketball teams see success with pay-per-view telecasts of some of their bigger games. The Los Angeles Dodgers lead the way among the handful of pro baseball clubs doing pay-per-view, selling pay-per-view packages of games to an audience that doesn't get Dodger games on free TV anyway. Dodger attendance traditionally is among the major league leaders, too. Then again, so is that of the Cubs, and just about every one of their games is on free, broadcast television. It just goes to show there is no standard formula for pay-per-view success – there's just success with the right event or failure with the wrong one.

Nobody knows that better than Roger Noll, the Stanford professor of economics who has made studying the trends that shape the economics of pro sports his life's work. Noll believes, plain and simple, that pay-per-view is here to stay and will grow, and that fan resistance to it will dissipate. It dissipated against paying for cable, despite cable's ever-increasing rates. Plus, with ballparks becoming overpriced palaces available to fans who can afford the high prices and high-priced amenities that come with them, mainstream, middle-class, blue-collar fans will be shoved out into TV land whether they like it or not – pay-per-view TV land. Attending games at stadiums, Noll knows, has become the privilege of the same several hundred thousand fans of each team in baseball, over and over again, rather than a completely individual 2 million or so per club. For those of you not in that number, pay-per-view is on the way. For those in that number, pay-per-view will become the option of choice when you're not at the game, because the teams already know you're willing to pay exorbitantly to get into the ballpark anyway.

Noll, however, stops short of believing the Super Bowl or the World Series will ever be on pay-per-view, as the WWF's Desjardin and the respective sports' moguls would like to see, despite their promises to keep such showcases off pay-per-view through the century. Noll simply feels it is too politically volatile for politicians to allow it to happen.

But they probably will anyway.

References

[1]   *Sport Marketing Quarterly*, Volume II, No. 2, 1993.

[2]   *Chicago Tribune*, sports section, Oct. 29, 1991, p. 1.

[3]   *Chicago Tribune*, sports section, July 6, 1992.

[4]   Letter from Congressman William Lipinski to fellow congressmen, July 20, 1993.

[5]   *Time Out*, newsletter of the National Sports Fan Association, undated.

[6]   *FCC Interim Report: Inquiry into Sports Programming Migration*, PP Docket No. 93–21, July 1, 1993, pp. 5–6.

[7]   *Chicago Tribune*, sports section, March 3, 1992.

[8]   *Chicago Tribune*, sports section, Aug. 24, 1993, p. 11.

[9]   *Chicago Tribune*, sports section, Oct. 30, 1991.

[10] *Cleveland Plain Dealer*, Sports, Aug. 30, 1992, p. 5.{fn}1. Speech at the American Marketing Association Sports Marketing Conference, May, 1992.

Fantasy Marketing

Perhaps in no way are fans' emotional attachments to the games they love more pronounced than in fantasy sports.

Mainstream marketers are latching onto so-called "rotisserie baseball," "fantasy football," and other sports adaptations that have exploded beyond the friendly, two-bit gambling competitions they began as a little over a decade ago. Through fantasy and rotisserie leagues marketed via mainstream media, marketers are giving fans opportunities to continue playing these games while simultaneously gathering their names in prospective customer databases of sports participants and rabid sports followers who could become amenable to purchasing these firms' goods and services.

These so-called fantasy leagues give fans the chance to do the one thing they've always thought they can do better than the pros: manage the game. These games have been created for all the armchair quarterbacks and couch-potato jocks watching sports on TV who believe they can outguess, outthink, and outplay the pro managers and coaches. On top of that, the next evolution has come alive – fantasy camps, where fans similarly get to actually train with and compete with and against their favorite stars.

These camps have become popular in several sports, but to date marketers have been able to best leverage the baseball version. Fans of all ages and professions have flocked to these camps for the opportunity to be close to the retired stars who are featured there. Fans pay upwards of $4,000 for a week for these opportunities and have no regrets. Seizing upon this, as we'll see later in this chapter, corporations have caught the fantasy-camp fever and are using them as vacation incentive rewards to motivate employee performance. And does it ever work.

In this chapter, we'll explore the history and origins of both fantasy leagues and fantasy camps. We'll examine how they are marketed and why they have become effective marketing tools for everything from boosting newspaper circulation to increasing business-to-business sales levels.

Newspapers have used fantasy and rotisserie league participation in exemplary fashion, inducing potential readers to open the publication daily and advertisers to participate as cosponsors and to share database information about consumers who are already bent toward sports participation and would probably fit their target customer profile. Sponsoring the league puts the advertiser in a good light with the consumer.

But more than anything else, by discussing this phenomenon we'll have a golden opportunity to see how events and games like these tug at the emotional heartstrings in the chests of fans who can't resist the opportunity to be as close or closer to the game than they ever have. Nothing goes to the emotional side of sports marketing more than fantasy marketing. And nothing goes to the heart of fantasy sports marketing more than rotisserie leagues and fantasy camps.

Rotisserie Leagues – All Aboard

How They Work

Rotisserie baseball drafts have become as much a rite of spring as spring training itself. The Rotisserie League Baseball Association in New York estimates that each spring somewhere between 2 and 2.5 million Americans – predominantly men – scour the spring training camp reports in daily newspapers, on ESPN, on their local TV news sports segments, anywhere and everywhere, for bits of information about how the players are doing.

If these fans are playing rotisserie according to its origins, they're basically seeking information on batting average, home runs, runs batted in, and stolen bases for offensive categories, and wins, earned run average, strikeouts, walks, hits surrendered, and saves for pitchers. Of course, knowing that a player is healthy and can participate is of paramount importance. Rabid fans are known to call team front offices if a player has missed a few games to get an update on his condition, short of being able to get the information anywhere else.

How their favorite team is doing is of no import. Rotisserie pits your primal competitive instincts above and beyond your hometown favoritism, as we'll also examine later in this chapter. To the avid participant, there is nothing like getting ready for the annual rotisserie draft.

Simply, it works like this: ten or 12 individuals (or teams, if you will) meet and select, as in a real sports draft, real players. Except these are real players on active major league rosters. There are many modifications, but the most common is 14 position players and nine pitchers. They can be from any and all the teams. In all likelihood, you'll end up with a first baseman from Baltimore, a catcher from the Mets, a relief pitcher from Philadelphia, and so forth.

Cumulative statistics are the basis for scoring. The team owners agree to toss a certain amount of money into the pot as a franchise entry fee, and the top three or four finishers divide it up after the season. The pot is enhanced during the season as teams pay fees for making trades with each other or ante up for claiming a free agent (someone who's on nobody else's roster).

This craze supposedly began in a rotisserie-grill restaurant in New York City in the late '70s – thus the bestowal of the "rotisserie" moniker. It has become the national scourge. Fans now expect their favorite teams to draft/trade/sign for the players who can help them win real pennants as they do themselves in rotisserie competition. "There's a rotisserie mindset out there," according to David Cone, who signed an $18 million free-agent contract in 1993 with the Kansas City Royals.

Much the same phenomenon has occurred in basketball and football. The same draft ritual happens, similar scoring structures are erected, and the same monies and trading and free agency stipulations are tossed into the hat.

Rumor has it that everyone from New York Governor Mario Cuomo to Buffalo Bills running back Thurman Thomas is in a rotissserie baseball league.

Marketers Discover Rotisserie Leagues and Fantasy Camps

With millions of fans playing, it didn't take long for major marketers to get in. Where millions of people are, marketers will follow, trying to exploit the emotional tug of whatever the attraction is.

How emotional is it? Would you believe I'm watching ESPN SportsCenter as I'm writing this?

Playing upon the fans' emotional attachment to their game, marketers have cashed in with sponsored leagues that help them build business and databases of customers. They have brought a sophistication to the games of rotisserie and fantasy baseball and football well beyond anything conceived of by the fans who founded it.

Still, the marketing thrust started with a dull thud – computer-savvy sports nuts devised programs to help rotisserie players do their statistics. With 23 or more players and eight or more categories to keep up with weekly, biweekly, and/or monthly, that was bound to happen. The services are regularly advertised in each sports' specific "bible" publication. From there though, marketing mayhem followed. Professionally marketed rotisserie leagues appeared that took advantage of fans' passions for their games and their lust for the information and statistics that go with it.

USA Today was one of the first publications to offer rotisserie participation. Around 1990, the newspaper started a database and a draft that offered statistics and player values (rotisserie players bid on athletes via drafts). You could make trades through an 800 phone number and tap statistics through on-line software. *USA Today*'s baseball game had 24-hour player statistical data available via computer or modem. And the paper kept score for the participants and published the names of league leaders during the season and, of course, the eventual champions and prize winners of the rewards graciously supplied by the cosponsors like Apex and Champion. *USA Today*'s NFL rotisserie game was dubbed "Sports Challenge Football" and promoted as "A Great Way To Play Football With Your Kids."[1]

USA Today published the "value" of each player alongside his name, so you knew how much of your $10 million starting purse you had to spend on each one. Of course, you didn't really have $10 million – but that was the "amount" each participant began with as he or she drafted his or her way through to a team of quarterbacks, running backs, and receivers. Each week the names of the players and their values were published to encourage trading. And each week, each participant willingly surrendered his or her name and other pertinent demographic information either through mail or telephone registration – all to the benefit of participating sponsors – and paid a modest fee for the privilege of having that happen to them. Each week, 1,800 winners received a prize of sorts. The overall season champ got $10,000.

In the *Toronto Star*, a "Star Ball" baseball rotisserie was promoted by a company called JBE Ltd. It had the top 100 finishers' names printed in the paper each week and gave out a $100 top prize and a $35 value pair of Blue Jays tickets. One grand prize winner received a $3,000-plus IBM home computer – just what every database-savvy rotisserie player needs. JBE Ltd. also promoted rotisserie hockey in hockey-crazed Canada.

Marketing Sophistication Grows

As the phenomenon grew to a fever pitch, the marketing pitches ticketed directly for information-crazed rotisserie players kept coming, too. The on-line services (Genie, Prodigy, CompuServe) began to offer statistics services and leagues for their computerphile registrants to generate more usage, participation, and fees from them, and to attract their friends to their services, too. On-line leagues enhanced their services' drawing power to an ever-increasing number of home computer users. A rotisserie presence only enhanced the services' offerings of detailed sports information, anyway.

So rotisserie grew from a restaurant birth in Manhattan to an American celebration, complete with its own special in 1994 on pay-per-view TV and with regular references from sportscasters and sportswriters everywhere. Drafts became parties and parties became midseason barbecues for making trades. Sports bars catered to the rotisserie trade with overdoses of TV monitors capturing games from all over the country. And the rotisserie trade patronized anyone and everyone, anything and everything that could supply a statistical edge, an inside tip, or a better handle on a player's real value.

Marketers capitalized on rotisserie fanaticism to the point that services like the Interactive Network were born. Interactive, out of northern California, wired an FM signal into homes along with the regular television signal. Through a modem and keypad, anyone in front of the TV could play along with the game in progress, whether it be football, basketball, baseball, or "Jeopardy."

Viewers got to call plays, regardless of what the coach actually called or what the team actually did. To top it off, they could compete nationally or regionally with other viewers doing the same, sending their "scores" into Interactive central via a built-in modem. For a few hundred dollars, the average sports couch potato or armchair quarterback became a participant. Prizes were awarded and winners' names posted on the Interactive Network to encourage more participation.

But when an ad agency and an interactive telephone marketing service hooked up to create, distribute, and administer "Dugout Derby," they invented the quintessential rotisserie marketing tool.

From Fun to Profits: "Dugout Derby" Epitomizes Rotisserie Fever

It is spring time – spring-training time, that is – 1990. And major-market newspapers across America are looking for ways to boost subscription revenues. Growth has been flat for years in the metro newspaper market. America has stopped reading and started to get its news and information more and more regularly from local TV, CNN, ESPN, the Weather Channel, et al.

But it is also that time of year when the estimated millions of rotisserie baseball buffs around America are sharpening up for their spring drafts, looking to improve their teams and finish in the money this season. They are studying every bit, scrap, database, and published or broadcast piece of information about baseball that they can possibly get their hands on. It's just that time of year.

One place America's rotisserie buffs turn to regularly once the season starts is their daily newspapers. Those box scores from the previous day's games are the first things they're checking: Who homered? Who stole a base? Who got a save? Or a win? How many RBIs for the "team" today?

America's metro newspapers know those fans are turning to those pages. Now, how can they make those fans regular subscribers? How can they convert rotisserie fanaticism into subscription revenue?

Enter "Dugout Derby."

The brainchild of Wakeman & DeForrest, an Irvine, California ad agency, and Phoneworks, a telemarketing service out of Hackensack, New Jersey, "Dugout Derby" hit 14 newspapers across the country in 1990, after a successful test run in southern California markets. To enter and play was simple: all fans had to do was select 13 players (nine position players, including a designated hitter, and four pitchers) and then dial an 800 number to advise the Wakeman & DeForrest computer who they were.

Each major league player had his name, statistics, and code number published. All fans had to do was call. Of course, to identify themselves and their teams, they surrendered their Social Security numbers, the one tool any marketer wants when designing research to create business pitches of their own.

On a weekly basis, fans could make twice-weekly trades through a 900 number to upgrade their teams. All in all, the game was simpler to play and administer for fans than standard rotisserie leagues; this was part of the plan to attract as wide a base as possible.

Prizes, of course, were offered weekly and for the season. While the weekly prizes were modest, grand-prize season winners could win a week-long cruise and $10,000 to spend on it.

The allure worked. Despite the work in selecting a team, despite the 900 calls to upgrade them, despite the depth of field in the competition that made it unlikely that you would win, all told some 225,000 to 250,000 fans registered, according to Bob Barbiere of Phoneworks.[1]

While some fans didn't complete the season or only played for a few weeks and lost interest, the bulk played for the entire season,

---

1. Interview, January 3, 1991.

trying to prove their rotisserie baseball worth versus a cross-section of fans from their region.

For the newspapers, it was a bonanza, according to Kevin Cherney of Wakeman & DeForrest, whose agency handled the team administration. Team registration was designed with questions and prompts to discover if players were subscribers or if they were interested in subscribing. If they were interested in a special subscription offer for "Dugout Derby" participants only, the information was immediately faxed directly to the participating newspaper for fulfillment.

"The success rate of that was tremendous," said Cherney, in an interview.[2] He couldn't give specifics, but he did detail that participating newspapers consistently closed on two-and-a-half to three times more potential subscribers than they did during usual circulation campaigns. The success formula was simple, too.

"You were a reader of the paper. You were playing the game. That equals built-in interest," Cherney explained. While subscription boosts varied from paper to paper, each paper did significantly increase circulation through "Dugout Derby."

Once they were subscribers and their Social Security numbers were captured, they became part of a promotion-minded database for other offers from the paper and participating marketers. For some newspapers, it became more than a subscription-driven promotion. They sold advertising space around their "Dugout Derby" sections and collected a portion of the revenues from the 900 calls made by players updating rosters and standings and making trades. The *Chicago Tribune,* for example, sold ad space in "Dugout Derby" sections to Molson, the Canadian beermaker, which sponsored a "Dugout Derby Corner."[2]

"The Tribune sold to Molson ad space it wouldn't have sold otherwise," Cherney said. That's because, he went on, "Advertisers know the demographics of 'Dugout Derby' players. They're upscale male sports enthusiasts. This gave advertisers guaranteed placement and exposure."

"Dugout Derby" did well enough that it induced Phoneworks and Wakeman & DeForrest to develop "Pigskin Playoff" for football and "Fairway Fantasy" for golf. "Pigskin Playoff" worked much the same

---

2. Interview, January 3, 1991.

way "Dugout Derby" did. "Fairway Fantasy," on the other hand, employed other elements. Prime among them was television.

To boost viewership and ratings for golf telecasts, "Fairway Fantasy" allowed golf-viewing enthusiasts to select in advance three PGA pros, with the fans themselves completing the foursomes. Through the course of CBS' televised golf tour schedule, fans played a different hole each week via an 800 number; their score was combined with the scores of the three pros they had elected to team up with. Substantial tie-in marketing from other sponsors brought down the cost of the program considerably.

But it's still "Dugout Derby" that is the best testimony to the fanaticism that reigns among fans for fantasy sports participation, for their opportunity to be the best coach potato or armchair quarterback they can be, and to be willing to pay for the privilege with demographic information about themselves, with money for 900 phone calls, and with their time, sweat, and effort.

Those elements are all there in the rotisserie player and fantasy participant, as they themselves attest.

Rotisserie – the Emotion of It All

Why do ordinary fans play rotisserie baseball? Mostly because they don't think there's anything ordinary about themselves. All of what you're about to read in this brief segment is true, especially my own observations and recollections about the emotions behind rotisserie participation.

But why fans play is simple. As Nathan Cobb wrote it allows "baseball fans to do what they always knew deep down in their hearts that they could do: run a team better than the people who actually do it for a living."[3]

Cobb, a long-time player himself, testified throughout the seven pages of running copy about rotisserie baseball to the extent of the participants' emotional involvement. In his initial season in a league, his activities included "7 player trades, 21 other roster moves, 964 miles of driving to and from league gatherings and $208.63 in long-distance telephone charges."

Lee Eisenberg, editor-in-chief of *Esquire,* is one of the group of scribes generally credited with helping create the first official league in a New York rotisserie-style restaurant in the late '70s. As he put it in a *New York Times* commentary in April 1990, "Rotisserie baseball is one of the reasons baseball is booming. It is responsible for fueling the astonishing interest that has developed in spring training. Last year, in the quaint and formerly idyllic ball park in Bradenton, Florida, more fans seemed interested in debating the rotisserie value of Jose Canseco than in watching the Pirates game."[4] The Pirates train in Bradenton. Rotisserie players train anywhere and everywhere – year round.

As Eisenberg continued, "Rotisserie fever is contagious. The game has touched off an explosion in services and publications expressly conceived to help the armchair general manager get an edge. . . . Network commentators . . . regularly refer to rotisserie baseball without further explanation. And if you have noticed a recent blizzard of arcane baseball statistics in every newspaper, you can chalk that up to the popularity of rotisserie baseball."

However, as both authors explain, the rub of rotisserie is in the allegiances for baseball that it shatters. No longer does it matter if you're a life-long Phillies fan or a Mets fanatic. Bleeding Dodger Blue as a fan no longer counts for anything. If you're a Mets fan, and one of your rotisserie pitchers from the Cardinals is going up against them that night, guess who you're rooting for that evening?

"That's the downside of rotisserie baseball: it messes up your loyalties," wrote Eisenberg, a life-long Phillies fan. "You say the Phillies got a chance to finish second?" he wrote in 1990. "Great, but I own half the (arch-rival) Cub pitching staff." He even remembers the fateful night in 1980 when he was rooting for Pittsburgh Pirate reliever Kent Tekulve to strike out Philadelphia legend Mike Schmidt so his rotisserie team could get a notch in the save column.

Emotions crunched, the rotisserie player delves into investigating the game and its statistics. As Cobb wrote, "How many box scores are you willing to read each day in order to get the same results you've already gotten in two different newspaper stories, even though you were watching those games on TV the night before? Answer: You can never read too many box scores."

Not only that, where else can you trade Barry Bonds for Orel Hershiser? Lee Smith for Barry Larkin? Cal Ripken for Kirby Puckett?

Or make any other deal that would be otherwise beyond the realm of human possibility on planet Earth. Would you have any other reason to call the Kansas City Royals front office, other than finding out the extent of David Cone's injury? And how do you react, as Cobb discovered, when your second baseman (in this case, Julio Franco) homers off of one of your pitchers (in this case, Wes Gardner)? It was "joy and despair," as he put it.

Then again, I have sat in on drafts and trading sessions that have gotten entirely out of hand. Drafts especially. Consistently, players try to squeeze someone into a slot for which he isn't eligible. True story: at a rotisserie draft, Sam Horn, who had never put on a glove in a major league game to that point, is drafted as a first baseman. Another participant protests. It is getting late. Everyone wants to leave. It's a Friday night and people have plans other than sitting around in a conference room at the office after hours. Clearly, Horn is not eligible at first base. He is a designated hitter only. But to expedite matters, the vote is 6-5 to let the maneuver stand.

The protesting owner sells his team and quits the league a month later. Others do the same in disgust over the course of the next few seasons as rules get bent and broken relentlessly. Rotisserie competition makes you remember that you were all friends when this started. Or maybe it makes you forget that as the stakes get higher, the fees rise and the emotions and frustrations take over and you can't understand why one of your opponents turned down that perfectly good, logical trade offer you made. What a jerk he is, right?

So, if you're emotional about sports, rotisserie is the quintessential emotional sports release. If you're a marketer, it's one great way to tap into it.

Instead of Rotisserie, How About a Fantasy Camp?

If rotisserie competition isn't your bag or if it gets you too stressed out, as it's been known to do to some, there's a new, different kind of sports fantasy participation exploding in popularity.

It attracts individuals from all walks of life – doctors, salesmen, engineers, and even writers. It attracts corporations from all disciplines, who use it as a motivation tool. It features not the current stars that

Figure 5.1. Retired Major Leaguer Gene Oliver instructs fans (consumers) at a White Sox Fantasy Camp. (Photo by Howard Schlossberg)

rotisserie-crazed fans use in their ongoing leagues, but retired stars whose skills have not degenerated as much as you might think.

It's called the fantasy camp, and for a mere few thousand dollars, fans can spend a week, or a weekend, training with and finally competing against the legends of the game. The allure of being that close to one's heroes is so powerful that these camps have taken off in popularity. Sales-driven companies use them relentlessly as incentive tools, rewarding their best performers with all-expenses-paid jaunts to warm-climate settings where the likes of baseball greats like Randy Hundley, Orlando Cepeda, Hoyt Wilhelm, Brooks Robinson, Harmon Killebrew, Lou Brock, Gene Oliver, and Ernie Banks, to name a few, await them.

And entertain them. And train them. And then compete with and against them. The fantasy camp has simply exploded into a national pastime of its own. Former Chicago Cub great Randy Hundley is credited with being one of the innovators in this genre, and he now administers fantasy camps for the general public for individual teams and MLB, as well as corporate concerns.

Figure 5.2.   White Sox Fantasy camp participant goes to the wall to practice making
a tough catch. (Photo by Howard Schlossberg)

As Mike Yaccino, his marketing director, notes, Hundley's camps began in 1983. "From the players' perspectives," Yaccino said in an interview, "it's like a reunion." For the campers, regular guys from all walks of life, it's heaven. They share locker rooms with the retired stars, and meals and social time, gleaning in their knowledge and becoming raptured with their lore.[3] And paying anywhere from $3,000 to $5,000 for the privilege.

Corporations have found the fantasy camp to be an ideal motivational award, an attractive way to generate sales performance. "Companies are at a point where they're looking for something new," Yaccino said. "It's on the verge of taking off big-time." In Hundley's first seven years in business, he handled 6,000 campers.

Andrew Cohen of Diamond Promotions, New York, also testifies to the drawing power of the camps he administers. He handles baseball, tennis, golf, and basketball, and can run women's camps. He'll do half-day and full-day camps, just to complement annual corporate sales meetings, or weekends and full weeks for individuals on vacation who spring for the attendance fee from their own pockets or for corporations rewarding their better performers.

As Cohen's programs go, you get to play in a real MLB facility and stay in a full-service resort nearby. Socializing opportunities abound with the retired stars. Competition lasts the length of the camp, first between campers and finally between the campers and the stars. Sacred memorabilia are taken home in the form of videos, photos, autographed souvenirs, uniforms, and personalized baseball cards.[5]

Cohen explained, in part, the allure of these camps. Anyone can take a vacation to Hawaii or Mexico, he said in an interview, "but playing tennis with Martina Navratilova is something they can't do on their own."[4] So when he noticed a lot of teams doing these on their own, he began to package and customize every aspect of them, from the venue to the sport to the travel to the retired-star participants. "I grew up with these people," Cohen said, so how could he or anyone else resist the temptation to participate with them?

As his promotional literature states, fantasy camps "are ideal promotional vehicles for enhancing interest and creating excitement around

3. Interview, August 1990.
4. Interview, August 1990.

a particular product, brand or company. They attract the desired target market by offering a unique experience – playing with sports legends before live audiences." Oh yes, spouses and families are usually and often welcome on these fantasy trips, making a complete vacation out of it for the participants and providing a built-in audience for the camp competitions. When the participants and their guests aren't playing or watching, they're videotaping or photographing each other with the stars and garnering autographs.

It's easy to structure the camps around sales contests and produce easy-to-measure sales results to budget against the cost of the camps for the prize winners, Cohen said. Camp participants need a certain level of sales performance to qualify, so if they're there, you know how much they sold in the designated period of time and how much that meant financially to the company, so the camp can be budgeted in as a cost of sales.

Camp participation can also be used as a sweepstakes device to promote consumer sales, with some lucky consumers getting a trip to a camp through a promotion that boosts retail sales of a given product.

"The pros love to do it, too," Cohen said, concurring with Yaccino. It puts them "back in the limelight," he noted. "They're real people, too. They're great guys." And when it comes to socializing with the participants, Cohen says, "they're not unapproachable."

Indeed, corporations like to put on these camps as sales incentives. "It gives them a chance to live out a fantasy," according to Joseph Annachino, then vice president of marketing at Orion Home Video, who used Hundley's camps to motivate sales from dealers carrying his products. After using Hundley, Orion exploded into other fantasy types of camps. Hundley's camps were used to help promote a natural tie-in, the baseball movies *Bull Durham* and *Eight Men Out*. Annachino, in an interview, said using the camp helped Orion establish a real point of differentiation between itself and other distributing studios,[5] a tiebreaker if you will when it came time for dealers to decide where to put their promotional bucks, in-store displays, and the like.

Annachino said the camps he's run are open to men and women equally, and that as an incentive, "Randy Hundley worked so well for

5. Interview, August 1990.

us that we'd use it again, even with a nonbaseball film tie-in. I cannot afford to have a dissatisfied incentive winner."

Al Schreiber, vice president at Festival Productions, the New York-based corporate-event production house, agrees with all the reasons the camp organizers give when asked why camps work. "They certainly appeal to certain jaded kinds of audiences that have seen everything," he said in an interview of their value. "It comes at them in a totally different way." Yet, he noted of their potential, "these things haven't been exploited to where they could be," and Schreiber believes it will be a while before they are.[6]

"They haven't been taken to the limit," said the 20-plus-year veteran of event marketing, who wrote *Lifestyle & Event Marketing* with Barry Lenson in November, 1993.

But the potential certainly has been realized. As Hundley's promotional materials state, fantasy baseball camps are "a travel incentive that will go to bat for you . . . [and] . . . provides incredible benefits such as motivation, teamwork, and loyalty. But the best single word to describe your company's involvement with a fantasy camp is camaraderie. . . . Your rookies will leave the program with a renewed enthusiasm toward their lives, their jobs, and an understanding that while we all age, we are still driven by the forces of competition and the challenge of excellence."[6]

The participants concur. Gregory White, then vice president with the St. Louis-based Wetterau Inc. food wholesaler, said that "What we found is it definitely motivated the retailers" who are Wetterau's customers – motivated them to move more of his division's private-label goods in the 2,900 stores it serves. It worked so well, he did it two years running.[7]

It helped distinguish the firm from competitors, White went on, noting, "Anything you can do to be a cut above your competition you really should take a long look at. It's a nice way to say 'thanks.' " And, added White, who participated in the camp with his retailer customers, "I never had so much fun in my life. I had more fun than I ever imagined."

How? Through close associations at the time with the likes of legends like Ferguson Jenkins, Hundley himself, Jose Cardenal, Larry Biittner,

---

6. Interview, August 1990.
7. Interview, August 1990.

Bill Campbell, Don Kessinger, Dave Kingman, Billy Williams, and many more. As Hundley's literature points out, "Any adult 30 years or older who loves baseball" is eligible for the camps. "You don't have to be a super athlete. . . . Our rookies range from 30 to 70-plus years of age. Median age is 42. A few play on organized teams and are in relatively good shape, but most haven't played organized ball for years, if at all."[6] In 1990, camp participation cost as much as some $3,000, but waiting lists abounded.

MLB itself picked up the craze and began marketing its own camp through Dream Week, Inc., out of Huntingdon Valley, PA. The week-long, $4,500 camp put regular 'Joes' up against the likes of George Foster, Steve Garvey, and Bob Gibson, with daily games, group evening activities, special parties and receptions, individual lockers, and individual instruction.

As Vince Rause, a writer from Pennsylvania, described a fellow camper's experience, "I was really rubbing shoulders with these guys, not just as players but on a personal level. [W]hen I get home, it's going to hit me – wow." Or, as another camper told him, "It really pumps your adrenaline to turn around and see those guys pushing you. [T]here you are high-fiving Bob Gibson, Curt Flood, or George Foster."[7]

USAir was the official airline for the Dream Week camp. The company also sponsors Dream Weeks for football, family getaways to spring training, and more.

It works so well that many companies are doing it. Hundley runs three types of camps – general public, special event, and customized (corporate). Companies from Edy's Grand Ice Cream to Upper Deck have used his services.

Like the rotisserie leagues, it's contagious. Sudafed sponsored a camp in 1992 featuring 15 of the country's most prominent female athletes, from figure skater Nancy Kerrigan to tennis great Chris Evert. Thirty-five male and female winners participated after winning a sweepstakes.

The camp made sense to Sudafed, which is a Women's Sports Foundation sponsor, and it gave Sudafed and its parent, Burroughs Wellcome Company, a chance to show off its commitment to health and fitness. The sweepstakes was run to promote the Sudafed brand through participating retailers nationwide.[8] And you can bet that

Sudafed built a considerable database of consumer names through the sweepstakes.

But as the firm said in its news release announcing the program and participants, "Sponsorship of women's sports programs visibly demonstrates the commitment by Sudafed to today's modern woman and the type of activity and entertainment that interests her. Sudafed benefits from the visibility and association with a cause that we feel our target consumers believe in."

Aren't fantasies wonderful – for marketers, that is?

Fantasy Fever Emulates Life – Catch It!

Build it and they will come!

It became more than a phrase that marked the hit movie *Field of Dreams*, in which the character played by actor Kevin Costner converts a portion of his Iowa farm into a baseball diamond, at great financial risk to himself and his family, so that a bunch of already dead baseball players can play again.

Upper Deck, the Carlsbad, California-based card marketer, seized the dream and the field, and took off. Not only did it sponsor a fantasy camp at the Dyersville, Iowa, field where the movie was shot, it put on a charity all-star game between many of its "Heroes of Baseball" old-timers tour stars and a celebrity team of athletes that helped raise thousands of dollars for local charities and brought in huge amounts of tourist traffic for the Dyersville merchants, who usually cater only to the local farming population.

Using the usual cast of characters including Reggie Jackson, Joe Pepitone, and Jimmy Piersall, Upper Deck brought in a team of Hollywood celebrities that included Steve Eastin, D.B. Sweeney, Richard Dean Anderson, and Kelsey Grammar.

If you think fantasy sports don't generate attention, think again. The event generated 74.7 million impressions, according to Burson-Marstellar's analysis of media coverage. Net print impressions from coverage of the event numbered 42.8 million. Broadcast impressions were reported at 19.1 million, including video press releases and the number of news items dedicated to the game at the 41 stations in 35 markets that covered the event to some extent.[9]

The report included evidence that the game generated some "350 implied celebrity endorsements" for Upper Deck thanks to the celebrities who wore Upper Deck uniforms. The report estimates that, by entertainment industry standards, endorsements of this type generally carry a $40,000 to $60,000 price tag. All of this was despite the fact that the all-star game and fantasy weekend was held some three years after the actual film was released to the general public. Upper Deck, in addition, was able to generate participating sponsorships from the Dubuque meat company, local Budweiser distributor Kirchhoff Distributing Co., local merchant Ertl Toy Store, and Coca-Cola. The local newspaper sponsored a school essay contest around the phenomenon, and local merchants promoted Upper Deck products in local media.

The fantasy camp was a $2,400 weekend that featured the usual amenities that make those fantasy camps so attractive to consumers. This one was a general, public camp that featured former big leaguers, of course, with the lure of the actual movie set for *Field of Dreams* as the catch.

In conclusion, fantasy camp and fantasy league marketing works. It attracts fans at the base, at the root of their emotional attachment to sports. It grabs their hearts. It allows them to be closer to the games they love by being closer to the athletes they admire or worship. And that is what they want – the opportunity to be closer to the games they love, somehow, some way.

Almost nothing does that better than fantasy camps and leagues. The camps also are excellent business tools for motivating sales forces; inspiring consumer purchases; generating customer loyalty and repeat business; drawing attention to your product, brand, or company; generating publicity; and even building databases of customers through contests and sweepstakes offering camp registrations as rewards or fantasy leagues with cash awards and other prizes.

It does work.

Build your fantasy, and they will come.

References

[1] *USA Today,* Sports Section, Aug. 24, 1993.

[2] *Chicago Tribune,* special advertising supplement, June 5, 1990.

[3] *USAir Magazine,* "Rotisserie: the Greatest Game for Baseball Fans since Baseball," February 1992, p. 101.

[4] *New York Times,* sports section, April 8, 1990.

[5] Diamond Promotions promotional literature, September 1990.

[6] Randy Hundley promotional materials, August 1990.

[7] *USAir Magazine,* "Catch A Dream," April 1992, p. 47.

[8] Sudafed news release, Aug. 3, 1992.

[9] Burson-Marstellar, "Upper Deck Field of Dreams Weekend Preliminary Analysis of Media Coverage to Date," Nov. 6, 1991.

6

Auto ...
and Other Racing

Where does Kodak go to get exposure to the consumers who use its film? It goes to the places where they gather and take more photos than at any other event – auto race tracks!

Why do package-goods companies have their logos and product emblems all over the cars and jumpsuits of auto racers? Because up to 40 percent of the audience at popular auto races is comprised of females – females who are the household decision-makers when it comes to the grocery store cart and what goes in it.

Racing – particularly auto racing – has become the premier place for marketers to flaunt their products and services, their logos and corporate emblems, and their association with winners, and to do it on tracks and ovals of all America and the world. It's their entree into new markets, their introduction to new customers, their reinforcing link to existing customers, and their ability to entertain key trade clients in a high-charged, exciting atmosphere.

How do companies leverage their presence in auto racing and other racing events? How do they raise awareness levels, increase their sales, generate product trial, schmooze key accounts, attract new customers, and solidify relations with existing ones through racing?

In this chapter, we'll discuss these questions and what sponsors get when they delve into a relationship with auto racing event rights' holders and individual racers and racing teams. We'll also see how hard it is to do a racing sponsorship properly and why it's important that both sides bring something to the table. The reach and exposure of auto racing is much more expansive than you think, and many firms have creatively and successfully leveraged their presence in these events and associations with individual racers and teams. Other companies – and the racers they went down the tubes with – haven't.

How and why will be discussed here. Fortunately, there are many ways to do it right.

Auto Racing – What's in It for Sponsors?

The headline said it all: "Wallace Edges Irvan in Budweiser 500."[1] It referred to June 5, 1994, the National Sprint Car Association event in which driver Rusty Wallace edged competitor Ernie Irvan in a race at Dover, Delaware.

It was the kind of publicity money can't buy – and, in this case, didn't. Budweiser didn't spend dime one to get its name in the paper that day, and you can be sure similar headlines appeared in similar metro daily newspapers that morning.

It's one of many reasons sponsors flock to auto racing. "Flock" is the operative word. If sports indeed attracts the $3.7 billion or more that some claim it does in annual sponsorship money from U.S. firms, then motor sports account for eight of the top ten events that draw that money, according to Ernie Saxton, publisher of *Motorsports Marketing News*. In fact, Saxton reports, the Indianapolis 500 alone has the promotional value of the next five largest events combined.[2]

Don't believe it? Don't believe the drawing power, the promotional power, the dollar power of auto racing? According to Saxton (see Table 6.1), out of the top ten sporting events in terms of overall promotion value, only two – tennis's Newsweek Cup and college football's Orange Bowl – were not auto racing events. Numbers one and two were the Indianapolis 500 and the Daytona 500 auto races, respectively. Between them, these two events attract more than $100,000,000 in promotional spending annually.

TABLE 6.1. The Top Ten 1992 Sporting Events in Terms of Overall Promotional Value

Event	Number of Sponsor Mentions	Dollar Value
Indianapolis 500	307	$72,396,500
Daytona 500	174	$28,264,025
Newsweek Cup	70	$13,216,445
Federal Express Orange Bowl	75	$12,490,000
Toyota GT Grand Prix	283	$7,333,315
Chevy Dealers Busch Grand National	266	$6,125,555
Mopar Summer Nationals (NHRA)	63	$5,395,835
Talladega (IROC)	53	$4,565,325
Motorcraft 500 K	532	$3,565,135
Toyota Grand Prix Long Beach	354	$3,536,420

Source: Ernie Saxton's Motorsports Marketing News/Joyce Julius and Associates.

Fans flock to the speed, power, and excitement of auto racing. The National Association of Stock Car Racing's (NASCAR) Winston Cup (tobacco companies are all over auto racing and other sponsorship opportunities considered to be "smoker friendly") attracts some 3.5 million fans in person and another 300 million via radio and television. All told, auto racing attendance exceeded 40 million in 1993. By the same token, Kraft/General Foods' Country Time drink mix sales doubled between 1988 and 1993, or roughly the same amount of time the product has tied into NASCAR racing through a sponsorship relationship. How does the brand leverage its presence?

While it can't absolutely link its sales boost to its relationship with the race series, Country Time knows that ticket giveaways through its product generate sales and consumer databases as fans scramble for free admittance. The brand creates awareness by sponsoring not only the races but the qualifying trial runs. And it complements its presence – and sponsorship – by hosting related events, like remote-controlled car races, that also increase the number of names in their customer database. During the telecasts of races, Country Time sponsors the remote camera that is mounted in a racer's car and simulates for television viewers the feeling of actually driving a competing car.

That kind of promotion is what helps build fan loyalty, otherwise known as "consumer loyalty," to your brands. In a study by the astute examiners at Performance Research in Newport, Rhode Island, the loyalty of racing fans shined through. Fifty-seven percent of the 1,000 fans interviewed told Performance Research "that they had a higher trust in products offered by NASCAR sponsors." By comparison, the study noted, only 16 percent of the general public holds higher trust in the products of Olympic sponsors and only five percent have a higher trust in the wares of World Cup soccer sponsors.[3]

The study went on to point out that 71 percent of the NASCAR fans either "almost always" or "frequently" choose products "involved in NASCAR" over products that aren't. By comparison, again, such comments are voiced by only 52 percent of tennis fans and 47 percent of golf fans. So if you think it's not important to reinforce your sponsorship with marketing communications in free-standing insert coupons or ads, in television and radio advertising, and in in-store displays, think again.

Performance Research describes the NASCAR fan as predominantly male (78 percent), married (73 percent), and with an average age of 42. They are homeowners (81 percent), with more than three cars per household, and a median household income of somewhere between $35,000 and $50,000.[2]

Yes, the stock car fan – and all racing fans – are a more upscale, refined audience than you might think. This is why, when it comes to motor sports, Budweiser is all over them. As its director of sports marketing, Mark Lamping, told the American Marketing Association's 1991 Sports Marketing Conference audience, where there's motor sports, there's Budweiser. No ifs, ands, or buts about it. Budweiser fully intends to have its presence at events where fans (i.e., consumers) are enjoying a beverage.[3]

Event promoters and track hosts are doing everything and anything to generate fan interest to attract sponsor attention – and dollars. The results can be fascinating.

Take the Charlotte Motor Speedway, host to some of America's biggest races, including the Coca-Cola 600, the Champion Spark Plug 300, and the Mello Yello 500. In the heart of the South, where motorsports reign, the speedway markets itself for sponsorship support and has created a new tier for fans who want special treatment,

Figure 6.1.   Yeah, a guy named Payton from another sport has himself a sponsored car. Photograph courtesy of Sports Club of America, Englewood, Colorado.

Figure 6.2.   Scott Sharp, the 1991 Trans-Am champion and his No. 33 team Duracell Camaro. Photograph courtesy of Sports Club of America, Englewood, Colorado.

fans that your brand is probably trying to reach, too. Its "600 Club" offers them, for $1,500 (and another $45 a month for food), family usage of the club, including its dining and entertainment facilities; priority seating on the reserved veranda; hospitality tent privileges; special parking privileges; a subscription to a regular newsletter full of insider information; and guest passes.

The 600 Club members, according to research by the speedways, are the upper-echelon fans. Sixty-two percent are male, 58 percent are married, and their average household income is nearly $40,000. The average age is 36, and the audience is nearly evenly distributed among 21-to-29-year-olds, 30-to-39-year-olds, and 40-to-49-year-olds.

NASCAR, trying to attract even more fans and their attentions, is offering "member" fans an opportunity to have their own names on the side of a race car – yes, their own names. According to the association, this was its way to reward its most loyal fans, who obviously can't afford to put their names on the side of a car the way large corporations do. However, the attractiveness to fans of such a program is sure to draw the attention of the companies that can afford their names on the sides of cars, too. If they're willing to spend whatever it takes to be on the side of a car, they might be willing to spend even less to pluck your event-associated brand off the shelf at the store.

But that's not all fans can buy. They don't have to look any further than their newspapers' free-standing inserts these days to be able to order NASCAR-licensed merchandise, including video and T-shirt combinations for as low as $14.95 as recently as April 1994.

Winston and Tide support their sponsorships with special merchandise offers as well. Winston marked its 20th year of auto racing sponsorship with, among other merchandise, a special edition collectors poster available for just $5 with a proof-of-purchase carton lid or, for smokers of legal age only, 10 packs' worth. Tide performed similarly with its laundry detergent, offering Tide race team caps, replica cars, and videos with product proofs-of-purchase and very nominal sums.

Even retailer Target got into the act, offering chances to meet champion Indycar driver Arie Luyendyk and his team and to see their car at Target stores, along with sweepstakes chances to attend a race in Indianapolis or Monterey. The foldover newspaper insert included special offers on in-store merchandise designed to drive customer traffic and a quiz on Luyendyk trivia and Indycar history in general.

In addition to driving sales and retail traffic, these promotions obviously allow the sponsor to accumulate even more database consumer names for future offerings and targetings, and the beginnings of a history of the types of offers they'll respond to.

Similar opportunities are offered by tie-ins, especially between complementary motorsport vendors. That's what happened in the summer of '94 when Sea-Doo, the personal watercraft supplier, tied-in with Chevrolet, Sunkist, and NASCAR for a massive promotion. "The Sea-Doo Watercraft Spectacular Sweepstakes" gave consumers opportunities to win the title sponsor's product as well Chevrolet S-Series trucks and other prizes. The promotion, built around Sea-Doo's popular and well-known "Everybody's Doin' It" slogan, gave consumers chances to "share the ride," according to Sea-Doo, by visiting participating dealers, purchasing participating products, and patronizing NASCAR events. Sunkist supported the promotion with special in-store displays offering entry chances. Entry could also be made at NASCAR events or at Chevrolet or Sea-Doo dealerships. Again, that direct marketing axiom – build the consumer databases with qualified leads – was filled.

Sea-Doo also sponsored consumer and dealer promotional tie-ins at the NASCAR Coca-Cola 600, held at the Charlotte Motor Speedway. National media buys supported the promotion. Sea-Doo was already the leading vendor in its category when it began the promotional tie-in and the firm planned a huge increase in promotional spending to support the summer-long event.

Does this stuff move fans? Consider this: according to a report in the *San Francisco Examiner*, the winning automaker in a NASCAR event usually converts quite a bit of sales out of it. Or, as one dealer told the newspaper, "Everybody relates to the fact that, 'Hey, that guy [the winning driver] is driving the same car I'm driving." "In our sport," claimed one of the NASCAR drivers, "you can basically buy what we race. . . . If we win on Sunday, Monday morning, that may help sales. If Chevrolet wins, they really do get recognition from it in this series."[4] No wonder sponsors flock to this sport.

They do the same for drag racing. Maniacal, fanatical drag-racing fans exhibit the same loyalty tendencies that NASCAR fans – let alone

CART (Championship Auto Racing Team) fans – do. Even McDonald's saw the family appeal of the sport in 1992, when it agreed to sponsor a National Hot Rod Association (NHRA) team, putting its golden arch logo on the cars and uniforms of all the participants. McDonald's, without being specific, said the hot rod fans are its customers, too, and even went so far as to try to prove it by opening a foodservice concession at tracks in Indianapolis and Gainesville, Florida. In return, the NHRA named Ronald McDonald Children's Charities as its charitable beneficiary.

Telecommunications supplier WilTel got into hot-rod sponsorship for reasons once outlined by Gil Broyles, its media relations manager: "Customers and employees alike have enjoyed attending races and watching (sponsored driver Michael) Brotherton's career develop. Brotherton is an extremely personable and articulate spokesman for the company. His pursuit of excellence, and the importance of teamwork in that pursuit provide an appropriate analogy for WilTel's way of doing business. And the fact that you don't find too many telecommunications companies among NHRA sponsors also fits WilTel's culture of doing things a bit differently than everyone else. We have played host to 300 to 400 customers at selected races in the past."[5] WilTel also sponsors female pro golfer Melissa McNamara. The firm publicizes and leverages both sponsorships through its corporate newsletter.

Audiences for drag-racing events can reach 300 million, including all media and at-event exposure. More than 100 companies put up more than $15 million in prize money for drag racing in 1992. These businesses ranged from the beer companies and automotive aftermarket suppliers you'd expect to telecommunications outfits and family restaurants. They're all attracted to the billboard out there on the track – namely, the car. Like their brethren in NASCAR and Indycar racing, some 80 percent of drag-racing fans say they are positively influenced to purchase a sponsor's product. Though the audience is 70 percent male, the female side is growing rapidly. Primary demographics range from 20 years old to 49, and household incomes range from $20,000 to $75,000, the latter attributed to 13 percent of the audience. Nearly three-fourths have college or high-school educations. They're huge customers of family-style, home-delivery, and fast-food food service; big buyers of video and camera equipment; and major patrons of convenience, auto parts, discount, and hardware stores, according to Bekins, which sponsors drag-racing events and teams.

Importantly for Bekins, these fans also travel a lot. If nowhere else, they go to drag races. Attendance was 4 million in 1992, and the number of U.S. events keeps growing annually. Drag racing is getting more and more media attention, from its own television shows and race coverages to specialty magazines and mainstream metro newspaper coverage.

Drag racing is a great marketing tool, according to the JOED Racing Team of Wauconda, Illinois. The team justifiably claims that sponsorship is a low-cost, effective alternative to general, mainstream advertising and backs it up, quoting the Chief Auto Parts chain as claiming that its number of female customers increases right along with female involvement with the sport. The team, says JOED, is your marketing tool, not only for its billboard value on the track, but for its members' value as personal spokespeople, endorsers, and representatives of your company at the track or at corporate functions, in trade relations, and in promotional appearances or in the use of their likenesses in promotional efforts.[6]

Indy . . . and Other Phenomenal Marketing Opportunities

Indianapolis. The Brickyard. These words are synonymous with greatness.

Legendary drivers. Outstanding performances. Overflow crowds. The riveted attention of a nation, if not the world. And now, more than ever, the riveted attention of worldwide marketers hopeful of striking it rich and delivering the message that will maintain their loyal customers and attract new ones among the millions riveted to the race – in person and through the media.

The Indianapolis 500 is the largest single sports promotional event, attracting some $72,000,000-plus worth of promotional dollars. Those dollars come in all shapes: corporate decals and logos on cars, driver and pit crew uniforms, the track itself, and electronic projections on television sets around the world in race updates and other informational overlays.

So many companies, particularly automotive aftermarket suppliers, bid so many dollars to be official suppliers to the race as part of their sponsorship packages. And the beer and tobacco sponsors are everywhere when it comes to motor sports, especially the biggest events in the genre.

While Indianapolis racing promotions range far and wide, and few have been overlooked, gaining most in popularity is the promotional vehicle that generates, if you will, fan frequency. The biggest problem in marketing a race is getting even the most devout fans to watch all of it because of its length and monotony. What many marketers have tied into in joint promotional efforts is telephone events that get fans to monitor the entire race, especially the first half of it. Like pro basketball, the real racing action comes at the tail end of a close event and truly does rivet fans.

But there are no natural timeouts in racing. Drivers take pit stops, and accidents or bad weather cause delays, but drivers can't signal a "T" and get everyone to stop for a moment while the television network crams in commercials. In fact, racing is so monotonous that networks can cram commercials in anytime they want, except at the every end, when they need to be ready to capture a winning flag moment or the tightness of racers just seconds apart. Even *at* a race, the action sometimes is truly in the grandstands or, at Indy, in the infield, where party-driven attendees have no idea what is going on in the race – and don't care either.

In that kind of atmosphere, you can see where promotions that garner fan attention for the entirety of a race that goes on for hours are imperative. And now they're coming in droves. For the 1994 Indy race, Ford, Kodak, and Valvoline hooked up in such a promotion. Their combined "Indy Power Drive" promotion, held during the two weeks prior to the race, allowed race fans to call an 800 number for race information updates, and, of course – the hook – a chance to win prizes from the sponsors.

Coordinated through Indianapolis Motor Speedway (IMS) and Indianapolis Motor Speedway Properties (ISMP), the toll-free number was expected to attract as many as 700,000 calls, considering that the race itself attracts 400,000 fans in person and draws 1 million to the Indianapolis area each May for qualifying runs and other related race events. To get the 700,000 phone calls projected, the sponsors distributed word of the line's availability to some 50 million homes through television and print advertising.

Fans calling in could access specific messages from any one of the sponsors, each of which was followed by a half-minute message with race update data. Then live operators cut in to offer callers sweepstakes entry opportunities. The prizes? An official pace car (a Ford Cobra Mustang, in this case), a trip to the 1995 Indy 500, remote-controlled replicas of Indy cars, and baseball caps sporting the Indy logo.

Of course, the marketing key is capturing information about the fans who call in, including key identifying and demographic information.

Think about it: 700,000 fans anxious for race information and thereby anxious for your sponsored message. And you get their name, address, and pertinent demographic information in exchange.

It worked so well, it was part of the package again for the inaugural Brickyard 400, an August 1994 race that brought stock cars back to the Brickyard/Speedway for the first time. The nationally televised event was expected to become the second-largest, one-day event in terms of attendance (behind its big brother, the 500). Pennzoil, Chevrolet, Delco Electronics, Budweiser, and General Motors Service Parts Operations were the joint sponsors; all were committed to strong on-site presence; cooperative ventures like the phone line, television, and print advertising; ticket disbursement and distribution; and general promotional activity.

The Phone Promo that Started It All

You can't know who's in first place at the halfway point of a race unless you've watched the first half of the race. With that premise, Gillette proceeded to run its "Halfway Challenge" promotion in 1990 during the NASCAR circuit. Viewers of nine races were given the opportunity to dial a 900 number at the halfway point of each race and let the sponsor know that they knew who was in first place at that point.

As many as 300,000-plus dialed in during each race, with a maximum handle of 225,000 in one hour during one race. Television viewers were so eager to respond to the promotion, they even spent the 90 cents it took to identify themselves to the sponsors on the 900 call. During each race, a randomly selected viewer was called back and awarded a Pontiac Grand Prix SE. Not only did the sponsor benefit with the accumulation of viewer names for the database, but race-tele-casting networks (ESPN, TNT, and CBS, in this case) each were rewarded with enhanced viewership.

In addition to the customer data base accumulation, Gillette also reaped good public relations value and exposure. Obviously, from the response, viewers didn't see it as a rip-off, according to one agency official who helped execute the promotion. In addition, to enhance the promotion and give viewers and fans something to cheer for, drivers leading at the halfway point were rewarded with a $10,000 check. The entire promotion was administered and in part devised by the same people who brought you "Dugout Derby" fantasy baseball, the newspaper circulation-enhancing promotion we discussed in Chapter 5.

Research done after the races revealed that the callers and the viewers of the extended race were primarily men aged 18 to 35, which is just what Gillette (the company behind Right Guard deodorant) wanted. The promotion paid off, too. Gillette reportedly garnered market share increases approaching triple digits in some markets where the promotion ran. With 300,000 calls accumulated during some races, Gillette accumulated well more than 1 million names for its marketing database. The promotion was so effective that it garnered a Golden Reggie Award for promotion excellence from the Promotion Marketing Association of America, and was repeated the following year, when it was upped to 12 races from nine with the 900 phone call price tag going up a nickel to 95 cents.

Grand Prix Me, Please

If you want to break through the clutter, make an impression, reach even more dedicated fans than those at Indy, then try the Toyota Grand Prix of Long Beach – California, that is.

Ranked by Ernie Saxton in the top ten of all sports events (and eighth among auto races) in terms of promotional value, the event is a gold mine. More than 200,000 annually attend; 63 percent of these are men. People in their twenties and thirties make up more than 60 percent of the audience. And if you think this is just the blue-collar crowd, forget it – nearly half have college degrees and some postgraduate education. An equal number, not surprisingly, classify themselves as professionals in the workplace, according to CART data compiled by Nordhaus Research, Inc.[7]

The three days of the event include not only the headline race itself, but a pro/celebrity race and a charity fundraising golf tournament. Television coverage is split between sister networks ABC and ESPN, but three weeks of radio, television, and newspaper publicity precede the race, generating the kind of positive glow in which sponsors like to bask. In fact, sponsorship of this event, according to the crack researchers at Joyce Julius and Associates, produced more than $26 million of equivalent media exposure for far less money actually spent. That is the largest single exposure equivalent Julius and Associates had ever compiled for a single event to that date.

Entertainment possibilities abound. Sponsors purchase hospitality tents and often have drivers and other nearby Hollywood celebrities attend to dazzle trade clients. Three-hundred-plus companies employ that route – everything from 2,000-person, mass party tents to more intimate 75-person tents. Special pit seating and elevated boxes also help sponsors enhance their guests' interaction with the race.

But it's not just Toyota and its dealers and customers who benefit from the sponsorship. Toyota is the title sponsor, yes, but secondary sponsors also shine. Coors, for instance, issued commemorative cans just for the race with a self-liquidating merchandise tie-in and moved (are you ready?) 1 million cases for the 1992 race – that's without being on the side of any racer's car.

Trippings and Trappings

It's easy to forget to do things right as an auto-racing sponsor, and in that regard Tom Amshay has forgotten more about such sponsorship than most people know. And that's exactly why he's angry about the state of auto racing sponsorship today.

A veteran racer, racing promoter, and racing sponsorship match-maker, Amshay believes that most racers don't present themselves properly and that most corporate marketers don't understand how to employ – let alone leverage – a racing sponsorship opportunity.

He has backed it up in a book – *Turning Horse Power Into Marketing Power: How To Use The Racing Industry As A Marketing Tool* – as well as in a syndicated column on racing sponsorship that appears in several auto-racing trade publications. He is currently in the process of developing and promoting a race car tour he hoped to get off the ground in 1995.

The Cuyahoga Falls, Ohio-based savvy marketer's main gripe on the racer's side is that "even the teams that have a marketing department of their own do not have a good grip of what marketing is about." On the corporate side, he continues, "the people in marketing departments do not understand how the racing industry works."[8]

Marketing of, to, and for auto racing by racers and corporate types alike is a different kind of animal and unfortunately, he believes, too many treat it that way. It has to be treated, instead, he says, like a part of the marketing program, fitted to the corporate and race team objectives and supported appropriately or commensurately. He strictly believes that – rather than just slapping a corporate logo on the side of a car, or around a track, or on racer and crew uniforms – in-depth, intense study needs to be completed about racing perceptions and the marketing levers that activate them.

Or, as he says, it's not enough any more, if you're a racer pitching a sponsor, "to show the prospect demographics, spectator and viewer numbers, and photos of all the big company and brand names visible at an event. That tactic is dwindling in effectiveness; mostly, because the companies generally mean it when they say they want proof that they're going to make money by sponsoring a team. Of course, it isn't possible to truly prove the sponsorship will turn a profit, until after the sponsorship is up and running."[9]

The problem – the root of the problem, that is – is that "corporations and racers don't know each other's businesses," Amshay says. First and foremost, for a team and a corporation to strike a happy marriage, they have to separate the team from the sanctioning association, which has entirely different motivations and goals. "A sanctioning body is in the business of putting on races, or sanctioning races," Amshay notes. "A racer may have to belong to a sanctioning body."[1]

---

1. Interview, February 1993.

Amshay's favorite scenario is imagining a corporate marketing meeting during which a hungry, young, would-be executive lion excitedly tells his marketing superiors that he has arranged for the corporation to have its name on the side of a race car. One of the superiors, noting the cost of the deal, asks what is in it for the company. When the young lion responds by reiterating that the company has its name on the side of a race car, everyone just stares at him, or through him, and he realizes he hasn't matched the corporate goals up to the marketing realities and marketplace possibilities of auto racing. All he's done is match up some money to a panel on a car.

Amshay notes that "most [corporate] marketing departments are regularly approached by reps from the racing industry [and] cannot see how a racing project can get marketing results." The problem is that "the shortage of skilled marketers within the racing industry has scared away a lot of companies."[10]

Too many racers, Amshay points out, have a "widespread misconception as to why companies get into racing in the first place," which he believes may be "due to the constant references to the term 'sponsorship' and its outdated suggestion that companies give money to support nonprofitable activities – for no other reason than to be nice." To get around that, he suggests, "[a] company coming into racing needs a good perspective of what the industry is about, so it can sort out who in the racing industry is for real and wants to help the company get its money's worth, and who might simply be good at selling the industry to you."[10]

While auto racing industry numbers are attractive (1,200 racetracks nationally, 200 sanctioning bodies, and some 350,000 drivers observed by hundreds of millions of fans in person and through the media), Amshay notes that the sanctioning bodies compete with each other for attention, media, and dollars – your dollars. Unfortunately, while much of the selling is done around these numbers, this doesn't promote long-term relationships between racers and sponsors. Many corporations see racing only as a short-term vehicle for corporate name exposure. Amshay maintains that four key principles – the reach, frequency, impact, and cost of auto racing – are the keys to selling it as a sponsorship package for a racing team. Those attributes build long-term relationships and success for all parties.

Beyond that, Amshay maintains, "Joe Average Consumer" on the street knows little about racing other than what he or she may have learned in the general media and also believes that sponsorship is just another form of charity in auto racing. Using auto racing as an entertainment vehicle for key accounts and trade clients becomes of immeasurable value then as a way to introduce them to the sport and bring them up close and personal to it in a thrilling, first-hand way. Pit visits and personal appearances with and from popular drivers make lasting impressions. Not only that, it's a great motivator for your own sales and corporate personnel. Because you sponsor the team, it's *your* team in a way, and the entire company can get behind it, promote it, talk it up, and root for it. It's untraditional and different, and therefore exciting and exhilarating. It can energize your people across departmental lines. Internal promotions, like ticket rewards for race attendance for employees, make for good sales and incentive tools.

But racing, Amshay maintains, also allows your company exposure to a dedicated audience and the possibility of national and regional promotions with television coverage that often approaches regional National Football League telecast ratings. Because races are so frequent, they allow repeat messages to be economically broadcasted – market to market and nationally – to that same dedicated audience. And the cost will be more economical than a straight media buy, with equivalent buying power that will astound you. (See Chapter 2 for detailed information on media equivalency buying power and other related research information.)

Plainly and simply then, as Amshay notes, "Before you go into racing, investigate it thoroughly."

Racers Who Are Better Investigators

Some teams have heard Amshay's calls. Others anticipated them. Among these are the JB Racing team and the Galles-Kraco team.

North Carolina-based JB is in the drag-racing business. Note that we didn't say just "drag racing." Beyond a winning car, JB knows the value of corporate marketing, endorsements, sponsorships, and licensing. In fact, JB is broken down into two divisions – the race car segment and the client services segment. The race car division is dedicated to winning races, and does. It won the 1990 World Championship in International Hot Rod Association (IHRA) competition. The client services division also is charged with winning – for the sponsors of JB Racing, although JB has eliminated using the word "sponsor" (the "s" word, as JB calls it) and now prefers "customer" or "client" instead.

JB sells customers and clients with a variety of methods. Top of the list is a first-rate, professional shop that says "big time." Second is the ability to present itself as a customer's marketing arm, not just a place to put a corporate decal. JB's marketing team has developed a mission statement for the team: "Prove to the marketplace that Pro Tour drag racing is a high-return strategy and that JB Racing is the logical choice for a no-hassle project that gets maximum results."[11]

JB claims to always be searching for new ways to add value to itself for marketers; much of this effort, it says, takes place off the racetrack. This includes team personnel and equipment appearances at client trade shows and corporate functions, public-service announcements on clients' behalf, and public relations appearances, including media interview availability. This goes a long way, team marketers say, toward providing customer satisfaction for clients (and clients' clients) and keeping JB ahead of the pack of competitor racers, both on and off the track. JB also develops public-service projects on its own to project its own corporate goodwill that clients can latch onto. In fact, WilTel-sponsored driver Michael Brotherton is part of the JB team, participating in client events such as personal appearances and visits with clients at or away from the track.

Albuquerque-based Galles-Kraco, meanwhile, employs up to 65 people spread between engineering, auto research and development, administration, and marketing. The team has a deep appreciation for what it takes to build a relationship with corporate marketers and helps them maximize their auto-racing sponsorship – it's where Galles-Kraco got as much as 80 percent of their revenue as late as the end of 1990.

What Galles-Kraco can translate that into for their sponsors is dynamite exposure: the firm estimates that it received as much as $40 million worth of equivalent media exposure. The team is more than willing to add the thrill of an in-car minicam that fans and sponsors – let alone the television networks – really love. Valvoline, Chevrolet, and Delco Electronics are among the sponsors reaping the glow of Galles-Kraco's success and getting to boast how they provide the team with equipment, parts, and expertise. Team driver Al Unser, Jr. of Galles-Kraco even had his 1991 entry named the "Valvoline Lola Chevy" in honor of his sponsor and its deep commitment.[12] As in any sport, winning helps. Six CART wins in 1990 produced double the sponsorship revenue in 1991 for Galles-Kraco.

Consultant Charlie Hayes, writing in *Ernie Saxton's Motorsports Marketing News* in May 1994, says using communication technology smartly is the new key to attracting sponsorship in the '90s. Quicker access to more updated information is crucial to racers trying to separate themselves from the pack, both on and off the track. "Racers," he told the industry in his essay, "we need to be racing business people."

He also advises racers seeking sponsorship commitments to negotiate like the businessmen they're dealing with. Put time constraints on marketers you pitch, he tells racers, to be sure that you'll at least get a response. Don't settle for an "I'll get back to you" response from a prospective sponsor, he advises. Let them know you need a response by a certain date and that if you don't hear from them by then that you'll be getting back to them. That way, you're at least sure that your proposal will be considered.

NASCAR – Why It Works

Auto racing may or may not prove to be the sport of the '90s. It would be hard to argue with NASCAR, which claims that its phenomenal licensed-goods sales growth rate makes it *the* sports license of the decade.

NASCAR certainly has its share of what its president, Bill Battle, says is the $700 billion spending power market of the 46.6 million Americans who comprise auto racing fandom. After organizing the circuit's diverse participants under one licensing banner, Battle has watched sales of its licensed goods soar from $60 million when he got it off the ground in 1990 to $300 million in 1993 to what was expected to be somewhere between $400 million and $500 million in 1994. And the growth is expected to continue to skyrocket upward. Licensees, skeptics, or companies that are out of the mainstream to begin with are now full-fledged supporters and well-known mainstream marketers, with more coming on all the time.

NASCAR's success formula for attracting them is simple. Unlike other sports, its 31 events have a 10-month season, yielding near year-long sales opportunities. In the nonracing months of December and January, sales of licensed goods sales – which make excellent holiday gift items – remain strong.

NASCAR events are held all over the country, and they do well even outside the traditional auto-racing strongholds of the Southeast. Average attendance is 134,000-plus per event (yes, that's per *event*) – double the average attendance for an NFL game. And fans spend days at events partying, buying merchandise up and down the trailer rows of vendors at the events, and watching the races, too.

Florida's Daytona 500 is NASCAR's crown jewel event, and for good reason. From audiences 30-plus years ago of 10,000 and purses you could count on one hand, the race now draws some 100,000 annually with hundreds of millions at stake. The 1993 event sold out just two days after the 1992 event was over. To top it off, fans drive an average of 230 miles to get there, and the event is estimated to pump some $1 billion each year into the Daytona Beach economy.

Considering all that, it's no wonder why McDonald's sells a thermal NASCAR mug – good for hot or cold beverages – for about $1.29 and refills it for customers for just 25 cents. The appeal drives initial and repeat sales for both coffee and soda pop. Speaking of coffee, Maxwell House is the official coffee of NASCAR. Some of News America's most successful free-standing national newspaper coupon inserts are the ones it ties into NASCAR; they reach the largest audiences and have the highest redemption rates. The weekly "NASCAR Country Radio Show" is syndicated by 25 stations.

NASCAR licensees, new and old, swear by the association's appeal and the loyalty of the fan base, which has diversified from blue-collar rowdies to white-collar businessmen seeking effective entertainment opportunities while promoting their brands along the trailer rows of licensed goods sales vendors on the uniforms of drivers and pit crews, along the walls of the track, in advertising in all media, in special promotional giveaways and premium offers of NASCAR-related licensed goods, and – of course – on the panels of the cars themselves.

The Racing Champions collectible miniature cars have exploded in sales since tying in with NASCAR, as have Maxx Race Cards, which became a contingency sponsor of the Winston NASCAR series. Companies leverage their presence at races not only through direct sales opportunities and signage, but on the track's electronic billboard and in the race program. And vendors like these get retail support for their products by tying in with retailers at these events and showing them the tremendous demand for these products among savagely loyal fans who will shop at their stores if they carry these NASCAR-licensed products. Many fans come to races just to party and shop along the trailer row at each event; many of these never even manage to get tickets to the race itself.

Licensed-goods vendors encourage retailers to separate or segregate NASCAR-licensed goods from other merchandise in their stores to drive sales by making it easier for rabid auto-racing fans to find the products and pour through them. NASCAR-related goods, say the licensees in collectibles and apparel, also motivate and excite their sales forces in their approaches to and work with retailers by giving them exciting information they can relate about traffic, sales, and customer loyalty.

Singularly, NASCAR and auto-racing fans may be the most loyal in sports. In Green Bay, Wisconsin, says NASCAR President Bill Battle, NASCAR-licensed goods outsell Packers merchandise. Because of a looseness and lack of harmony in NASCAR before this decade, licensed goods sales were disorganized and flat at best. But with the parties uniting under the NASCAR banner, sales are exploding and are projected to continue that way. Battle would know – he personally united colleges under his Collegiate Licensing firm, satisfying the needs in the national marketplace for that segment.

"It isn't a southeastern sport," Battle says of auto racing. "It's an international sport." And you can expect he'll drive it all over the world.

Auto Racing Isn't the Only Racing

But auto racing isn't the only kind of racing or racing sponsorship. If your customer demographics match up to interests in running, biking, or any combination thereof, you may have identified lucrative sponsorship opportunities for yourself and your company – opportunities that exist in environments as relatively free of media-message clutter as might be possible, in an atmosphere where your would-be customers are more receptive to your message.

Bicycle Racing

Bicycle racing – with the exception of the Tour de France (or the "Tourdy France thing," as Bo Jackson once called it in a Nike commercial) and the Olympics (if American racers are doing well) – doesn't attract much interest in the United States, but it is enormously popular elsewhere around the world, especially in Europe. (Sound like another sport you might be familiar with, known as "futbol" around the world but as "soccer" here?) Dirt biking, short track, and long-distance bike racing all offer sponsorship opportunities of great economies of scale to astute marketers who can make them part of their mainstream marketing mix.

Motorola, the global communications giant, receives wonderful – and absolutely free – publicity from its sponsorship of a biking team that competes in international events, including the Tour de France. Newspapers from Santa Fe to Chicago to London feature stories and photographs of Motorola team members with specific mentions of the corporate team name. The team has an international cast of racers, a support crew that includes Olympic speedskating champion Eric Heiden, and races all over the world. Lending notoriety to the team and the company was the stellar 1993 performance of American Lance Armstrong, which yielded considerable press coverage in the United States. His winning performances on the European tour only strengthened Motorola's corporate battle cry of "Quality Means the World to Us" featured in its marketing communications programs.[13]

To show Motorola's international marketing bent, the team not only has a multinational makeup, but its guide and publicity materials are printed in multilingual formats. Motorola also markets and uses as premiums licensed team merchandise, including T-shirts, sweaters, hats, and other clothes, as well as water bottles, golf balls, posters, and desk accessories.

Why is Motorola excited about biking? Well, research from the U.S. Cycling Federation, *Bicycling Magazine*, the Bicycle Institute of America, Sports Marketing Surveys, and Medalist Sports reveals that cycling represents a $3.5-billion market in the U.S. alone and identifies the sport as America's second-favorite activity. The research estimates that 93 million Americans – and twice that many Europeans – participate in bicycling. The sport's popularity is further seen in the 50 million Europeans and the 2.8 million Americans who attend bicycling events each year.

But that's nothing compared to the media exposure. According to the research, more than 28 billion impressions are created by the coverage of biking in Europe; some 1.7 billion more are made in the United States. Only soccer, the research estimates, extends on a broader scale worldwide.

The demographics are also appealing. In the United States, according to the research, 87 percent of the audience is between the ages of 18 to 44, and 63 percent are classified as professionals. Fifty-five percent are males. Average household income is an impressive $55,000 annually. In Europe, 80 percent of the audience is between the ages of 25 and 54, 60 percent of them are male, and some 60 percent earn between $25,000 and $40,000 annually.

Among extended sporting events (as opposed to one-day events like the Indianapolis 500), the Tour de France is the third most popular event in the world, after the Olympics and World Cup soccer. One hundred and twenty countries get television coverage of the race, and 3,600 journalists cover it. In France alone, twenty-two million cycling fans line the roads and streets to observe the race, and race officials estimate that on a daily basis, 1 billion people pick up media information about the event.

And if winning is everything, and if it truly enhances fan (customer) attention, sponsor sales, and sales opportunities, then Motorola benefited greatly from bicycle racing in 1993. In 32 international events, the team reached the medalists' podium 11 times, including nine first-place finishes. Motorola has been with the team since 1986, and its performance against intense international competition on the race course has improved steadily. So has Motorola's performance in business globally, it might be said.

Budweiser saw the opportunity, too. Its 1993 Roostmaster Shootout, held in Colorado under the banner of its Bud Dry brand, featured some of the world's best in that sport. Over the Memorial Day weekend, Bud Dry basically took over the touristy town of Durango. The day after the event, Bud Dry sponsored a massive cleanup of the race venue, rewarding volunteers who helped out with a few premium items and refreshments and garnering the goodwill glow that goes with such an effort. With the support of industry-specific sponsors like Prime Ticket television; local racing merchants, restaurateurs, and outfitting retailers; an airline carrier; nutrition supplement vendors; and other media partners, Budweiser was able to produce a killer event for a galvanized audience more than ready for and receptive to its marketing communications messages.

But biking may be hitting the United States in the biggest way ever through the Tour of America, a seven-stop, distance-touring event with big-name, big-time sponsors; well-known riders; and large, enthusiastic audiences. The Tour is comprised of seven races, three of which form the Million Dollar Thrift Drug Triple Crown of Cycling. Sponsors include gigantic companies, from CoreStates Bank to Kmart. In fact, Motorola's Lance Armstrong captured the grand title prize after winning all three events. International Cycling Promotions handles the tour, which has international credibility because it allows racers to accumulate world-ranking and event-qualifying points.

Sponsors spread the word of their participation in many ways, and not just on the racecourse, where their signage is visible to on-site and television viewers alike. Amid the picnic-like atmosphere of the courses and in the Lifestyle Expo at each event, sponsors offer samples of their products. They support their sponsorships with event-oriented advertising in print and on radio and television. Their executives are interviewed about it in the media, and their sponsorship packages include public-address announcements of their participation. They also advertise in the official tour magazine and entertain key clients and guests at the event.

Customized sponsorship benefits are also available. Kmart, for instance, through a "Fast Wheels" program, reaches school-age children by distributing packets that include a video and a discussion guide in schools and encouraging class projects on biking. Such activities allow Kmart to bask in the glow of solid community relations activities.

Thrift Drug does likewise. The Pittsburgh-based retailer sponsors an opportunity for amateur cyclists to take a lap on the actual race course just prior to an actual cycling race. Charity-driven, the event raises thousands of dollars for the American Diabetes Association. Tie-in sponsor Aplus Mini Markets supplies postlap refreshments for the charity fundraising riders. As with the Kmart promotion, the glow of positive community goodwill and the sense of giving something back to the community through the popular event come shining through.

Subaru takes a different, but no less effective tact – a sort of "event within the event" approach that awards a cash stipend to the first three riders to reach a certain point of the race during each lap during one of the more grueling tour stops. Called the Subaru Power Peak, the promotion creates additional media interest and exposure.[14]

Other participating sponsors, including Coors Light, Nuprin, and Aplus Mini Markets, sponsor similar activities.

For all this, and more, the Tour of America and its sponsors feel the potential is headed nowhere but up. The festive atmosphere of the events provides ideal hospitality opportunities. The number of sponsors involved so far are few and far between contrasted to mainstream pastimes, making the sport free of clutter right now, with the ability to stay relatively free even as it grows.

And because, as the event organizers say, the event "comes to the people" (as opposed to the other way around with mainstream pastimes), it makes for an ideal, in-your-backyard exposure opportunity. Courses often run through metropolitan streets and neighborhoods. One event attracted up to 500,000 spectators along the course. These backyard opportunities have sponsors scrambling for support activities.

The First Union Grand Prix event of the Tour in Atlanta features amateur time trials, junior time trials, a sweepstakes, a bike expo, and a block party, among other events. The Thrift Drug Classic in Pittsburgh includes a jazz festival, a bicycle seminar, a photo exhibit, and an outrageous eating contest. Celebratory festivals, recycle-a-cycle events, kids races, educational programs, family fun rides, charitable fundraising events, and an in-line skating event are also part of sponsors' plans to raise awareness, entertain clients, boost sales, distribute product, generate trial and sampling, and show goodwill toward the community.

Cycling has exploded in popularity in America. In the last ten years, the number of professional race events here has grown from one to 45, and the sport has become among America's most popular. Like auto racing, it has become an ideal venue for television advertisers seeking "equivalent media exposure" with logos and decals on bikes, bikers, crews, and tracks. But if the enormous growth opportunity of bicycling isn't enough for you, maybe triathlons will fill the bill with their combination of running, swimming, and bicycling.

Triathlons

Triathlons, like their competitors, come in all shapes and sizes today, and so, subsequently, do their sponsors. From consumer products to specialty sport vendors, from women to kids, triathlons, like bicycle races, are a relatively untapped but growing sponsorship opportunity.

The heavily diversified women's sport clothier Danskin has capitalized on what it sees as a fitness and competition trend among its core customers by sponsoring its Danskin Triathlon Series for women, attracting everyone from local fitness buffs to world-class competitors. The six-stop tour, which is entering its sixth season, ends in a championship competition. Its appeal is simple. "Since it is an all-women event," according to world-class triathlete Michelle Jones, "it's less intimidating and allows for a real feeling of camaraderie, while the distance (12.4 miles or about half a traditional triathlon) affirms the sense of accomplishment for all those who compete in the event."[15]

Danskin marketers know that sponsoring this event puts them back in touch with the direction in which their core customers are headed – toward competitive fitness events. What was once a dancewear manufacturer has become an outfit supplier to participants in all kinds of fitness events, from triathlons to mountain climbing. Danskin's triathlon series has been a success for no other reason than in its first year the field was composed of first-time event participants.

Danskin promotes itself and women's fitness through the tour sponsorship, which features displays of women of all ages and backgrounds to show the significance and universality of women's fitness. Needless to say, Danskin has become a hero – make that "heroine" – to its customers, participants, and trade clients alike through this series. The Susan G. Komen Breast Cancer Foundation is the charitable beneficiary of the tour.

At the other end of the spectrum though is an event like the IronKids Bread Triathlon series, for children from ages seven to 14. Sponsored by Rainbo Bread, a Campbell Taggart (Anheuser-Busch, how about that?) company, the event culminates in a national championship meet and has been running continuously since 1985. Distances are adjusted downward for kids to a 100-meter swim, a 3-mile bike ride and a less-than-a-mile run. But because "Every Finisher is a Winner" is the event theme, all participants get pins, T-shirts, and bicycle and swim caps.

In addition – and this is key – Rainbo gathers customer names through registrations (as does Danskin through its women's series) and maintains a dialog with them through its Kids Club educational program. If you think it doesn't work, think again: in its first eight years, the event attracted 20,000 participants, a considerable number for an event out of character for many kids that age, who are usually more enamored with mainstream sports or Sunday soccer leagues.

Subsponsors, market to market, also reap rewards and benefits. They can get signage along the race route, official race publicity release value, public-address-system announcements on-site, and product sampling opportunities. Rainbo allows subsponsors to participate in as many as three qualifying-event markets. For the national championship meet, Rainbo guarantees national and local television exposure as well as sampling, race packet insert opportunities, complimentary accommodations, VIP and hospitality tent credentials, and admission to the postriathlon party.[16] Another subsponsor tier offers more extensive product sampling and the opportunity to be the official, exclusive supplier to the race in your product or service category.

Marathons

Of course, you may want to stick to sponsoring racing in its purest and oldest form: plain old running. There is much opportunity available there as well. If you want to eliminate the swimming and bicycling and just stick to the footwork, there's always the ever-popular marathon sponsorship opportunities, and with the national television exposure and media attention and world-class participant attraction these events are getting, they too are developing into the clutter-free sponsorship opportunity that their brethren racing events have become.

The New York Marathon, with its 28,000 participants from 50 countries, is fast becoming among the most prestigious of these marathons. The event plays to the hearts of America's estimated 8.5

million recreational runners and the other 4 million who run competitively on a regular basis, according to MRI Doublebase and New York Road Runners Club research. These runners are generally aged 18 to 44, nearly half are in America's top income brackets, most have strong educational backgrounds, and nearly two-thirds are managers and/or professionals.[17]

To reach them through the New York Marathon, sponsoring companies get category exclusivity for a clear communications environment, on-course signage, product sampling, program advertising, publicity, media coverage, hospitality privileges, and event awareness-raising promotional participation. Just observing the race and all that surrounds it is testimony to that.

A John Hancock/asics banner is broken by the winner at the finish line. BFI recycling bins line the race course. Telecommunications provider NYNEX posts mileage markers throughout the course. Seiko timers adorn the course as well. Trevira carpeting helps cushion the run across the Queensborough Bridge portion of the race. A Mercedes-Benz is the women's pace/lead car. Kids in asics jackets wearing BFI caps offer Vermont Pure Natural Spring Water to runners along the course. Chemical Bank signage reminds participants, fans, and casual observers that the institution is helping raise money for the event. Advil-sponsored first-aid stations line the course. And what would a sporting event like this be without Gatorade refreshment along the course? Everyone from Blimpie (submarine sandwiches) to Coca-Cola to Borden to Dole offer refreshments at the Family Reunion Festival associated with the race.

Maybe you ought to be running to racing sponsorship opportunities. Or is that racing to running sponsorship opportunities? But, as with all sponsorship opportunities, beware and be wise. Risks are inherent. Things can go wrong (see Ben Johnson). Opportunities can go astray if your target market isn't included in the fan/participant profile of the events, so do your homework. Don't just hang your name on a banner on the course – that's not leveraging a sponsorship, that's hanging a banner. Do something good that will have you thought of in a positive light by race participants and observers that are, or could be, your customers.

First Interstate Bank did it right in 1990, as reported in the August 1990 issue of *Bank Marketing*. Through a simple sponsorship of a local but hardly small (Orange County, California) triathlon in 1990, the bank got the attention of local opinion leaders; basked in the glow of aiding local charities through monies donated from the race; got more goodwill by arranging an "event within the event" via a corporate relay for the very corporations whose business they have, want to maintain, or attract (let alone the individual employees' accounts); generated employee enthusiasm and support by rewarding them for promoting the event and attracting business through it; rewarded participants with premiums and prizes in a sweepstakes held in conjunction with the event; got even more goodwill through a postrace party for participants; encouraged national employee participation in the race (150 took part); and, finally, generated 2,000 qualified business leads out of the race (as it does each year).[18] Closing on any one of those opportunities helps offset the cost of the sponsorship and the investment in leveraging it. The goodwill of the race and its associated events is almost impossible to measure.

Summary

As with any sponsorship opportunity, sponsoring a racing event is just as much a matter of properly matching corporate objectives and goals to event patron demographics as it is meeting and matching corporate goals and objectives.

Racing can accomplish that for a sponsor because many of its events are still relatively uncluttered when it comes to getting out a marketing communications message. Your message hooks in directly to fans dedicated to the event and appreciative of your sponsorship thereof. It yields qualified sales leads. And it establishes an aura of community goodwill that is hard to beat. It can be – and usually is – localized to help a company establish a local link or strengthen an existing one.

Racing comes in all shapes and sizes, but auto racing is not only a huge opportunity, it is a sometimes misunderstood one. Marketers must realize that it and other forms of racing – from bicycles to foot races – are not just a permit to hang a banner on a track or a course. Leveraging the sponsorship is critical, whether accomplished with premium giveaways and sweepstakes to build customer databases, charitable cause tie-ins to strengthen community goodwill, first-class hospitality at a first-class event that customers and employees will appreciate with future enthusiasm and business opportunities, or media exposure in events that are tailor-made for television cameras, giving your well-placed, well-designed banner or signage real pop to millions of people.

This is why package-goods companies sponsor race cars, why McDonald's sponsors a drag-racing team, and why racing teams are delving into more sophisticated marketing approaches, letting prospective sponsors know that all of the aforementioned opportunities are available to them through sponsorship of their teams.

Especially if their team wins.

References

[1] Paddock Publications, *Daily Herald*, Sports Section, June 6, 1994.
[2] *Motorsports Marketing News*, Ernie Saxton Communications, Vol. IX, No. 4, April 1993, p. 1.
[3] Performance Research study, January 1994.
[4] *San Francisco Examiner*, Sports Section, May 9, 1993.
[5] Letter from Gil Broyles, manager, Wiltel media relation, Aug. 14, 1992.
[6] JOED promotion kit, October 1993.
[7] Toyota Grand Prix official information kit, 1992.
[8] *Marketing News*, March 15, 1993, p. 13.
[9] *Motorsports Marketing News*, Ernie Saxton Communications, Vol. IX, Issue 9, September 1993, p. 2.
[10] *Turning Horse Power Into Marketing Power*, Chapter 1, pp. 1-4.
[11] *Fast Facts and Hi-Speed Strategies*, JB Racing Service newsletter, November 1990, pp. 3-4.
[12] *Albuquerque Journal*, Dec. 10, 1990, Business Outlook section, pp. 1-2.
[13] 1994 Motorola Cycling Team Guide.
[14] *Tour of America Sponsorship Report*, p. 6.
[15] Danskin press release, May 1994.
[16] IronKids Bread Triathlon Sponsorship Program, 1992.
[17] New York Road Runners Club official guide, 1994.
[18] *Bank Marketing*, August 1990, pp. 26-29.

7

Soccer in America and the World Cup Tournament

World Cup Soccer: It is bigger than the World Series. Bigger than the Super Bowl, that bastion of American sporting events.

World Cup Soccer: It is bigger than the NBA finals, the Olympics (winter or summer), and the Stanley Cup finals.

World Cup Soccer: It attracts the biggest television audiences of any event, anywhere. It sells out every game. It draws the world's most raucous fans, hands down.

World Cup Soccer: It is the penultimate event of the world's most popular game. It epitomizes all that is *fan* in *fanatic* and seizes the imagination of a worldwide audience.

So how come the world's most popular game can't sustain professional-level league play successfully in the United States, where as many as 16 million people, many of them kids and teenagers, are registered players?

So much is on the line now because in 1994 America played host to the world's biggest sporting event: the World Cup soccer tournament. While there was no doubt that the tournament's first-ever visit to American shores was successful in and of itself (in terms of television revenue, ticket sales, and economic trickledown for venue merchants), it is the aftermath to which everyone is paying attention.

Will professional soccer finally catch on in this country? Or is American soccer fated to be a temporary fascination for millions of youngsters who eventually grow up to be football, basketball, baseball, or – dare we say it? – hockey fans. Soccer's fate in America was on the line when the World Cup was held here, and sponsors who tied in to the event knew that. While those sponsors (who reportedly paid as much as $20 million and up to World Cup USA for the privilege) knew that internationally they would garner benefits with soccer-crazed folks, their fate with the coveted American audience was much less clear. Is it worth it to be a soccer sponsor in the United States, the World Cup notwithstanding?

Considering that a Soccer Industry Council of America study, as shown in Table 7.1, indicates some 2.5 million officially registered players are from college age on down, and, as shown in Table 7.2, reveals that the higher you go in U.S. household income the more soccer participants you find, perhaps it is worth it.

In this chapter, we will examine the World Cup and the benefits of being officially associated with it. American and international perceptions of the sport will be presented, and the state of soccer will be laid out. Who plays, and why? Who watches, and why? Who sponsors, and why? What, how, and why do they gain from it? MasterCard's participation as the exclusive credit-card sponsor will be examined in detail and its sponsorship program analyzed. The world's most widely accepted credit card garnered success from treating the World Cup as the special event that it is, rather than viewing it as a one-shot opportunity to hang banners in stadiums around the United States where an international audience was watching every boot, shot, dribble, tackle, yellow card, and save.

If those terms don't sound familiar to you, or if you associate some of them with other sports, you are not alone. The American audience, despite the World Cup and the $4 billion that was expected to trickle down to American merchants because of it, is still barely knowledgeable about the sport. Soccer's inability to adjust to American tastes – as other sports have done – is the reason for this, although there is some movement afoot to adjust the game to American tastes so that a

TABLE 7.1. Soccer Participation in the United States (1991)

Organization	Total Registration
Soccer Association for Youth	83,151
American Youth Soccer Organization	358,114
U.S. Youth Soccer Association	1,714,539
High Schools	350,102
	(boys and girls)
NCAA	Men's programs: 581
	Women's programs: 348

Source: Time Warner Sports Merchandising, from a 1992 Soccer Industry Council of America study.

pro league can survive, let alone thrive, in this country in the post-World Cup halo.

But television networks still can't find enough advertising time in this nonstop game. Fans, especially adults, find the lack of scoring to be unexciting and uninspiring. Maybe that's why the higher-scoring indoor version of soccer has proven attractive to fans in the United States on a limited, market-to-market basis. With scores like 17-10 and 15-13 instead 0-0 or 1-0, the games are much more provocative.

But don't let the attention given by Americans to the 1994 World Cup fool you: the game still has a long way to go in this country before it becomes the next football or baseball or basketball, let alone the next hockey. In fact, basketball – even without Magic Johnson, and Larry Bird – is ever so close to creeping up on and surpassing soccer as the world's most popular game, at least in the views of some experts. Those opinions and their supporting arguments will be presented in this chapter, as the complex world of soccer unfolds on these pages. "Complex" is the key word – it's why America hasn't yet embraced the world's favorite sport. Or is that "perplexed"? Let's see.

The World Cup – Its Dimensions

"The world will collectively put their lives on hold" for the World Cup Soccer Tournament, says Ralph Irizzary, vice president of merchandis-

TABLE 7.2. Soccer Participation in the United States by Household Income

Income	Participants per 100	Number
Less than $25,000	5.2	4,870,000
$25,000-$49,999	7.8	5,804,000
$50,000+	7.1	3,893,000
Totals	6.5	14,567,000

Source: Time Warner Sports Merchandising, from a 1992 Soccer Industry Council of America study.

ing at Time Warner Sports Merchandising, the licensing agent for World Cup USA.[1]

To what extent? To this extent, according to the 1993 predictions of World Cup USA Chairman and CEO and U.S. Soccer President Alan Rothenberg: 32 billion people, worldwide, would watch the event's 100 hours of television; 1.5 million people would specifically come to the United States just for the World Cup Tournament; 900,000 game tickets had already sold out instantly when made available in two separate offerings; and live attendance at the games would total some 3.5 million.[1]

Comparatively, Rothenberg noted, the Summer Olympics in Barcelona, Spain, in 1992, drew a television audience of 16 billion cumulatively for 200 hours of broadcast time. Ticket sales for the 52 games in nine cities for the 1994 World Cup Tournament in the United States were the briskest in TicketMaster history, he claimed, for any event, sports or otherwise.

"Now the World Cup comes to America for the first time," or so it said in Time Warner Sports Merchandising literature. "World Cup USA 1994 promises to be the most significant event in sports history and the biggest soccer festival of all time. The sleeping American giant will awaken to take its place as a force in world soccer and become the definitive showcase for the sport the immortal Pele called 'the beautiful game.' "

There is no doubt these gentlemen were right – soccer exploded in the United States with the arrival of the World Cup Tournament. Its ability to sustain that momentum is critical to the formation of a pro

1. Speech at National Sporting Goods Association annual convention, August 2, 1993.

league here, however. Is soccer in the United States ready for the big time, the prime time, as its purists and fanatics claim that it is? Let's examine what these experts call the "state of soccer" in America and the game's potential for sustained professional growth.

Soccer in America – Anything but *Futbol*

According to Jeff Bliss, a World Cup USA 1994 licensing executive, "There will never be a war while the World Cup is being played because there would be no media coverage."[2]

In fact, according to Bliss, interest in the World Cup is so intense that it's "win or die. It's not just a matter of life and death. It's much more important than that." Non-Cup matches from Europe to South America have seen hooliganism, brawls, riots, and deaths, but no one was sure how the World Cup would be received in America. Because of the United States's proven drawing power for international sporting events (witness the 1984 Summer Olympics in Los Angeles); its facilities; and its outstanding infrastructure for handling audiences, transportation, and mass communications, World Cup organizers were persuaded to locate the 1994 games here.

It is private-sector support that will drive the World Cup here, through sponsorship agreements with the world's best-known marketing names, from Coca-Cola to MasterCard to American Airlines. With the sponsors' promotional support, World Cup USA 1994 planned to create "walking billboards," according to Bliss, to garner $1 billion in sales by distributing licensed tournament merchandise and clothing for up to two years preceding the tournament through channels as traditional as retail mass merchants and as innovative as television's home-shopping networks.

"We really do want those walking billboards," Bliss stressed. The licensing of those materials will "really . . . help us achieve our overall goals," especially by creating free advertising – or at least ads paid for by millions of others.

The goals, however, went beyond the World Cup Tournament's success alone, according to Hank Steinbrecher, executive director of

---

2. Speech at American Marketing Association Sports Marketing conference, May 6, 1992.

the U.S. Soccer Federation (U.S. Soccer), headquartered in Chicago. In his remarks to the American Marketing Association's June 1992 Sports Marketing Conference audience, he laid out many of the goals for the tournament itself and for the future. First and foremost, he said, was to "get our sport *branded* in our society."

Steinbrecher, no novice to sports marketing due to his previous associations with the likes of Quaker Oats and its Gatorade sport drink brand, knew that "most people don't see sports as an entertainment industry," even though that's what it is. Gatorade did during his tenure there and "grabbed a niche," in sports. Now, because "soccer competes in the sports industry," says Steinbrecher, "we in soccer intend to have our share" of the sports and entertainment market.

Very simply, U.S. Soccer examined the U.S. soccer market, found a problem it could turn into an opportunity, and did just that. In 1990, U.S. Soccer had only one sponsor, Anheuser-Busch, which was a long way from connecting with soccer's principal audience – kids and teens.

"We were not in business, we were in sports," Steinbrecher admitted. The turning point for U.S. Soccer came with the adoption of the positioning, "Soccer is the universal game of family and health." And so the corner got turned.

Now more than 15 million Americans are registered soccer players. Thirty-eight percent of them are female. U.S. Soccer is unifying soccer organizations and associations across the country. Of the 15 million-plus participants, 40 percent, says U.S. Soccer, play "25 or more days a year." More than eleven million are under 18, making soccer the number-three participatory sport in that age group, behind basketball and volleyball.

Nearly 7 million participants are under 12, making soccer the number-two participatory sport in that age bracket, behind basketball. The number of high-school players in America nearly doubled to more than 370,000 between 1981 and 1992, making soccer the fastest growing sport at that level. There are 591 men's and 533 women's NCAA soccer programs. By comparison, football has 553.

Are you getting the message? U.S. Soccer is.

"Our mission is to build and grow the spectator and participant base of our sport," Steinbrecher asserts these days. His organization has unified – and will continue to unify – splintered soccer organizations, giving sponsors better marketing targets.

"We believe soccer in the U.S. today is the greatest, untapped entertainment sport," Steinbrecher contends, citing his organization's 300-percent revenue increase between 1990 and 1992 and its alliances with marketing partners such as M&M, Coke, MasterCard, American Airlines, and others. "We have been very aggressive," he asserts, in developing the national team and its following as well as youth programs nationwide.

The U.S. National Team is a good example of what U.S. Soccer is shooting for – and accomplishing. Even with its World Cup qualifying effort for the 1990 tournament, a few years ago the U.S. National Team was playing to domestic audiences of some 5,000, even against premier opponents. Those numbers zipped as high as 50,000 plus and averaged 35,000 in 1992. The 1993 U.S. Cup Tournament, in which the United States, Brazil, Germany, and England played round-robin matches throughout the United States, drew just under 48,000 per game. The tournament games were played in five different cities, four of which were World Cup 1994 venues.

• As Steinbrecher preached, participation has been the rule to grow by. As youth participant registration shot up, so did success. Six different U.S. age-group and gender teams qualified for their respective world championship tournaments. And the U.S. women's team captured the initial women's World Cup Tournament in China in 1991, a testimony to how seriously the sport was being taken in this country and to the level of competitor capable of being produced in this country.

Then again, maybe none of this should come as any surprise. After all, the 1984 Summer Olympic Soccer Gold Cup game in the Rose Bowl in Los Angeles drew an audience of 101,000. Soccer, says Steinbrecher, accounted for 40 percent of ticket sales revenue for the 1984 Olympics in Los Angeles, even with the minimal media play it got compared to that given to other sports.

Soccer has rocked the world and it was expected to rock the United States similarly. The 1990 World Cup Tournament, held in Italy, had a cumulative television audience of 26.7 billion and a championship game audience of 1.06 billion, making it the most-watched sports event in history, according to U.S. Soccer data. And the 1994 tournament in

America was expected to top it handily, with projections of a 2 billion-plus viewing audience for the final championship game in Los Angeles.

The U.S. Cup tournament that prefaced the 1993 World Cup featured what U.S. Soccer said was an 80-country television audience and the issuance of 1,500 sets of credential for international journalists. As a Federation Internationale de Football Association (FIFA) executive said at the time, "No one should say Americans don't like soccer. They like it if you have the right teams. Nowhere else in the world could you average 47,000 fans for such games. This was the most important step in the history of soccer in this country."[2]

Marketing World Cup 1994 in the United States

In a country where it has been historically difficult to successfully market professional soccer, the best-known names in marketing and business were on board as official sponsors for the World Cup 1994. Among them: Canon, Coke, Fuji, General Motors, MasterCard, McDonald's, Snickers, and Gillette. These firms paid up to $20 million for the privilege of associating their brands with the tournament. As to the tiered sponsorships Rothenberg spoke of in his talk to the National Sporting Goods Association in the summer of 1993, they ranged from the estimated $20-million level down to the estimated $7-million range for the likes of American Airlines (official air carrier of the tournament), Adidas, Sheraton, Sprint, and Upper Deck. A $2.5-million tier was also available. Each tier carried different levels of permissible licensing and sponsorship activity. Local organizing committees had sponsors whose contributions ranged from $700,000 to $4 million, according to a report in *The Sports Lawyer,* a bimonthly publication of the Sports Lawyers Association.

These sponsors faced a particularly challenging situation in marketing World Cup soccer, despite 52 televised games and the scope of the massive international audience. Soccer's 45-minute-half format and its nonstop clock do not lend themselves to traditional television advertising as well as other major sporting events, which have natural breaks. Baseball has its between-innings breaks. Basketball and football have timeouts (for teams and for television) and quarterly and halftime intermissions.

Yet the World Cup USA 1994 sponsors and advertisers rose to the challenge with localized promotions in the various markets and a willingness to settle for television exposure that was limited to flashing their logos on the screen during the action. Traditional commercials were aired before the games, during halftimes, and during the postgame wrap-ups. Of the 52 games, 41 were aired on cable's all-sports ESPN network; its sister station, the ABC network, televised the other 11, including the finals from Los Angeles.

The facts that the audience for these games was huge and that nearly 16 million Americans play soccer are well known. But what are their attitudes? How does America feel about soccer? Why has the United States always been "a country that historically has had difficulty maintaining the sport on a professional level?"[3] Just what are these high-profile, big-spending sponsors spending their money on anyway? We already know the rest of the world loves soccer. What about Americans?

American Attitudes and Pro League Prospects

The draw that determined first-round World Cup 1994 venues and round-robin opponents was not the most popular in the history of televised pretournament events. In fact, live coverage of the pairings announcements on ESPN drew a less-than-resounding rating, although the Spanish-language Univision network reported more encouraging numbers, testimony to the international flavor of the tournament. Granted the draw was performed on a fall Sunday afternoon when National Football League games were ongoing, but still . . .

There is a gray, blurry line surrounding American attitudes on soccer: indoor professional teams like the Milwaukee Wave of the National Professional Soccer League (NPSL) have drawn above-average crowds of some 8,000 per game to their Bradley Center home. The sport's popularity in the state and the team's ability to market smartly to local youth organizations and schools has helped fuel the numbers.

Other leagues have faltered altogether. The National Professional Soccer League now plays to markets as diverse as Chicago, Canton,

Dayton, and Harrisburg, but Americans still don't go out to see the sport in overwhelming numbers. Professional leagues have shut down, consolidated, and merged. Ad campaigns were launched here prior to the 1994 World Cup that were designed to convince "the American public that football can be played with a round ball," according to a 1993 Reuters wire service report. The American public, despite its 16 million soccer participants, still needs to be educated about the game.

Yet, as Steinbrecher and Rothenberg allude to constantly, U.S. National Team games versus world-class opposition increasingly drew healthy crowds as World Cup 1994 drew closer. Today soccer camps and entrepreneurs attract youths hungry for instruction and workouts.

U.S. Soccer still insists that it will establish a pro league here in the United States, which was one of the main reasons the FIFA even considered granting this country rights to the World Cup Tournament in 1994.

Will it work?

Not if *Chicago Tribune* sports columnist Bernie Lincicome has his way. In two 1990 columns he set the tone for World Cup and pro league soccer prospects here: "What soccer needs is a beer frame," he wrote in his August column, responding to a fan letter complaining about low-scoring soccer games coming between the game and fan interest. When the U.S. team unceremoniously bowed out of the 1990 World Cup Tournament in Italy, Lincicome commented that the team had "saved us from going through another soccer scare."

Well, it did for a while. Then the World Cup came here and the scare became a reality. The games sold out, all 52 of them, and talk of a pro league lingered and strengthened.

But the perceptions remain. Aleks Mihailovic, a Yugoslavian-born American citizen, has been a soccer coach, trainer, businessman, and clinician for many years. He has played and coached the game at both amateur and professional levels. Today he teaches and trains soccer players through his Chicago-based Soccer Made In America program. He travels the country teaching the sport and developing training materials for it. When it comes to soccer, Mihailovic has seen it all. He told *The Chicago Tribune* in a 1991 interview what he thinks the game needs to succeed. Those elements still hold true.

"In South America and Europe," Mihailovic said, "players are taught to hold on to the ball and take a player on. This is what we need to teach our players: how to take on a defender consistently and just blow right by him with finesse. American soccer players receive the ball and get rid of it. We have to allow young players to create things. Then, and only then, will the score cease to be the main focus of the game. It is the moves, the fakes, the feints, that will keep people interested in the game even if the score is 0 to 0. . . . It is hard for me to be patient with people who say soccer is boring."

Still, Mihailovic sees problems building the sport in this country: "In the United States, our players don't have a consistent foundation. Many of them have never really been taught the correct execution of a movement. This happens because many of our coaches don't know how to read their players' movements." And until they do, Mihailovic's message to American coaches is that "all you will be doing is reinforcing bad habits in your young players."

So, yes we have millions and millions of young soccer players in this country. And, unfortunately, we have so many of them doing things wrong that the game may not have a chance to succeed because its participants here can't appreciate the right way to do it since they've never learned the right way. That's if Mihailovic's analysis is correct, and there's no reason to believe his long-honed expertise is off target. What's the use of enjoying a 0-0 soccer game if you can't appreciate the skills that made it happen? Would you appreciate a 0-0 National Football League game?

This, and the sarcasm expressed by the likes of Lincicome, are at the heart of why pro soccer has never caught on in the United States. Yet Rothenberg plans to make it happen sometime soon, although the FIFA was hoping it would start up immediately after the 1994 World Cup.

The Sports Lawyer report in late 1993 said the league projects attendance averages of some 25,000 per game and hopes to build "soccer role models" to build fan interest. But, the report concluded, while "short-term successes (World Cup Tournament) are quite evident . . . what remains unclear is the long-term reaction to the World Cup and soccer in the United States." There is truly no way to gauge whether a new pro league will be a success, unless you go by the success of previous leagues, which have been slim to naught.

Even soccer's staunchest defenders admit that changes are needed to attract the American audience on a full-time, long-term basis. Rothenberg, not long after the 1990 World Cup Tournament, told FIFA that rules changes are needed to encourage more scoring. In a statement that "rocked the soccer world," according to the *Chicago Tribune*, FIFA President Joao Havelange "suggested that the games be divided into quarters instead of halves to accommodate the commercial demands of television."[4]

Regardless of how the pro soccer league shapes up, Rothenberg will run it. He is part of a group recognized (and now partly financed) by U.S. Soccer to start up such a league. Other hopefuls' plans (including one tied into a real-estate development deal and another that was the brainchild of the American Professional Soccer League's brain trust) have been dashed. *USA Today*, however, reported late in 1993 that that league only averaged some 5,000 in attendance. The major stumbling block to getting the league going at all is paying the star players. Stars in soccer-crazed Europe make several hundred thousand dollars a year, and it will be difficult at best to get them to give that up for far-lowing-paying stardom here and no guarantee of big audiences and big television ratings.

Yet other experts and pundits challenge the wit and wisdom of U.S. Soccer and its attempts to bring pro-league soccer to America. The well-traveled Frank Deford, late of *Sports Illustrated* and *The National* fame in the world of sports publishing and one of our most respected sportswriters, told the American Marketing Association's May 1992 Sports Marketing Conference audience in a keynote address that basketball might supplant soccer as the world's most popular game. Speaking at the same conference a year earlier, David Downs, ABC's vice president for sports programming, told the audience that soccer was simply nothing more than a game enjoyed in this country by kids who would grow up to be football and baseball fans – that the World Cup would be a hit here, but after that . . .

Still, Rothenberg remains optimistic and steadfast. In an August 24, 1993, *USA Today* commentary, he wrote that World Cup 1994 will "initiate the conversion of soccer participants to soccer spectators" in this country. "Because of its impact, the 1994 World Cup will serve as an integral, initial step to maintain and cultivate soccer as a spectator sport in the USA. It is evident that the World Cup is an excellent vehicle to accomplish this goal. This event will aid the increased demand for the great game of soccer, and I say 'increase' as there is a strong demand for the quality in this country already."

"The North American Soccer League," he went on, "created a foundation for the sport of soccer, promoting participation at all levels." And he's right, except the league had been dead for years when he wrote that.

In response to his opinion, *USA Today* television and sports business columnist Michael Hiestand commented that soccer "has had a great future for a couple of decades now" as a spectator sport in this country, but that future has obviously not materialized. Calling the World Cup's arrival here "the Holy Grail" for soccer boosters, he predicted that those same "boosters will find their Grail will result in little more than the thrill of the chase.

"Here's why: If everybody who watches a sport first had to play it in competition, there wouldn't be any female football fans. Auto racing events would have empty grandstands. . . . People become fans so they can kibitz and kvetch: to criticize game plays they could never make, to psychoanalyze personalities, to conjure parallels to the past. To do that, you need a mental file drawer strewn with ripe tidbits on traditions and rivalries.

"Until U.S. sports fans fill those drawers with soccer stuff, the sport just has a great future."[5]

Soccer International: Do You Want to Sponsor *This?*

September 16, 1991: Four people are shot and 47 injured in fights between fans at the Brazilian soccer league championship game in Rio de Janeiro. The fights start three hours before the game.

June 13, 1993: In a review of Bill Buford's book, *Among the Thugs,* the *Chicago Tribune* cites passages referring to British soccer fans as hating foreigners, and stealing and/or destroying everything in their path. Buford describes, at one point, the "stage-by-stage metamorphosis of a crowd turning into a murderous mob."

June 18, 1990: News reports link sex and soccer to AIDS. Some of the AIDS cases in Edinburgh (which has the highest number of AIDS patients in Scotland) are traced back to Scottish drug abusers who became infected while attending the 1982 World Cup. Even worse: many were prepping for their trip to the World Cup Tournament in Italy that year.

December 18, 1992: Prostitutes traveling with the Romanian national soccer team admit to Reuters that they see a great source of profit in this relationship and accompany the team on many of their travels, particularly those out of the country.

December 18, 1993: A member of the German national team, which had just defeated the United States in an exhibition game, tells the media: "Germany is a soccer nation. Soccer is probably more important than politics."

December 5, 1993: *Chicago Tribune* reporter Phil Hersh describes Dutch and English soccer fans as having "battled for the title of the world's most reprehensible."

March 21, 1991: A *Chicago Tribune* feature story headline reads: "Argentine Soccer: a Way of Life – and, Sometimes, Death."

May 14, 1993: A *Chicago Reader* feature story headline reads: "When the World Cup Comes to Soldier Field . . . Will the World's Most Violent Fans Come, Too?"

Is this the game you want to associate your brand with? Is this the game you want to associate with? Is this really a game?

MasterCard: One Company's Sponsorship Leveraging . . . or, How To Get a Kick Out of Soccer . . . or, How to Put a Kick into American Soccer

Two-hundred-billion-dollar-plus MasterCard, the world's most widely accepted credit card, was a top-tier sponsor of World Cup USA 1994. It is believed the New York-based company spent upwards of $20 million just to get in.

MasterCard spent that much or more than that leveraging its sponsorship. This is in line with what marketing advisors recommend: that official sponsors spend somewhere between 100 percent and 150 percent of its sponsorship fee on leveraging its sponsorship to protect it against ambush-marketing attempts and to maintain its official status in the eyes of its would-be customers.

In a series of seminars held in all nine U.S. venue cities for the World Cup 1994 Soccer Tournament, MasterCard's Vice President for U.S. Promotions, Mava Heffler, personally urged retailers to participate and to back up their participation by powerful marketing campaigns segmented to attract consumers from local markets as well as foreign fans who would be following their favorite teams around.

MasterCard had all the numbers, all the hype, all the support of U.S. Soccer and World Cup USA officials, and all of its powerful marketing guns lined up. Its goals? To drive retailer promotion for and acceptance of MasterCard and to promote its use by consumers through multifaceted marketing support.

MasterCard used existing marketing programs and created new ones. Its well-known and widely accepted MasterValues program, which invited customers and retailers to use and accept the card, was tied into the World Cup sponsorship. Programs were designed to be venue specific (from host city to host city), retailer specific, and industry specific (from restaurants to mass merchants to hotels).

MasterCard was clearly counting on grass-roots drivers for soccer success. As Heffler said, "Soccer in this country is coming from the bottom up. . . . the parents get involved." Heffler wasn't too concerned about ambush attempts, saying, "We're first. We're loudest. We're out there establishing relationships. Any competitors who get in, well, imitation is the sincerest form of flattery."[3]

Heffler continued that MasterCard was taking this seriously: "One thing about sponsorship," she said, "It's not what you have, but what you do with it." What she'd like to have done with it was reach an audience. Hank Steinbrecher, in a 1993 speech at a MasterCard seminar, described this audience as participatory. "We'd rather have 16 million play than 50 million watch on a Monday night with a beer in hand," he prescribed, tightening the audience profile for Master-Card's projected retail participants.

In any event, the games meant money for merchants in the various venues in the form of souvenirs, meals, and visitors. There would be thousands of people spending millions of dollars. Chicago alone expected 500,000 visitors for the games there – 5,000 of whom would be media members that would report back to their local communities – and some $200 million in economic impact.

With Pele, perhaps the world's greatest soccer player ever, in tow as spokesperson and endorser, MasterCard trumpeted its official theme

---

3. Interview with Mava Heffler, Feb. 24, 1993.

Figure 7.1.   Mava Heffler, who drove MasterCard's 1994 world Cup participation.
Photogrph by Brad Hall, Brock Photo/Graphics, Courtesy of Mastercard International. New York, New York.

for its World Cup promotional campaign: "Welcome the World to the United States." MasterCard estimated that the typical visitor to a World Cup venue city would spend about $200 per day on meals, lodging, and shopping. MasterCard wanted its merchants to attract most if not all of that by promoting its card. MasterCard and World Cup officials anticipated some $4 billion in sales in the United States related to the tournament, on top of the $1 billion that would typically be spent here on soccer-related purchases.

MasterCard's MasterValues program was a success. By offering special values for consumers who plunked down their MasterCards at participating retailers and increases for the retailers, it generated a 30-percent sales increase between Thanksgiving and Christmas in 1993.

MasterCard came back with similar programs for the 1994 World Cup. In addition to MasterValues, it offered a special program targeted to malls that included a MasterCard/World Cup booth to promote card usage and the distribution of special World Cup souvenirs. It taught restaurateurs how to promote retention of customers. It taught grocers how to promote the World Cup to increase sales. It showed fast-food proprietors how to augment sales through the card, noting that credit-card holders spend 80 percent more with credit cards than they do when using cash in a fast-food facility. It showed merchants how to participate by using its Maestro Card, a debit card with 66 million cardholders worldwide that is finding increased acceptance in lieu of credit cards.

Specifically, each program was tailored to augment sales in each individual World Cup venue. MasterCard wasted no time promoting the fact that the nine venue markets were among America's most populous.

Most importantly, each marketing thrust was promoted as having benefits that MasterCard and MasterCard alone could provide.

Here's how some of the specific programs worked:

MasterCard at the Mall

At leading malls, particularly those in the World Cup host venues, a MasterCard booth enabled shoppers to get a World Cup premium item simply by stopping by and showing receipts for purchases made with their MasterCards. A sweepstakes entry was also available to win a photograph taken with international soccer legend Pele, who would appear at the mall booth at the end of the promotional period. Fifteen winners at the participating malls had their photos taken with him. The premium items ranged from pins to posters to T-shirts, depending upon the amount of purchase displayed on the receipts.

Direct mail, radio, mall signage, and youth soccer communications and public relations supported the campaign. A percentage of sales in the mall made with MasterCards were donated to youth soccer programs as well. Youth soccer organization volunteers were employed to help run the booths, and the volunteers had their photos taken with Pele as an incentive.

MasterCard at the Mall worked so well, in fact, that at one Dallas-area appearance by the great Pele, some 35,000 were estimated to have shown up.

Merchant Sweepstakes

Participating merchants were encouraged to display MasterCard promotional materials at the point of sale to encourage card use among consumers. Registering to participate made them eligible for prizes ranging from tickets to the games in their venue to cash to World Cup memorabilia. Merchants participating included retailers, restaurateurs, and hoteliers.

A special mystery shopper program, supported by radio advertising during the games, notified consumers and retailers about a MasterCard World Cup team roaming the venue city seeking people using their MasterCards and the retailers who were accepting them. The team was waiting to award them with special premiums and gifts on the spot.

MasterValues

The long-running, successful program that helped boost MasterCard usage and sales during holiday periods also came to World Cup. All 100 million MasterCard holders in the United States received special statement stuffers informing them of the special values that awaited them if they used their MasterCard at participating retailers. The same program boosted sales made on MasterCards by as much as 30 percent during the Thanksgiving-to-Christmas period in 1993.

MasterValues comprehensively covered the retail spectrum, including categories from food to fashion, health to gifts, travel to entertainment centers, and home to office. Participating were the likes of 800Flowers, Burlington Coat Factory, Camelot Music, Colony Hotels and Resorts, Coconuts Music and Movies, FootAction, Hertz, Radisson Hotels International, Opryland USA, Pearle Vision, LensCrafters, Lens Express, Venture, and Sharper Image.

Local merchants, on a market-to-market basis, also participated in the MasterValues program with special discounts and offers.

According to Mava Heffler, MasterCard's "very strong" national and local merchant support and participation built what she called a "special-events strategy" to leverage its participation as a sponsor of the World Cup Tournament 1994. Point-of-sale, city-specific, segment-specific, and mall-specific programs guaranteed MasterCard a highly positive, tournament-related aura. Whether or not the company would continue on though as a sponsor of soccer had not yet been determined, Heffler said in an interview a few months before the World Cup 1994 Tournament.

In summary then, MasterCard's World Cup Soccer sponsorship "welcomed the world" to the United States for the 1994 tournament. It specifically targeted not consumers but the channels by which it markets its cards – its issuing members and particularly retailers, to energize them to promote and drive MasterCard usage. Its message was basic: the World Cup's economic impact would be huge – something like $4 billion for the run of the tournament. While soccer was a sport whose 16 million American participants were primarily kids, MasterCard's targeting of merchants and members was critical to drive card usage, because while the program had grass-roots elements, kids aren't the ones who pull out MasterCards in the mall or anywhere else. In reality, the program's theme was "welcoming the world's money to the United States."

MasterCard made it easy for the retailers to participate. The window and counter decals they distributed to drive MasterCard use at point of purchase had retailer sweepstakes entries on the back of their peel-off strips that the retailers simply filled out and turned in in order to be automatically entered in a trip-around-the-world sweepstakes. The mystery shopper program reinforced it all by rewarding Master-Card usage on the spot at retail and hospitality venues in World Cup host cities. MasterCard's strategy was supported promotionally by statement inserts and radio advertising for MasterValues, MasterCard at the Mall, and a MasterCard Welcome Center in World Cup host cities that provided travel services, special discount offer notices, and promotional materials.

MasterCard will examine the possibilities of tying in with pro soccer in this country after the World Cup tournament. Certainly, its participation with youth soccer has paid handsome dividends.

"This isn't just about soccer," Heffler said in summing up Master-Card's participation. "This is about the biggest event in the world."

In summary, the biggest sports event on the globe is still having trouble securing the sport's future in the United States, the market in which so many global firms crave to be established. Whether soccer will fly in this country is anyone's guess, but a Harris Poll released just after the 1994 Winter Olympics (some four months before the World Cup Tournament) showed that only 25 percent of Americans were even aware that the tournament was a soccer event and only 18 percent knew it would be played in the United States.[6]

These numbers, however, were greeted with cautious optimism by World Cup USA 1994 officials, who were glad they had trended up and not down since a similar survey three months earlier. In addition, the number of people expressing an interest in attending or viewing a World Cup game increased with each new survey.

Not a Deterrent

Those survey numbers didn't discourage sponsors, either. In addition to MasterCard's comprehensive program, Sprint of Kansas City, Missouri, became official telecommunications provider to the games, with plans to leverage that presence.

According to its consulting firm, Performance Properties Inc. of Greenwich, Connecticut, Sprint entered the World Cup Tournament with a focused program of integrated marketing efforts. These included: "The Sprint Soccer Poll," with international judges ranking the world's top 10 teams; a geography education program in Hispanic schools; sponsorship of U.S. Soccer's "Yellow Pages" of soccer businesses and associations in the United States; a "Sprint Soccer Ambassadors" program featuring members of the U.S. national team; a sweepstakes program at the games; a World Cup Soccer prepaid calling card (which attracted a lawsuit from MasterCard); and direct mail to "soccer-involved families."[7]

This comprehensive program was designed to reach consumer and business targets, domestically and internationally, leveraging what Performance Properties called the "42 million involved family members" of soccer in this country. In addition, as official telecommunications provider to the tournament, Sprint had an exclusive opportunity to display its services and products at each of the nine host U.S. cities. Specifically, Performance Properties said Sprint was targeting suburban families and what it described as "first- and second-generation ethnic families that regularly use international calling services."

The Big Question remains, however: Will all of this marketing impetus enable soccer to stick in the United States as a world-class, pro-level sport, or will it remain the domain of kids and teenagers who ultimately grow up to reject it? Will those 16 million registered kickers and 42 million so-called involved family members in this country support it at the pro level, or just keep on kicking?

Only time will tell.

References

[1]   Time Warner Sports Merchandising official promotional literature, 1993; and Rothenberg speech at NSGA convention, Aug. 2, 1993.
[2]   Official U.S. Soccer promotional literature, 1993.
[3]   *The Sports Lawyer*, November/December 1993, p. 3.
[4]   *Chicago Tribune*, Sports section, "U.S. Domes Could be Homes for the '94 Cup," June 20, 1990.
[5]   *USA Today*, "SportsViews," sports section, August 24, 1993, p. 7C.
[6]   *Chicago Sun-Times*, "Little Interest in World Cup in U.S.," February 28, 1994, p. 111.
[7]   Performance Properties Inc. newsletter, November 1993.

8

Futuresports . . . You Ain't Seen Nothin' Yet

How much longer will the fans take it and still come to the ballparks, buy the licensed merchandise, watch the games on TV, and generally be loyal sports customers?

How much longer will they take the escalating prices, the (to them) out-of-whack salaries and the seemingly endless greed that they perceive to be driving sports? They don't comprehend player strikes or owner lockouts. They can't even fathom multi-million-dollar salaries. Ticket prices have skyrocketed to the point that most fans don't go to games anymore – most attendance, particularly at baseball games, is the same several hundred thousand going again and again, according to Roger Noll, a Stanford University economics professor who has studied the phenomenon far and wide. Increasingly, tickets and boxes go to corporate sponsors.

Stadiums have become palaces with high-priced seats (even the so-called "cheap seats" are not very "cheap"), value-added amenities, expanded concessions, expensive parking, and luxury-priced suites or skyboxes that reap in the gazillions that the owners need to keep up with escalating player salaries.

Routine, everyday, average fans have been driven out and are ultimately looking at pay-per-view as their option of the future for viewing sports – even events like the Super Bowl and the World Series. It's coming as sure as you're reading this.

"Maxing" revenues is the byword in sports, and owners and moguls will go to every end to achieve it. Starting with the stadiums and working out into "fandom" from there, owners, teams, and leagues are marketing a value-added experience not only to individuals who can afford them but – more often – to corporations that want to latch on as sponsors, entertain their trade customers, offer event trips and tickets as database name-building sweepstakes prizes, and associate their companies, services, and products with the excellence and championship aura of these leagues and teams so idolized by fans.

Despite it all, despite the escalating prices and costs, the fans keep coming back – or trying to. They fill the stadiums. They fuel the television ratings. They scan the sports pages and magazines. They play rotisserie and fantasy sports in ever-increasing numbers. They buy about $12 billion worth of licensed sports merchandise annually. They continue to state that being close to their heroes and favorite teams is the payback that they seek for being loyal fans, and they appreciate the good companies that make that possible for them – or so they say in survey responses.

Why fans remain loyal, as well as the state of the palaces that pass for stadiums and arenas today and how they're marketed to help owners max out revenues, will be explored here. The reasoning behind these routes and the growing sophistication and comprehensiveness of sports marketing will also be examined.

Going to the Game Just Ain't What It Used to Be

As evidence that the owners are forcing common fans out of the parks and into pay-per-view stances, let's examine the marketing of the stadium. The key is the pricing of seats and amenities, the creation of the amenities, the skyboxes, and the subsequent virtual renovation of stadiums into amusement complexes and virtual shopping malls, where sponsors and advertisers grab at fans with their messages, and soon will be doing the same *electronically* during the games (not during timeouts, either) to fans watching on TV.

Yes, the electronic, super-imposed on-screen message is coming, between pitches in baseball, between plays in football, etc.

Owners continually leverage the powerful emotional attachment fans have for teams to forge these money-making palaces and attract to them the sponsors and advertisers who also want to leverage that attachment. We'll talk more about how powerful that emotional attachment is later in this chapter. But it is the foundation on which these palaces are built and marketed, and upon which most sports marketing promotions are built.

Building the Stadium

There are two pillars upon which new stadiums get built: economic development benefits to the area and the prestige of having a team in that area (otherwise known as "your city ain't nothin' without a pro franchise"). These hooks are debatable but powerful. One thing remains certain: The new stadiums and arenas help owners max out revenues by giving them not necessarily more seating but more expensive seating (particularly skyboxes) and more expensive amenities (like in-seat food service).

Extensive studies prepared by teams, their consultants, and government agencies show that the economic development benefits enjoyed by cities that build new arenas and stadiums or allow their construction are in the millions annually.

Like where, you ask? Well, in the 1980s in Indianapolis they added the Hoosier Dome right in the middle of downtown, got the support of local major businesses for it, and became the amateur sports capitol of America – host to the Pan American Games and the U.S. Olympic Festival, among other events. The Hoosier Dome also helped draw the Baltimore Colts to Indianapolis in a now-famous midnight escapade and is estimated to have created somewhere in the neighborhood of 100,000 jobs and a tripling of the city's tax base.

After the Superdome was constructed in New Orleans in the '70s, a University of New Orleans study showed that during the stadium's first ten years of existence it created $13 in economic benefits for every dollar that Louisiana taxpayers had paid to build it. In Baltimore, the new Camden Yards complex, where the Orioles play, will yield $1.1 billion in "value-added benefits" to the state, according to the Maryland

Stadium Authority. The Truman Sports Complex, which houses Kansas City's football Chiefs and its baseball Royals, has supposedly yielded some $9.2 million in tax benefits to the state of Missouri and $237.7 million annually to the Kansas City-area economy. According to one study, "Every employee of the two organizations generates another three employees elsewhere in the economy. And for every dollar's worth of income paid in the form of wages and salaries by the Chiefs and Royals, another $1.30 of income is generated for other workers in the economy."[1]

Despite those impressive numbers, there is disagreement and dissent. Distinguished, award-winning columnist Jim Murray of the *Los Angeles Times* syndicate, in a column questioning the standards by which communities vie for teams and the underlying motivation for new stadiums, stated that "no one ever computed exactly how much a franchise contributed to a local economy."[2] The Heartland Institute, a public-policy think tank, says that the 13 publicly financed stadiums it studied were all losing money – and that the New Orleans Superdome was the leader. Of course, not every new stadium and arena lives up to its preconstruction promise.

Toronto's Skydome, playpen for baseball's Blue Jays and the Canadian Football League's Argonauts, came in some $260 million over budget, with interest alone totaling $35 million. The City of Toronto and the Province of Ontario were partners in the construction, and they aren't smiling, even though the Blue Jays regularly pack the place with up to 50,000 fans in a stadium that includes an overhanging hotel and restaurant (items that are getting to be new ballpark staples).

Of course, the idea behind these playpens is development – economic development. Sometimes it happens, and sometimes it doesn't. The Richfield Coliseum, once home of the NBA's Cleveland Cavaliers, never did attract the development the original developers hoped for – businesses and residences that would stretch from Cleveland on one side and greater Akron/Canton on the other. The Cavaliers are moving back into downtown Cleveland with a sweeter deal as part of the new Gateway development there.

In the midst of a bustling downtown, stadiums and arenas are supposed to provide revitalization. In more rural and suburban settings, they're supposed to spur development. Opinions differ on whether stadiums and arenas achieve these goals. The Chicago White

Sox contended that up to $100 million in economic trickledown would be felt by merchants in the area of their new ballpark, which was financed mostly with monies from a new hotel tax. The Texas Rangers, on the other hand, anticipate development around their new classic stadium, The Ballpark, in Arlington, Texas.

Above all else though, the one thing that spurs development and economic trickledown is a winning team, which puts fans in the seats and brings their money to the neighborhood. No amount of steel and concrete can guarantee that. But stadiums and the teams that occupy them remain intensely emotional issues.

No less than eight times the barren Suncoast Dome in St. Petersburg, Florida has been used as a ploy by teams threatening to move out of their hometowns. The White Sox did it and got a stadium. The Mariners did it and got money-healthy Nintendo to buy them and keep them in Seattle. The Giants lured new ownership out of the San Francisco closets by threatening to move to St. Petersburg. And on and on. Each time, politicians got involved, promising fans they'd keep their beloved teams at home regardless of the cost and giving teams concessions in taxes, facility rent, and the like rather than let the teams move. Keeping the pro sports franchise intact indeed is one of the greatest vote-getting tools ever invented. So what if it costs the state or the city treasury a bundle?

But not every team gets what it wants. Illinois drew the line at building a new stadium or upgrading the existing stadium for the Chicago Bears, who have sought to build their own elsewhere in the community. (Of course, the Bears didn't threaten to move to St. Petersburg.) And the Cubs will desert Wrigley Field to be able to play more than the 18 night games a year they're currently allowed. Such a move would enable them to maximize television prime-time advertising and ratings for national superstation WGN, which, like the Cubs, is owned by newspaper magnate the Tribune Company, which clearly doesn't care if the Cubs win or lose as long as they draw fans and advertising and ratings. To maximize all that, the Cubs will announce a new facility before the decade is out. Just watch. This will also enable them, like it has so many other teams, to maximize revenues through increased seating, in-stadium amenities, and – most importantly – those gloriously profitable and high-priced luxury skyboxes.

Truly, the new stadiums and arenas are palaces. The Detroit Pistons's home is even called "The Palace." Food-service options now include upgraded seating sections with wait service, where the server electronically records your order on a hand-held device and debits or charges your account, as the case may be. Several minor league teams have even resorted to this value-added, revenue-building tactic.

But that's not all. In New York, the Mets were reportedly talking to the Nickelodeon people about opening a family amusement area at Shea Stadium during games. Denver's new Coors Field has bike racks for the riding enthusiasts who peddle to the games. The Skydome in Toronto offers dinner views of the park, hotel rooms with views of the diamond, and even a swinging Hard Rock Cafe in right field. The new baseball parks have less foul territory, so fans feel closer to the game. Baltimore's new Camden Yards offers wider, more comfortable seats with more leg room, a restaurant behind the right-field scoreboard where diners *al fresco* can watch the game, and twice as many washrooms for both men and women than old Memorial Stadium had.

And for all this the teams go to the bank. For playing in the Georgia Dome, for instance, the NFL's Atlanta Falcons received $6 million in return for a 20-year lease agreement and another $4 million a year in luxury box revenues. Estimates peg their additional annual revenue at more than $10 million just for moving in.

But not everything is so peachy. To keep up appearances, teams provide modest "family sections," where alcoholic beverages are prohibited and ticket prices are supposedly "family-priced." One family member got carried away, though, when "The Ballpark" opened in Texas – she fell over the upper deck rail while posing for a photo and wound up in a local hospital in serious condition. Chicago's new Comiskey Park has been criticized routinely for the severe slope of its upper deck, which has given many a fan vertigo.

Then again, today's ballparks have ATM machines, virtual shopping malls, and the aforementioned restaurants and hotels. Is it any wonder that corporate sponsors and advertisers are flocking to splendid palaces, even to the point of paying for the privilege of putting their names on them, while fans are paying more and more for the privilege of being exposed to these marketing communications messages? Yes, people pay for the privilege of being advertised to. Kinda makes you wonder, doesn't it?

Marketing the Ballpark

Like grocery stores and retail outlets, stadiums and arenas have become merchandising and promotion arenas. Signage, couponing, and even survey researchers are suddenly all over the place, just as they are at retail outlets. The bottom line: sponsors and advertisers go where the people are, where the customers are – or at least where they want to be.

How? It goes beyond signage. There are premium giveaways of everything from sunglasses to bats and hats, sponsored by corporate advertisers. Beefed-up gameday programs feature direct-response ads from sponsors or coupons for discounts. New seating sections, like the family sections, the picnic sections and the kids' amusement sections in the concourses, are sponsored by corporations.

Heck, the latest stadiums and arenas bear the names of the corporate sponsors themselves. In Chicago, the new home of the Bulls and Blackhawks is the United Center, named for Chicago-based United Airlines, whose payment for the privilege helped offset the construction fees. In Phoenix, it's America West. In Minnesota, it's Target. For the Washington, D.C. area, it's the USAir Arena. In Sacramento, the Kings play in the Arco Arena. The Lakers are in the Great Western (Bank) Forum in Los Angeles. Why do stadiums do this? Because estimates peg the value of such name-planting at about the $5 million mark, which in some cases means that, in equivalent advertising, they're obviously paying much less than that for the privilege, although the various sponsors and arena developers won't reveal the cost of the deals.

What all this does, in addition to the marketing and cost advantages, is put a goodwill spin on the company for sponsoring the facility where the local heroes compete. While immeasurable in sales dollars, that goodwill aura should translate to increased sales. It also looks good to the hometown fans that the local corporation made such a move (for examples, Chicago-based United, Denver-based Coors (Coors Field), and Phoenix-based America West).

It's not just ballparks and stadiums. ProKennex, the tennis equipment manufacturer, donated enough to have the ProKennex Tennis Building at the new San Diego U.S. Olympic Training Center named for itself, a particularly smart move now that tennis is a medal sport at the Olympics and the new training center is the first in the United States in a year-round warm-weather climate.

In the stadiums and arenas, however, the high-pitched advertising continues full throttle with no slowdown in sight. In the new ballparks, designed to present the feel of old ballparks, ads reign again on the outfield walls and scoreboards, some bigger than life. They were designed to look as though they were part of the stadium, not an add-on.

Yet, this advertising is being debated, too. Tobacco companies are increasingly finding resistance to their billboards and signage around stadiums and arenas. They are banned at some parks, as are hard liquor companies, even though teams need their monies. (Yet, ironically, beer companies aren't banned.) At the new Jacobs Field in Cleveland, which has drawn great praise for its architecture and design, smoking is not allowed, even though a tax on cigarettes helped raise some of the monies to pay for the construction. Cleveland is not the only place where taxes on taboo products have helped build stadiums in which the products, and advertisements for them, are banned from the facilities.

Still, teams, facilities, and sponsors continue to search for the ultimate signage. In rotating signage and the soon-to-be-unveiled rotating electronic signage, they may have found it along with a maximized expenditure of an advertising budget.

Dorna USA's rotating courtside signs have become the rage. You see them in the arena and on TV, but they've caused as much controversy as they have provided friendly intrusion. The rotating signs are now everywhere – along scorer's tables, along the stands in foul territory, and behind home plate (where TV cameras pick it up on every pitch) – in more and more stadiums and arenas all the time.

The ads are simple – usually just the corporate name and logo – and graphic rather than electronic. They started in Europe and moved into the United States in the '90s. To calm the storm, Dorna and other rotating signage providers work with facility managers, leagues, teams, and television networks to be sure that they aren't providing advertising that competes with team or league sponsors. During nationally televised games, this situation is generally avoided by turning the rotating signs off, and showing only signage displaying the name of the host team. And the rotating signage is becoming part of the sponsorship packages to avoid ambush marketers that aren't team or league sponsors getting on the rotating signage system.

Critics of the system say it's distracting and detracting to the integrity of the facilities and the games. However, it achieves awareness levels that are huge contrasted to those reached by other advertising techniques – some 33 percent higher, according to a study contrasting it to other in-arena signage.

Now the next evolution of rotating signage is coming – electronic rotating signage. Electronically projected onto your television screen, it provides the same rotation and exposure as the in-arena brand but reached the home television audience only. Like the in-arena rotating signage, careful consideration has to be given to avoid conflicts with official sponsors and advertisers, and ambush marketers.

If you watched the World Cup 1994 Tournament events held in the United States, you saw games that had no natural timeouts using electronic graphics to enhance advertiser and sponsor presence during the game action. Advertiser logos and names were superimposed transparently over the screen and the game clock while announcers reminded viewers who the sponsors were that were making the commercially uninterrupted broadcasts possible.

Now electronic rotating signage will embellish this approach (if "embellish" is what you want to call it, especially if you're a sports purist). In their hunger to maximize revenues, leagues and teams will grasp at this new advertising opportunity, just as television networks have commercialized everything from game summaries to scoreboards to announcements of pitching changes during ballgames. Eventually, if this is played as can be expected, you'll not only be able to see the ad but order the product or service as the game is in progress.

For the privilege of viewing all this advertising, which is advertised as being the advertising that breaks through the advertising clutter, fans pay a hefty price.

The High Price of Going to the Game

Plain and simple, it's just getting too expensive to go to the games. Everywhere you look, teams are raising prices the same way politicians are giving themselves pay raises.

Want to go to a Chicago Bears game? Seats between the 20-yard lines cost $40 in 1994, up from $35 in 1993. Going to the 1996 Atlanta Olympics? A ticket for the opening and closing ceremonies will run you $600 (they cost $500 at Barcelona in 1992). To sit in the coveted bleachers at Wrigley Field in Chicago, you'll pay $10. And you've usually got to get those tickets well in advance.

On average, according to Chicago-based *Team Marketing Report*, it cost $168.68 for a family of four to attend an NBA game. That price includes two beers, four hot dogs, four soft drinks, two souvenir caps, two programs, parking – and the tickets. In 1993 alone tickets jumped eight percent, to an average of $27.12 per. The New York Knicks, as could be expected, are at the high end of the scale, at some $232.62 for a family of four to attend a game. The Chicago Bulls, despite Michael Jordan's retirement, raised ticket prices to an average $36.45 for their last season in Chicago Stadium before moving into the United Center.

In October of 1993, according to *USA Today*, a small beer cost $3.28 at an NFL game, up 7.2 percent from the previous season. Hot dogs had gone up 6.6 percent, and a ticket, at an average of $28.68, was up 3.5 percent. For a family of four, according to *Team Marketing Report*, it cost $173 to attend an NFL game.

The cost of attending games was depressingly similar in structure and increase when looked at from sport to sport and event to event. (See Tables 8.1 through 8.6.) Keep that pay-per-view television guide handy – you're going to need it.

It's getting to the point that teams and leagues are really going to get desperate. Lawyer and National Sports Institute Director Martin Greenberg of Milwaukee's Marquette University, told the *Chicago Tribune* in January 1992 that "even if it means turning stadiums into shopping malls, professional sports teams have to look at alternative means of producing big dollars to survive at the escalating salary levels of today. The alternative is to price fans right out of the game."[3]

But when "cheap" seats are $15 to $20, the "average fans are disenfranchised," according to Team Marketing Report Editor and Publisher Alan Friedman.[1]

---

1. Speech to American Marketing Association's Sports Marketing Conference, June 1991.

TABLE 8.1. 1991 National Football League Ticket Price Changes

NFL TEAM	1991 AVE. (RANK)	1990 AVE.	% +/-
Atlanta Falcons	$24.67 (14)	$20.00	23.3%
Buffalo Bills	$27.67 (9)	$27.67	0
Chicago Bears	$28.50 (7)	$25.50	11.8%
Cincinnati Bengals	$25.63 (11)	$25.63	0
Cleveland Browns	$22.00 (22)	$22.00	0
Dallas Cowboys	$28.33 (8)	$26.50	6.9%
Denver Broncos	$24.67 (14)	$24.67	0
Detroit Lions	$18.17 (28)	$18.17	0
Green Bay Packers	$20.00 (26)	$20.00	0
Houston Oilers	$23.67 (17)	$22.40	5.7%
Indianapolis Colts	$22.33 (21)	$22.33	0
Kansas City Chiefs	$20.33 (25)	$19.33	5.2%
L.A. Raiders	$23.33 (19)	$21.00	11.1%
L.A. Rams	$21.67 (23)	$21.67	0
Miami Dolphins	$25.33 (12)	$25.33	0
Minnesota Vikings	$25.00 (13)	$23.00	8.7%
New England Patriots	$29.67 (5)	$29.67	0
New Orleans Saints	$23.67 (17)	$23.67	0
New York Giants	$24.50 (16)	$24.50	0
New York Jets	$22.50 (20)	$22.50	0
Philadelphia Eagles	$30.00 (3)	$30.00	0
Phoenix Cardinals	$30.00 (3)	$30.00	0
Pittsburgh Steelers	$29.25 (6)	$23.25	25.8%
San Diego Chargers	$19.67 (27)	$19.67	0
San Francisco 49ers	$35.00 (1)	$30.00	16.7%
Seattle Seahawks	$27.00 (10)	$27.00	0
Tampa Bay Buccaneers	$20.75 (24)	$18.00	15.3%
Washington Redskins	$32.50 (2)	$27.50	18.2%
NFL AVERAGE	$25.21	$23.96	5.2%

Courtesy of Team Marketing Report, Chicago, Ill.

TABLE 8.2. Team Marketing Report, 1991 National Football League Fan Cost Index™ for family of four.

Team	Ave. Ticket	Draft Beer	Soft Drink	Hot Dog	Parking	Program	Cap	FCI™	% Change vs. 1990
S.F. 49ers	$35.00	$3.25 b	$1.50 b	$1.75	$10.00	$5.00	$9.00	$197.50	11.9
Dallas Cowboys	28.33	3.00 c	2.00 e	2.00	7.00	3.00	18.00	184.33	4.1
Wash. Redskins	32.50	3.00 a	1.25 a	1.50	6.50	2.00	12.00	181.50	12.4
Philadelphia Eagles	30.00	4.25 b	2.25 e	2.25	4.00	3.00	10.00	176.50	0.3
N.E. Patriots	29.67	3.50 c	2.00 c	2.00	10.00	2.00	8.00	171.67	0
Chicago Bears	28.50	3.25 c	1.75 c	3.00	7.00	2.50	10.00	171.50	10.3
Phoenix Cardinals	30.00	n/a *	1.50 b	3.00	5.00	2.00	10.00	167.00	5.7
Pittsburgh Steelers	29.25	3.00 c	1.50 c	1.50	5.50	2.50	10.00	165.50	19.0
Buffalo Bills	27.67	3.00 d	1.50 c	1.75	5.00	2.00	10.00	158.67	0.6
L.A. Raiders	23.33	3.50 a	2.00 c	2.25	10.00	3.00	12.00	157.33	11.2
Seattle Seahawks	27.00	3.25 b	1.50 b	1.75	6.00	2.50	8.00	154.50	1.6
New York Giants	24.50	3.90 c	1.80 b	1.95	5.00	3.00	10.00	151.80	0.3
LEAGUE AVE.	25.21	3.04	1.51	1.85	6.05	2.84	9.73	151.55	4.7
Maimi Dolphins	25.33	2.00 a	2.00 e	2.00	10.00	3.00	6.00	149.33	2.8
Denver Broncos	24.67	2.50 d	1.00 a	1.50	5.50	3.00	10.50	146.17	0.3
N.Y. Jets	22.50	3.90 c	1.80 b	1.95	5.00	3.00	10.00	143.80	0.3
Cincinnati Bengals	25.63	3.00 e	1.00 b	1.00	4.25	2.50	9.00	143.75	0
Atlanta Falcons	24.67	3.25 e	1.25 c	1.50	3.00	3.00	9.00	143.17	13.2
Minnesota Vikings	25.00	3.25 c	2.00 c	2.00	6.00	2.00	5.00	142.50	4.8
Tampa Bay Bucs	20.75	3.25 b	1.50 a	1.75	7.67	3.00	12.00	140.17	11.7
L.A. Rams	21.67	3.25 b	1.75 a	2.00	5.00	5.00	8.00	139.17	6.9
Indianapolis Colts	22.33	2.50 c	1.50 c	1.75	5.50	2.00	11.00	138.83	0.4
Houston Oilers	23.67	3.00 a	1.40 a	2.00	4.00	3.00	6.95	138.18	5.5
New Orleans Saints	23.67	2.75 c	1.00 a	1.50	8.00	2.00	7.00	136.17	2.3
Cleveland Browns	22.00	2.75 c	1.00 a	1.60	4.50	2.00	10.00	132.40	0.4
Green Bay Packers	20.00	2.00 b	1.25a	1.50	4.00	2.50	12.00	128.00	1.2
Kansas City Chiefs	20.33	2.00 a	1.25 b	1.75	6.50	3.00	9.00	127.83	3.2
Detroit Lions	18.17	2.75 a	1.25 a	1.75	5.00	3.00	12.00	125.17	0
San Diego Chargers	19.67	3.00 c	0.75 a	1.50	5.00	5.00	8.00	124.67	0

Legend for drink sizes: a=12oz; b=14oz; c=16oz; d=18oz; e=20oz; *beer is not sold at Sun Devil Stadium
All information © 1991, Team Marketing Report, Chicago. Fan Cost Index and FCI® are registered trademarks of Team Marketing Report, Chicago.

TABLE 8.3. 1992 National Football League Fan Cost Index for family of four.

	Avg. Ticket	Beer	Oz.	Soft Drink	Oz.	Hot Dog	Parking	Program	Cap	1992 FCI	Pct. Chg.
Atlanta	$28.07	$2.50	14	$1.50	12	$1.50	$6.00	$3.00	$9.00	$159.26	12.6
Buffalo	$28.71	$3.00	18	$1.50	16	$1.75	$5.00	$3.00	$12.00	$168.84	11.9
Chicago	$29.41	$3.25	16	$2.50	16	$3.25	$7.00	$2.50	$12.00	$183.13	7.5
Cincy	$24.78	$2.25	12	$1.00	14	$1.00	$4.25	$3.00	$8.75	$139.37	-0.7
Cleve.	$26.24	$2.75	16	$1.25	12	$1.75	$6.00	$3.00	$10.00	$154.44	10.5
Dallas	$26.71	$3.50	14	$2.00	20	$2.00	$5.50	$3.00	$18.00	$177.34	n/c
Denver	$27.76	$2.50	16	$1.25	12	$1.50	$5.00	$3.00	$10.00	$158.02	n/c
Detroit	$25.00	$2.75	14	$1.25	12	$1.75	$7.00	$3.00	$12.95	$156.39	17.6
G. Bay	$25.13	$2.25	12	$1.25	12	$1.75	$5.00	$3.00	$7.50	$143.02	11.3
Houston	$29.45	$3.25	16	$1.50	16	$2.00	$4.00	$3.00	$12.95	$174.22	19.6
Indy	$26.48	$2.50	16	$2.00	20	$1.75	$6.50	$3.00	$11.00	$160.40	3.0
K. City	$22.62	$2.25	12	$1.25	14	$1.75	$6.50	$3.00	$14.00	$147.50	15.0
Raiders	$25.94	$3.50	12	$2.00	14	$2.25	$8.00	$3.00	$12.00	$165.76	-1.2
Rams	$27.67	$4.25	12	$1.50	16	$2.25	$6.00	$3.00	$13.00	$172.18	5.3
Maimi	$28.42	$2.00	12	$2.00	20	$2.00	$10.00	$3.00	$10.00	$169.67	4.9
Minn.	$25.00	$3.25	18	$2.00	18	$2.00	$7.50	$3.00	$7.00	$150.00	5.3
N. Eng.	$28.42	$3.50	16	$2.00	16	$2.00	$10.00	$3.00	$12.00	$176.70	6.0
N. Orl.	$24.07	$2.75	16	$1.00	14	$1.50	$10.00	$3.00	$12.00	$151.79	18.5
Giants	$28.74	$3.90	16	$1.80	14	$1.95	$6.00	$4.00	$12.00	$174.74	17.5
Jets	$25.00	$3.90	16	$1.80	14	$1.00	$5.00	$4.00	$12.00	$160.80	11.8
Phila.	$35.00	$4.00	18	$1.50	12	$2.00	$4.00	$3.00	$9.00	$186.00	5.4
Phoenix	$27.69	$3.00	12	$1.50	12	$1.75	$4.00	$3.00	$10.00	$160.77	-1.8
Pitt.	$25.84	$3.25	16	$1.75	16	$1.50	$5.00	$3.00	$10.00	$154.87	2.0
S. Diego	$29.07	$3.25	16	$1.50	16	$2.00	$5.00	$3.25	$8.00	$161.78	15.3
S. Fran.	$35.75	$3.25	14	$1.75	14	$1.75	$10.00	$3.00	$12.00	$205.00	3.8
Seattle	$26.59	$2.75	12	$1.50	14	$1.75	$4.50	$3.00	$10.00	$155.36	1.6
T. Bay	$24.03	$3.25	15	$1.50	14	$1.75	$5.00	$3.00	$13.00	$152.62	n/c
Wash.	$35.70	$3.00	12	$1.25	12	$1.75	$6.00	$3.00	$8.00	$188.79	8.3
LEAGUE	$27.32	$3.06		$1.61		$1.83	$6.21	$3.06	$11.12	$163.70	7.1

*T

Note: NC indicates no change from last year's FCI.

TABLE 8.4. Team Marketing Report, 1991 National Football League Fan Cost Index for family of four.

Team	Avg. Ticket	Draft Beer	Soft Drink	Hot Dog	Parking	Program	Cap	FCI	% Change vs. 1990
Lakers	$47.11	$3.75 b	$1.75	$1.75	$6	$5	$16	$257.94	15.8
Bulls	29.40	3.25 c	2.00 c	2.50	9	4	12	183.10	12.0
Pistons	27.07	3.50 c	1.50 a	1.75	5	4	12	165.29	2.5
Spurs	26.00	2.50 c	1.50 c	1.50	4	4	12	157.00	9.8
Celtics	24.80	3.50 a	1.50 a	2.00	15	3	5	151.20	9.6
Rockets	22.71	3.25 c	1.75 c	1.50	X	3	14	145.01	20.6
Blazers	24.36	2.75 c	1.25 b	1.75	4	3	10	144.93	3.7
Nets	21.50	2.90 a	1.80 a	1.95	5	3	13	143.80	6.6
AVERAGE	22.52	3.05	1.51	1.84	5.29	3.21	10.21	141.75	7.7
Suns	21.67	3.00 c	1.50 c	2.00	3	3	12	139.67	5.2
Warriors	22.25	3.00 b	1.25 a	2.00	5	3	10	139.00	6.8
Hawks	20.00	2.50 b	1.75 c	1.50	6	5	12.15	138.30	11.1
Clippers	20.40	3.50 a	2.00 c	2.25	6	3	10	137.60	1.9
Cavs	21.43	3.25 c	1.75 c	1.75	5	3	8	133.21	9.8
76ers	19.67	3.00 c	1.50 b	1.75	4	2.50	13	132.67	n/a
Sonics	19.57	3.50 c	1.50 b	2.00	4.50	2	12	131.79	5.0
Kings	19.67	2.75 b	1.50 a	2.00	4	3	10	128.17	0
Hornets	22.44	2.25 c	1.00 c	1.50	3	4	5	125.28	1.4
Mavs	19.38	2.75 c	1.50 c	1.50	4	3	10	125.00	0.8
Jazz	22.57	3.00 f	.75 f	1.50	3	3	5	124.29	-0.5
Bullets	19.75	3.00 b	1.60 c	1.65	5	2.25	8	123.50	15.9
T-Wolves	17.56	3.00 d	1.50 b	2.00	1.50	3	12	121.75	0
Nuggets	17.43	3.00 e	1.50 c	1.75	3	3	12	121.71	0
Bucks	18.14	3.00 c	1.50 c	1.75	6	2	10	121.57	5.6
Packers	19.50	2.75 c	1.50 c	2.00	4	3	5.50	118.50	18.2
Heat	18.25	3.25 c	1.50 b	2.35	5.30	3	6	118.20	12.4
Magic	15.00	2.75 b	1.50 c	1.50	4	3	9.95	108.40	1.4

Notes: Key to drink sizes: a=12oz, b=14oz, c=16oz, d=18oz, e=20oz, f=8oz.
X: Parking included in ticket cost for Rockets.
For the NBA, FCI, premium-priced seating areas of less than 200 seats were not included in determining average ticket prices. Average ticket prices were calculated by adding the different ticket price levels and then dividing that sum by the number of price levels. Teams were asked to supply draft beer and soft drink prices for the smallest size sold and cap prices for least expensive caps.

TABLE 8.5. 1992 Major League Baseball Fan Cost Index for family of four.

	Avg. Tix.	Beer/ Ounces	Soda/ Ounces	Hot Dog	Parking	Program	Cap	1992 FCI	Pct. Chg.
Atlanta	$8.40	$3.25/20	$1.25/16	$1.50	$5.00	$2.50	7.00	75.10	10.23
Baltimore	9.65	3.00/18	1.00/14	2.75	5.00	3.00	8.00	86.61	23.10
Boston	11.67	2.91/14	1.50/14	2.00	10.00	2.00	7.00	94.48	4.85
Calif.	8.02	3.25/14	.75/12	2.25	5.00	2.00	10.00	79.60	8.65
ChiSox	11.70	3.00/12	1.50/14	1.50	6.00	3.00	10.00	96.81	18.71
Ch. Cubs	10.87	3.25/16	1.00/12	1.75	10.00	3.00	10.00	96.98	16.30
Cincin.	7.20	2.25/12	1.00/14	1.00	5.00	3.00	10.00	72.28	8.24
Cleveland	7.70	2.75/16	1.25/12	1.75	4.50	1.75	9.00	74.30	7.62
Detroit	8.96	3.00/14	1.35/12	1.80	5.50	1.50	10.00	92.96	-0.66
Houston	8.26	3.00/12	1.50/12	2.00	4.00	2.00	12.00	85.02	15.64
Kan. City	9.20	2.25/12	1.25/14	1.75	5.00	4.00	10.00	86.29	26.83
L.A.	9.15	3.25/14	1.50/14	2.25	4.00	2.25	10.00	86.60	16.29
Milwaukee	9.27	2.75/12	1.50/14	1.75	5.00	1.50	12.00	87.57	13.55
Minnesota	8.93	3.50/18	1.25/12	2.00	3.00	3.00	7.00	78.70	6.14
Montreal	8.67	2.71/12	1.46/16	1.67	5.84	4.17	12.52	91.85	12.77
NY Mets	10.89	2.95/12	1.25/12	1.75	5.00	2.00	8.00	86.46	0.03
NY Yanks	13.28	3.36/14	1.25/13	3.00	6.00	3.00	10.00	101.61	13.95
Oakland	10.04	3.00/14	1.25/12	2.00	5.00	4.00	10.00	92.16	3.36
Philadelphia	8.20	3.25/14	1.50/12	1.00	4.50	2.00	10.00	77.81	8.84
Pittsburgh	9.23	3.25/16	1.75/16	1.75	4.00	2.00	8.00	81.41	11.26
San Diego	8.54	3.25/16	1.00/12	1.50	4.00	2.00	12.00	82.67	12.99
San Francisco	8.98	3.25/14	1.75/14	2.00	6.00	3.00	9.00	87.41	4.80
Seattle	7.98	2.75/12	1.50/14	1.75	5.00	3.00	8.00	77.41	4.60
St. Louis	9.11	2.00/12	1.00/12	1.40	4.50	2.00	10.00	78.54	13.39
Texas	8.93	3.00/16	1.50/16	1.50	5.00	3.00	7.00	78.73	9.82
Toronto	12.90	2.50/12	1.34/16	1.66	12.52	4.17	11.69	112.83	5.73
LEAGUE	9.41	2.94	1.31	1.81	5.51	2.61	9.55	85.85	10.37

TABLE 8.6. 1993 Major League Baseball Fan Cost Index for family of four.

Team	Avg. Tix	Beer	(oz.)	Soda	(oz.)	Hot Dog	Parking	Program	Cap	1993 FCI	FCI Rank	% Change	Tix. Rank	% Change
Atlanta	9.76	$3.50	20	1.75	16	1.75	5.00	4.00	12.00	97.06	9	12.7	10	16.2
Baltimore	11.12	3.25	16	1.00	14	1.75	5.00	3.00	15.00	102.96	5	24.6	6	15.2
Boston	11.67	3.25	14	1.50	14	2.00	15.00	1.00	10.00	104.18	3	10.3	5	0
California	8.02	3.25	14	0.75	12	2.25	5.00	2.50	12.00	84.60	22	0.0	25	0
Chicago W.S.	11.70	3.00	12	1.50	14	1.75	6.00	3.00	10.00	97.81	8	1.0	4	0
Chicago Cubs	11.74	3.50	16	1.25	12	2.00	11.00	3.00	10.00	103.94	4	7.2	3	8.0
Cincinnati	7.95	2.25	12	1.00	14	1.00	5.00	4.00	12.00	77.31	28	7.0	27	10.5
Cleveland	8.70	4.00	16	1.25	12	1.75	5.00	1.75	10.00	87.30	15	17.5	20	13.0
Colorado	7.91	2.50	16	1.50	16	1.75	4.00	3.75	12.00	81.12	25	n/a	28	n/a
Detroit	9.42	3.50	14	1.50	12	1.75	6.50	2.00	14.95	92.17	11	11.1	12	5.1
Florida	9.73	2.00	12	2.00	20	2.00	4.00	3.00	10.00	98.83	7	n/a	11	n/a
Houston	8.26	3.25	12	1.50	16	1.75	4.00	2.00	10.00	80.52	26	5.8	23	0
Kansas City	9.20	2.25	12	1.25	14	1.75	5.00	4.00	10.00	86.29	18	0.0	14	0
Los Angeles	9.15	3.50	14	1.50	14	2.50	4.00	2.50	12.00	88.60	13	1.1	16	0
Milwaukee	9.80	2.75	12	1.50	14	1.75	5.00	2.50	12.00	91.69	12	4.7	9	5.7
Minnesota	9.16	3.50	18	1.25	12	2.00	4.00	3.00	8.00	82.63	24	2.4	15	2.6
Montreal	8.63	2.60	12	1.20	16	1.40	6.40	2.50	12.00	80.14	19	6.2	22	0.4
NY Mets	10.89	2.95	12	1.25	12	1.75	5.00	2.00	8.00	86.46	17	0.0	7	0
NY Yankees	13.48	3.25	14	2.00	14	3.00	5.00	3.00	11.00	113.43	2	11.6	2	9.8
Oakland	10.49	3.00	14	1.50	14	2.00	6.00	4.00	12.00	99.97	6	8.5	8	4.5
Philadelphia	8.20	4.00	18	1.50	12	1.25	5.00	2.00	11.00	82.81	23	6.4	24	0
Pittsburgh	8.80	3.25	16	1.75	16	1.75	4.00	2.00	12.00	87.70	14	5.1	19	4.7
San Diego	8.70	3.25	16	1.00	12	1.50	4.00	3.00	12.00	85.31	21	3.2	20	1.9
SF Giants	9.31	3.50	14	1.25	12	2.00	6.00	3.00	9.00	67.23	16	0.9	13	3.6
Seattle	7.98	2.75	12	1.50	14	1.75	5.00	3.00	12.00	85.41	20	10.3	26	0
St. Louis	9.11	2.00	12	1.00	12	1.40	4.50	2.00	10.00	78.54	27	0.0	17	0
Texas	8.93	3.00	16	1.50	16	1.75	5.00	6.50	10.00	92.73	10	9.4	18	0
Toronto	13.73	3.60	12	1.60	16	1.70	12.00	3.20	11.20	116.11	1	2.9	1	6.4
	Ave. Tix	Beer (oz.)		Soda (oz.)		Hot Dog	Parking Program		Cap	1993 FCI		% Change		% Change
League Ave.	9.57	3.09		1.39		1.80	5.76	5.76	11.01	90.87		4.3		1.7

Research – Discovering What Really Drives Fans

When you see the means to which fans will go to be closer to the teams and heroes they idolize, you see the power of the emotional pull of sports – and the reason to market through it. Understanding those emotions and the actions they produce can make the difference in marketing through sports.

Increasingly, sports marketing research is augmenting and pinpointing the drivers of success in sports marketing in increasingly sophisticated ways. From equivalent media values attached to sponsorship packages to lifestyle identifications with a sponsor by sports fans, sports marketing research continues to do a better job of quantifying what counts – and what doesn't. Everyone knows it works. Knowing *why* is getting to be the big thing. That's why sports marketing research continues to proliferate and has become a specialty of many research houses, from Performance Research in Newport, Rhode Island, to Joyce Julius Associates in Ann Arbor, Michigan, that are trying to grasp the what and wherefore of sports marketing promotions and fan reactions thereto.

If sports marketing is the sponsorship that produces the goodwill, awareness, and sales that corporations seek, then sports marketing research is the data that produces those promotional schemes. It justifies making the effort and quantifies the results.

The research isn't much different from what goes on in traditional marketing research in business. It's just that sports marketing never had a real body of research of its own. The movement has spurred increasing sophistication that allows continued peeks into consumer lifestyles. These lifestyle factors impact consumer interaction with sports and the opportunities for marketers to reach consumers through sports. Measurements of fan attitudes about sports, about the sponsors of sports, about the value of sponsorship, and about the impact of sponsorship are emerging. More and more companies are relying on such data and are developing the formulas that will make their sports marketing efforts better and better.

Prospective sponsors are discovering more and more that they can identify the relative value of an event both before and after it happens as well as identify the right prospects to reach through a sports marketing effort – and whether a given event offers those prospects.

One of the more compelling marketing formulas that has been developed belongs to Coca-Cola, and it has shared it with the world, so to speak, in its efforts to quantify sponsorship value before an event. Stuart Schwartz, manager of business affairs for Coca-Cola USA, has developed a progression of formulas in helping his company determine appropriate rights fees.

"Coke used to have a price tossed at it and then made a decision," Schwartz told the International Events Group conference in 1994. Not any more. Based on a method developed by the DDB-Needham ad agency, Schwartz's formula helps determine the potential impact of an event both qualitatively and quantitatively. Simply stated, that formula is *impact per dollar equals impact divided by dollar cost*. It is folded into an overall formula that includes factoring in the property purchase price; trademark, sampling, and other exposure impressions; consumer attitudes and behavior; and shareholder value.

For Coke and Schwartz, measuring the event's performance, shareholder value, and the face value of the property keys the final analysis and the price Coke determines is the right one for its sponsorship participation. Impact measurement includes media mentions (or relative advertising value), venue signage, and incidental signage exposures, based on interviews with what Schwartz defined as "exposees," with questions measuring pre- and postevent attitudes and perceptions, trademark recall, and product awareness. The yield, Schwartz says, is "actionable information" that can be immediately plugged into the aforementioned working model to figure the value of the event and the appropriate rights fee.

Another key for Schwartz is the return on investment, which includes cash flow from incremental sales attached to the events *minus* the cost to purchase and *activate* the event (that is, to support and promote it relative to your sponsorship position). Most experts recommend 1.5:1 spending in such regard; some even advocate a 2:1 ratio. Of course, for a first-time event, this type of attitude and behavior measurement is more difficult.

Schwartz likes to unbundle the various components of the rights associated with the property and establish separate values to them. If the separate values (signage, promotion, licensing) add up individually to more than the value of the event in and of itself, he knows he's got a winner.

Finally, Schwartz figures what he concludes to be the deal's value by adding his sum of the unbundled rights to the cash flow of product sales associated with the event and *subtracting* what was the originally estimated value of the deal. If that yields a number less than zero, then Schwartz has discovered what he calls a "value gap" and knows what to recommend to Coke officials responsible for deciding whether or not to take on the sponsorship.

Joyce Julius and Associates, meanwhile, has its own patented method for discovering the value of a sponsorship, and it's as simple as measuring the value of your media exposure through the sponsorship against what it would've cost you to purchase equivalent media advertising time or space. Well, it's not that simple, but the yield is, and it's often astounding.

Julius's *Sponsors Report*, which reports the results of its findings to clients, noted in September 1993 that during a rain delay at the Federal Express St. Jude Classic golf tournament, Ram, a maker of umbrellas, received 1:38 worth of exposure time, equivalent to $147,000 it could've spent on a 30-second commercial. Competitor MaxFli umbrellas got 1:14 or $111,000 worth of exposure, according to Julius.[4]

Julius has made its mark in auto racing and now measures similarly in many sports and events. In a stunning revelation for Volvo Tennis, the automaker was able to find that for the $5 million it was investing in sponsoring and promoting the men's tennis tour annually, it was receiving close to $35 million in equivalent media expenditure. That's a 7:1 ratio. And Joyce Julius has the research and methodology to show such results to its clients.

But perhaps the newest and most significant development is attitude and lifestyle consideration and measurement. Leading the way in this new measurement genre is a partnership of companies specializing in measurement and analysis thereof. The Yankelovich research group and the Lifestyle Marketing Group of New York are measuring how fans react to an event and the promotions around it, including factors like perceived image of the sponsor and the event, and demographic information ranging from income bracket, leisure-time activities, vocation, age, and sex. The key is the company's ability to turn around such data, analyzed and shaken every which way from Sunday, virtually overnight.

Professor William Sutton of the University of Massachusetts developed a similar system while serving as an executive for Virginia-based DelWilber Associates, a sports marketing and consulting firm. Now popularized to the point of becoming an art form, Sutton's technique sends laptop-computer–laden researchers out into the stands before an event to gather answers to a bevy of questions similar to those asked and analyzed by Yankelovich/Lifestyle. Sutton's teams would typically ask people why they were attending an event – especially basketball and baseball. The number one answer, usually, would be "because of the quality of the competition." Factors such as "weather" or "the tickets were free" often checked in ahead of any special promotional considerations associated with the event. Sutton's computer-driven teams could have the information analyzed and tabulated before the end of whatever sporting contest they were deployed. The Lifestyle/Yankelovich effort will turn information around overnight.

As quick, on-site information grabs, these techniques are useful and innovative. Their value will increase as they maintain their longevity and their body of data builds to year-to-year comparative levels, better enabling sponsors and event promoters and producers to deduce and track fan attitudes and behaviors.

One attitude is certain, however: we fans love our sports, and we ain't bailin' out – just yet.

Here We Come – Catch Us if You Can

No matter the cost, no matter the city, no matter the game, we keep watching sports in person or on television. Somewhere, there's always someone to pay the freight, whether it's Major League Baseball or in-line skating hockey. Attendance numbers and TV ratings are generally trending upward, especially for the major sports, but it's what's behind those numbers that drives the games and the marketing thereof.

Some of America's most notable observers of and participants in sports have their opinions on why we keep showing up, why and how we worship sports and sportsmen, and how we show the attitudes that marketers are trying to latch onto to move their products and services. From basketball coach Bob Knight to sponsorship guru Lesa

Ukman, everyone has an opinion on what works, why it works, and how we feel about it.

We Love the Games

President Clinton had an unusually busy day on Monday, April 4, 1994. That afternoon, in Cleveland, he opened the baseball season and inaugurated the Indians' new ballpark, Jacobs Field, by throwing out the first pitch. That night, in Charlotte, North Carolina, the former governor of Arkansas watched the University of Arkansas win the NCAA basketball championship.

Being there for the big events was high on Clinton's agenda that day, as it is for most of us every day in relation to sports. It is that kind of emotion that lets fans look past the seamier side of sports, the illegal activities that players often get involved with, and the often gaudy prices that they have to pay to be involved with it intimately. For whatever the reason, fans say it's worth it.

As syndicated columnist Lewis Grizzard put it in relation to college football: "Congress can waste your money, the President can lie to you, and your kid can wear an earring and watch MTV, but if your alma mater is 8-0, who's sweating the small stuff?" [5] Our emotions just run that strong, regardless. However, Secretary of Health and Human Services Donna Shalala, then chancellor of the University of Wisconsin, tempered that a bit, saying, "Athletics, if done right, creates a sense of community. It helps foster a sense of good will. It's not a substitute for quality undergraduate education, but it can bring people together."

At Wisconsin, it brought them too close together in 1993. After the Badgers' stunning 13–10 upset of Michigan, fans attempting to storm the field in celebration instead stampeded into a tragedy. Several people were crushed in the resulting melee. Of the 80 fans that were hurt, seven were injured critically, according to news reports. Unfortunately, that type of behavior is all too typical among fans in celebrating their teams' successes. Fans try to emulate their conquering heroes, who often wind up in headlines as much for what they do off the field as what they do on it. Looting and violence in relation to sporting event celebrations is all too common. If sports patrolled and policed themselves better – and perhaps demanded more retribution from malcontents – some psychologists say fans would respond accordingly. But the sports don't, at least not until after the fact, and the fans obviously don't see why they can't act like their heroes and get into the same types of trouble.

Attitudes like these are among those that marketers are playing into when they market through sports. By the same token, fans are willing to pay the price. For the Chicago/New York NBA playoff series in 1994, fans paid up to $750 to ticket scalpers to attend games. Fans pay premiums for collectibles, too. The highest price ever paid for such a collectible other than a trading card was the $363,000 someone forked over at auction for Lou Gehrig's 1927 flannel road jersey. And for anywhere between $7,500 and $35,000, you can get the likes of Joe Pepitone or John Madden to speak at your function. And the *Chicago Tribune* reported in 1990 that memorabilia from Michael Jordan, Patrick Ewing, and Wayne Gretzky sold for more at an auction than did a valuable print of Abraham Lincoln.

When it comes to trading cards, the research firm Market Facts found that, for 10 percent of adults, cards were their gift of choice, particularly if they shared a household where a 17-year-old or younger resided. More females (12 percent) than males (7 percent) surveyed were planning on making such purchases.[6] (See Figure 8.1.) The firm also found, however, that men (61 percent of respondents) were the primary card collectors, but households with 17-year-olds or younger are the primary card-collecting households. Baseball (72 percent) cards are the number one card collected. While men dominate in card collecting overall, a higher percentage of women collect basketball and hockey cards.

People travel to games and attractions, too. For $625, through a company called Sports Tours, fans can travel to the Baseball Hall of Fame in Cooperstown, New York, take in a game in Detroit, Toronto, and/or Pittsburgh while they're at it, and also manage a stop at scenic Niagara Falls. Such tours, trips with players during their offseasons, and special trips to see teams play on the road are commonplace.

But the common gripe is that prices have hit their limit and fans are being priced out or pushed aside for corporate sponsors and clients who can afford blocks of season tickets or the increasingly popular and pervasive skyboxes. On January 15, 1992, the venerable *Chicago Tribune* sportswriter Jerome Holtzman told WSCR-AM sports talk radio

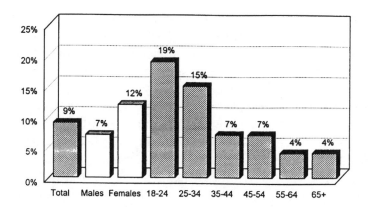

Figure 8.1. Percentage of adults planning to purchase trading cards as holiday gifts.
Source: Market Facts research. Arlington Heights, Ill.

in Chicago that the average fan was being priced out, in good part because corporations were buying up the seats.

Was he right? Well, it used to cost $50 just to see the Quebec Nordiques (the Nordiques?) play. Wrigley Field bleacher seats have escalated in price, and you have to get them six months in advance. And it's not just the big four (hockey, baseball, football, basketball) sports that have these problems.

Roger Cox, a contributing editor to *Tennis* magazine, griped that "in a detestable marketing decision that favors corporate clients over everyday tennis fans, the U.S. Tennis Association has done away with mail-order sales of individual tickets for the U.S. Open, meaning more bucks for USTA and tough luck for the average fan. . . . Gone was the option of picking only those sessions I wanted to see. In its place was a choice of four inflexible package plans, each wedded to specific day and night sessions. . . . The new plans clearly were conceived with corporate businesses, not individual fans, in mind. Businesses buy tickets to give away to favored clients, whereas individuals buy them for personal use. . . . But the package plans bundle day and night tickets together. To see those first two days this year, I have to buy tickets to five sessions (the first three days and two nights) at a cost of $84. What am I supposed to do with my unwanted tickets?"[7]

The marketing of the game – or the games – is becoming a disservice to the common fan. The corporate sponsor who can pay the freight is increasingly the beneficiary and target of the new sports marketing, which those sponsors try to turn into sales and market share by promoting their association with the sport. Increasingly, the corporate sponsor holds the key for the common fan to get close to the game and closer to the sports heroes they worship.

Or, as NBA Commissioner David Stern notes, "Sports is in an enviable position to be at the intersection of a phenomena . . . making it the single most significant way to market products and services around the world and in specific domestic barriers. . . . In many ways, we [the NBA] are ahead of the organizational flow at the world's corporations as they try to deal with this phenomenon." Sports has this opportunity, Stern claims, because it can tie into anything, from the cause-related to the product-related to the service-related.[2]

The sports marketer, according to Frank Deford, is "working on the happy side of life." Of society in general, Deford says that "we have become professional spectators. . . . We keep going out to sports events, for good or bad teams. People wear clothes to prove they're spectators."[3]

Deford is expert at defining how important sports has become to society. He has noted that in 1972, when Pete Axthelm filed a great story from the Munich Olympics about the hostage tragedy there, Axthelm's editors at *Newsweek* wanted to know why he didn't have something about the gymnastics competition in the lead of his story. College athletics has been scandal-ridden for decades, Deford has pointed out, yet the fans still fill the stadiums and arenas.

Where Deford does it with insightful anecdotes, *Team Marketing Report* Editor and Publisher Alan Friedman does it with statistics and numbers. Friedman seconds William Sutton's conclusion that the number one reason people go to a game is the appeal of the visiting opponent. Promotions rate eleventh. "Promotion ain't the answer," Friedman quips. He sees the upgrading of facilities and new amenities like branded food-service products helping to drive fan participation and improve the experience and atmosphere. "The move away from

2. Speech to the American Marketing Association's Second Annual Sports Marketing Conference, May 7, 1992.
3. Speech at the American Marketing Association's Second Annual Sports Marketing Conference, May 7, 1992.

free TV will be accelerated," Friedman believes. He feels that this will drive revenue somewhat but restrict fan access to teams and eventually hit a tradeoff point where its pervasiveness will halt.

Like others, Friedman sees the facility as the key. The rotating signage will continue to proliferate as a revenue builder. More facilities will take on corporate names. And the skyboxes just keep on coming.

Where does that leave the average fan?

It may leave him or her on the outside, hungry for more – for that unattainable seat, that highly priced front-row ducat, that thrill of the experience of being there, close to the game and the team and the players. Corporate marketers, acting through their sponsorships, leverage this, giving away everything from licensed merchandise to tickets as new conduits to satisfy the emotional link that fans crave.

That emotional link runs strong. Very strong. Both ways. A group called "Fans of Abner" has sprung up to let owners know that they want a say in the game. They want it to stay affordable to the average fan (which it already isn't), they want television to stay within the fan's grasp, and they want sanity and continuity in the game.

Fat chance.

Indeed, in a poll published in *Team Marketing Report*, 78 percent of fans said it's not right if they pay extra to watch on television what they get now for free. Eighty percent said they are not influenced by sponsorships when it comes time to make product-purchase decisions. Only 26 percent said it sometimes figures into their purchase decisions. Sixty-nine percent said they see through the corporate motives and that the companies are only out to get more sales, not to make sports more accessible to fans through sponsorships. Yet 77 percent realize that if it were not for sponsor advertising, sports wouldn't be possible on the tube. But seventy-four percent are more impressed with companies that sponsor local sporting events like Little League baseball.[8]

And when it comes to the benefits of sponsorship, *Editor & Publisher* magazine, reporting on an International Events Group survey, said that of 30 major metro newspapers surveyed, only 20 regularly mention sponsors in covering events. Eight said they don't mention sponsors and the other two don't have a policy. Sponsorship may have benefits, but now it looks like it needs a public relations campaign.

Don't tell that to Lesa Ukman, the International Events Group chief executive and founder. Ukman, whose 12-year-old company tracks sponsorship, publishes newsletters and directories about it, and consults on the subject, believes sponsorship will be the fastest-growing discipline in all of marketing. Why? It offers integration opportunities in a total marketing package. It's public relations, advertising, direct marketing, database building, exposure, awareness, and research all rolled into one. It transcends industries. It allows football to tie in with ailing kids, baseball to make an alliance with missing children's relief, and basketball to link up with education. And it allows marketers supporting those sports and those causes to bask in the glow of all of them. As a tiebreaker, associating with these causes and events could be the difference between a consumer picking your product and a competitor's when all other things are equal in the marketing mix.

Ukman also believes sponsorship's nonintrusive nature in comparison to advertising makes it preferable to consumers and fans, and should therefore make it preferable to sponsoring companies and event rights holders too.

And so the power of sports continues. In Kansas City, $40 million in pledges were raised in three months in 1993 when it appeared that the baseball Royals were headed out of town. Yet, as Deion Sanders says, "There are some things you just can't market. . . . Baseball is boring. You could fall asleep up there in the stands."[9] Peter Gent, a former football player who is now a novelist, says that today's players are richer than ever financially but poorer emotionally than ever before, less satisfied with their jobs. The pain they'll live with the rest of their shortened lives hasn't hit them yet. As the top-flight sports merchandise manufacturer David Beckerman, president of Starter, says, "It is business, and when you watch [it on] the tube, it no longer is the joy."[10]

Perhaps no one more than Bob Verdi, *Chicago Tribune* columnist, put it better when it comes to describing the emotions of fans and the attitude of the teams towards them. Writing in September 1992 about a baseball work stoppage, Verdi wrote:

> Fans generally donate themselves to the cause at an early age, even before they dive heart first into the pool of ticket buyers. You watch games on television and read newspaper stories, a contribution to

America's sports fixation that is priceless, in every sense of the word. The teams for which you root pay nothing for this blind devotion, which swells demand beyond supply. Owners who own and players who play get rich as you spend for their privileges – emotionally, then monetarily, then both . . .

. . . It's a one-way street with toll booths, traveled by millions of you . . .

. . . The Red Sox have drawn more fanatics than 1986 [their last World Series appearance] to Fenway Park every season since. Being loved means never having to say you're sorry for not returning the favor . . .

. . . Only when the games resume will baseball remind one and all that it needs you, the fan. And you'll be back, like homing pigeons . . .

. . . "It's scary," Mike Ditka said about how important sports are to fans.

The problem is, who's scared?

References

[1] *Marketing News*, American Marketing Association Publications Group, " . . . on Sports Marketing," April 29, 1991, p. 10.

[2] *Daily Herald*, Paddock Publications, sports section, December 3, 1993, p. 16.

[3] *Chicago Tribune*, sports section, January 18, 1992.

[4] Joyce Julius and Associates, "A Second Look," *Sponsors Report*, Vol. 3, No. 3, September 1993, p. 1.

[5] *Daily Herald*, Paddock Publications, Arlington Heights, Ill., "Ways of Life Face Off in College Football," September 10, 1993, p. 2.

[6] Market Facts Telenation poll, December 3, 1993.

[7] *Tennis*, "The USTA is Closing the Open," August 1992, p. 20.

[8] *Team Marketing Report*, January 1992, p. 6.

[9] *USA Today*, sports section, April 14, 1994.

[10] *Daily Herald*, Paddock Publications, business section, Aug. 2, 1994, p. 1.

Questions and Exercises for Discussions and Further Research

Chapter 1: Sports Marketing—An Overview

Make a list of sports you think will emerge as hot sponsorship properties in the next decade and write a paragraph under each entry explaining why you selected that sport.

What are the elements that make a sport or a property hot for sponsorship?

How could your (prospective) company get successfully involved in sponsorship?

Why are hockey teams emigrating from the sport's Canadian birthplace to the United States while pro basketball franchises are finding homes in Canada?

Write a marketing plan that a small-town, small company could use to sponsor a small, local event for a budget of $10,000.

Chapter 2: Ambush Marketing

Think of and describe an ambush marketing campaign not mentioned in this book.

What are the legal considerations you must evaluate in designing an ambush marketing campaign?

What do those elements have in common with those of a successful ambush marketing campaign?

Design an ambush marketing campaign for a non-Olympic sponsor that competes with official sponsor Coca-Cola.

Research report: Who invented ambush marketing? How was it first applied?

Chapter 3: The NBA Takes Over the World

How does the NBA help companies market multinationally?

How does the Continental Basketball Association benefit from its developmental relationship with the NBA?

Argue for or against: The NBA (basketball) will overtake soccer as the world's most-popular sport.

How do multinational companies help the NBA do its marketing?

Just for fun: the best Dream Team is I, II, III . . . and why.

Chapter 4: Media as You've Never Seen It Before

Make up a list of ten new pay-per-view events you think would be successful and a one-paragraph explanation for each choice.

What are the elements that make up a successful pay-per-view event?

Write a one-page summary of your version of proposed legislation governing pay-per-view.

Why didn't the Olympic Triplecast work?

Case study: Research and write a report on how Dodger-vision works and why it's successful.

Chapter 5: Fantasy Marketing

Design a fantasy sports marketing campaign.

What are the benefits of a fantasy sports-marketing incentive program?

Why is fantasy sports marketing so successful?

Design a nonsports fantasy marketing campaign.

Who invented fantasy sports? Fantasy sports marketing?

Chapter 6: Auto . . . and Other Racing

Why and how has auto racing become one of the hottest sponsorship properties?

Design a marketing plan for a packaged-goods product tie-in with—or sponsorship of—auto racing.

What are the pratfalls that could befall a marketer in an auto-racing sponsorship relationship?

Besides auto racing, what racing sport would you tie your (prospective) packaged-goods product into, and why?

Considering the level of competition between horse racing and gambling casinos, what is the future of horse racing as a sponsorship property?

Chapter 7: Soccer in America

What has restrained soccer's growth and popularity in the United States?

Can soccer become in the United States what basketball is becoming in the rest of the world? Why or why not?

Why was World Cup '94 so successful in the United States?

If you were MasterCard, how would you quantify the results of your World Cup '94 sponsorship?

What are the differences between American and European attitudes about soccer?

Chapter 8: Futuresports

List the elements you would include in the design of a new stadium or arena to make it fan-friendly.

Case history research report: Should new stadiums and arenas be publicly funded? Have existing stadiums and arenas delivered a return on investment?

What is the marketing difference between today's new stadiums and those built 30 and 40 years ago?

Describe the demographics of today's typical sporting event attendee.

Who buys more event tickets—corporations and sponsors or individual fans?

Index

Aaron, Hank, 5
ABC (network), 88, 93, 94, 131, 157
Abdul-Jabbar, Kareem, 96
Adidas, 156
advertising, 23, 66. *see also*
    ambush marketing; media
    coverage; signage
Advil, 145
Albert, Prince of Monaco, 72
Amateur All-Star Baseball Inc.
    (AABI), 18, 19
ambush marketing
    defined, 29
    impact of, 29-33
    NHL vs. Pepsi/Canada, 33-40
    rotating signage and, 179
America West, 177
American Airlines
    ambush marketing and, 30, 32
    sponsorship, basketball, 63
    sponsorship, soccer, 153,
        155, 156
American Express (AMEX), 29, 30-
    33, 41, 43-47
American Medical Association, 5
AMEX. *see* American Express
Amshay, Tom, 131, 132, 133, 134
Anderson, Richard Dean, 116
Anheuser-Busch, 10, 23, 143, 154
Annachino, Joseph, 113

antitrust exemptions,
    professional sports, 83, 89
Apex, 102
Apex-One, 22
Aplus Mini Markets, 142
arenas. *see* stadiums and arenas
Armstrong, Lance, 139, 141
asics (company), 145
Association of Independent
    Television Stations (INTV), 86, 87
Atlanta Braves, 14
Atlanta Falcons, 176
AT&T, 5, 68, 71, 72
attendance
    auto racing, 137
    baseball games, 14-15, 171
    basketball games, 19, 74
    football games, 20
    soccer games, 159
Australia, NBA expansion, 56-57
automobile purchasing decisions,
    women and, 9
automobile racing
    Daytona 500, 120, 137
    Indianapolis 500, 120, 127-29
    marketing and, 119-20
    sponsorship of, 3, 4, 64, 120-
        27, 123f, 131-36
    telephone promotions, 129-30
    television commercials and, 128

203